Fuelling the Empire

Fuelling the Empire

South Africa's Gold and the Road to War

❧⚜❧

John J. Stephens

WILEY

Published in the UK in 2003 by John Wiley & Sons Ltd, The Atrium, Southern Gate, Chichester, West Sussex PO19 8SQ, England
Telephone   (+44) 1243 779777

Email (for orders and customer service enquiries): cs-books@wiley.co.uk
Visit our Home Page on www.wileyeurope.com or www.wiley.com

This publication is designed to provide accurate and authoritative information in regard to the subject matter covered. It is sold on the understanding that the Publisher is not engaged in rendering professional services. If professional advice or other expert assistance is required, the services of a competent professional should be sought.

Other Wiley Editorial Offices

John Wiley & Sons Inc., 111 River Street, Hoboken, NJ 07030, USA

Jossey-Bass, 989 Market Street, San Francisco, CA 94103–1741, USA

Wiley-VCH Verlag GmbH, Boschstr. 12, D-69469 Weinheim, Germany

John Wiley & Sons Australia Ltd, 33 Park Road, Milton, Queensland 4064, Australia

John Wiley & Sons (Asia) Pte Ltd, 2 Clementi Loop #02-01, Jin Xing Distripark, Singapore 129809

John Wiley & Sons Canada Ltd, 22 Worcester Road, Etobicoke, Ontario, Canada M9W 1L1

British Library Cataloguing in Publication Data

A catalogue record for this book is available from the British Library

ISBN 0-470-85067-1
Typeset in 10/13.5 Photina by Mathematical Composition Setters, Ltd., Salisbury, Wiltshire
Printed and bound in Great Britain by TJ International Ltd., Padstow, Cornwall
This book is printed on acid-free paper responsibly manufactured from sustainable forestry in which at least two trees are planted for each one used for paper production.

DEDICATION

To the memory of my father: he loved a good story and told me many from the old days …

CONTENTS

CONTENTS

ACKNOWLEDGEMENTS

This book would not have been possible without the encouragement and support I received from Sally Smith, my executive editor at John Wiley and Sons. Were it not for her initial responsiveness and positive suggestions, the whole idea of this book might still have been languishing at the back of my mind. It was our first history project together and, as always, I found working with her a tremendous joy. But I owe a debt of gratitude to many others also.

Researching a book like this always presents a tremendous challenge. In this, I was greatly assisted by the unstinting and enthusiastic attention of a number of librarians and their assistants. First on this list must be Cathy Erasmus, the chief librarian of the Harold Strange Library of African Studies in Johannesburg. She and her assistant, Linda Boswell, managed to meet all my numerous requests and found some amazing materials, some of which I feared might be impossible to get, given the often vague and general nature of my requests. Cathy is a fount of knowledge and information on works on South African history and especially that of early Johannesburg.

I was also the beneficiary of very friendly advice and courteous service by various kind assistants in the library of the Chamber of Mines in Johannesburg, the main reading room of the Johannesburg Central Library and the reference section of the Mogale City Library. Dr. Janet du Plooy of the latter library warrants a special word of thanks for her very helpful information and the fact that she arranged for me to have untrammelled access to the archives of the Mogale City Museum. In my delicious ramblings through the archives of the museum, I was very kindly and very ably assisted by the ever-helpful Christa Eksteen. I also wish to express my sincere thanks and appreciation to Francois de Jager, a friend of long standing, who generously consented to lend me his closely cosseted copies of a number of out-of-print history books, much of which I found helpful and duly found their way into the body of this book. Lending out one's treasured books I have always found to be a less than rewarding transaction, but I am happy to report that I have returned each and every one of them, still in the pristine condition I received them.

Due to my devotion to detail, I found it difficult to decide what to leave out and what to put in, while still trying to maintain a close narrative. In this choice, I was guided by the advice of both Sally Smith and my son Philip, who consented to read the very rough first draft and proved remorseless in his criticism. Many of the improvements in style can be attributed to their efforts, although I alone can be held responsible for the many deficiencies that undoubtedly remain.

Because of a very tight production schedule, everybody connected with the production team had to pull out all the stops to complete the project on schedule. My thanks and congratulations go to everyone on the team for their grand effort and the success they achieved. In this regard, I do want to mention the name of Amie Tibble, the production editor who was responsible for the smooth running of the whole process and the not inconsiderable task of coordinating the efforts of so many people.

A special word of thanks is also due to Martin Key of The Magic Word Company. He had the rather formidable task of copyediting the final manuscript. It had to be done within a very tight time framework and he managed to do the job with great competence, insight and thoroughness. I was fortunate in having a copyeditor with such experience and knowledge.

Finally, most of a work like this is done sitting down in front of a computer and just hacking away. That is a devotion to duty which I sometimes think is deserving of some special decoration. However, in this case the accolades must go to my long-suffering wife Rina. She was always there for me, as she has always been: to act as sounding board for ideas, to give encouragement when my spirits flagged and sometimes, simply to get me to sit down and get on with it. She does not need to read the book. She has already heard every word that is in it and a good deal more that didn't make it.

ACKNOWLEDGEMENTS

She disclaims all interest in history, however, which is a pity, otherwise I would have told her even more ...

It is now traditional to say that all the mistakes, incorrect reporting of facts, silly comments and foolish opinions are all entirely my own and nobody else should be blamed for them. I hereby solemnly repeat that assertion, but not for the sake of tradition; there is simply no one else to blame.

INTRODUCTION

For the good that I would, I do not: but the evil which I would not, that I do.

        – St. Paul to the Romans – *Romans 7:19, The Bible, King James Version*

Empires are not inherently evil; they have merely had a bad press. They are the creations of highly organized societies of people that, from a particular confluence of circumstances, imperatives and opportunities, act collectively to impose their influence over vast regions of the planet and the people who inhabit them. Being of human creation, they display in their histories all the good and evil of which humans are capable.

All empires require fuel to come into being, to grow and to persist, but what precisely fuels them is not always clearly perceived. Empires are often thought to result from no more than people's greed, avarice and lust for power, but successful empires require more than such base motives. Empires based solely on such motives would not last long. Which is not to say that such motives are absent in successful empires, only that in order to grow, flourish and persist, they require much more than mere avarice.

In ancient times, the Roman Empire, although fuelled by the immense riches it derived from its far-flung Empire through exacting tributes and levying taxes, established such a successful sanctuary of peace within its borders that cities queued up to join. In the end, the Pax Romana in Western Europe was not so much destroyed by barbarians who attacked Rome, as by the thousands living outside the empire that streamed across its borders seeking sanctuary from attacking hordes. It became such an unmanageable mess, that the fabric of the Empire eventually frayed due more to the inability of the administrative machine to keep it together than to the inability of the military machine to protect it. Their empire was fuelled by treasure, but maintained by peace, law and order.

As it was with the Romans, so it was with all later European empires, including the British Empire: they were fuelled by economic advantage. The British Empire was not built because of a deliberate, coordinated plan to establish a world empire but rather, it came into being as a result of complicated factors operating over a long period of time, all of which originated from Britain's drive to trade with the world at large.

Britain, as most European powers, regarded its imperialist policies as a benefit to itself and to the colonial peoples. Many Europeans truly intended to bring the advantages of European civilization and the light of Christian religion to backward peoples, while trade benefited both sides. They had no qualms, under the circumstances, that the home country benefited most. The empire was thus seen as a vehicle for good, and in the colonies there is ample evidence of the good that it did. But the evil that all too often accompanied empire building overshadowed much of the good that might have been intended.

In the beginning, for example, the Spanish Empire in South America was fuelled only by gold; especially gold that was already mined and in its metal form. The Spanish Royals commanded 'get gold despite all hazards'. Fabulous treasures, but especially shiploads of gold were thus plundered from the indigenous cultures and shipped to Spain. The Spanish Empire building forays into South and Central America were no more than extended bank robberies and mayhem on a grand scale. Obtaining great quantities of gold was clearly always an important objective of their efforts at empire building. Gold certainly does fuel empires.

But gold and treasure played no direct role in the European colonization of South Africa. The southern tip of the African continent did not seem to hold any economic advantage for colonization or promise of gold. Initially it was colonized to serve not as a repository of treasure but merely as a necessary facility on the way to treasure – the treasure of trade with the Far East and India. Nevertheless, the gold of South Africa, the greatest gold deposits that would yet be discovered, were there; they were merely very well hidden in the eastern highlands of the sub-continent, where Europeans had never set foot.

That, then, is the story of this book – how South Africa's gold came to be discovered and its role in growing and sustaining the British Empire. Very importantly, it is also about how, but especially why, the discovery of such immense riches led to the tragedy and human suffering and the first modern war: the war that ended the 19th century and started the 20th century in an orgy of bloodletting, but still served only as the curtain raiser for much more devastating conflicts in Europe.

The South African War started late in 1899 and lasted for a mere nine months as a conventional war, but further hostilities, in the form of guerrilla warfare, would last for nearly two further years. It broke the thirty-year Victorian peace and served as the testing ground for new, high-tech weapons. It was closely observed by Germany, France and the other European powers who were anxious to see what effect the new weaponry would have on battlefield tactics and strategy. They wrote and published detailed military evaluations of each battle, but still they were not sufficiently prepared to avoid using these weapons to stage an even greater tragedy: the First World War.

The turbulent history of empire building and colonization in South and Southern Africa weaves a rich and interesting tapestry of people, places and events. It is a very human story. It tells of people filled with idealism, courage and determination, conquering all obstacles in their way. It also tells of people caught in a maelstrom of events they did not understand, could not control and did not know how to deal with, but who still survived. It is a tale also of greed and fear and hate. Bigotry, ignorance and arrogance all play their part in this human drama. But eventually it is a story of the human spirit. A story of how, despite setbacks, trials and tragedies, the indomitable human spirit survives and eventually prospers.

The book follows the story of the European colonists at the tip of Africa and how the seeds of the later conflict with Britain were sowed and nurtured by events and circumstances which were present virtually from the beginning. The road to war is indeed a long, but fascinating one. The road starts in the Cape Colony, from the inheritance of the Dutch East India Company and the later take-over by Britain. It then winds its way inland, following the Dutch colonists in their swaying, creaking, white-tented ox-wagons over the waving grasslands of the interior and over the precipitous, rugged mountains of the eastern seaboard. It is woven through much of their travels and travails and their eventual settlement north of the Vaal River. The impact they had on the lives of the indigenous peoples of the continent was dramatic. And that too was an important step on the road to war. Most of that road had been built before the discovery of gold in the Transvaal; only after its discovery would it become the highway to tragedy.

The story of Transvaal gold did not start with the discoveries on the Witwatersrand. There is an older and even more colourful prologue to gold mining on the Rand. It stands in the tradition of the 49'ers and the Australian gold diggings. Indeed, many of the same salty and colourful, hard working, hard swearing, hard drinking characters make their appearance first in California and Australia before showing up in the warm, humid and densely wooded creeks, gulches and ravines of the spectacularly mountainous eastern Transvaal. However, although the fields were rich in gold, the economic impact was not great. It would not yet be fuel on the fire of the British Empire. Before South Africa could become a desirable addition to the empire in its own right, a few further elements were required.

First, in the western part of the country, one of the major diamond fields of the world was discovered. The city of Kimberley arose as if conjured up from the sparse veldt. From a necessary facility, South Africa started to look more like a colonial proposition for Britain, but also to other European powers. The diamonds of Kimberley would prove to be a necessary prerequisite to the success of gold mining on the Witwatersrand. There the necessary capital base was accumulated; capital that would be required to get at the heart of South Africa's gold. Most importantly, the Kimberley experience formed and moulded the financial and business acumen of most of the men who would later be deprecatingly dubbed 'the Randlords' by an unappreciative London press.

Only then could the curtain rise on the main event – gold. The problem was not discovering gold on or near the Witwatersrand – everybody knew it was there. It was found all over the region, but where could it be found in payable quantities? Payable gold was discovered on the Witwatersrand by a lucky Australian prospector, George Harrison. The Witwatersrand is really a 40-mile long, 10-mile deep, rocky promontory with, at many places, white waters gushing from its northern face. It rises from the surrounding high inland plateau, unsurprisingly called the highveld, to nearly 6,000 feet above sea level. On this lofty, treeless savannah, they started building the city of gold, evocatively called Igoli by the Zulus, who would flock there in their thousands to work on the mines. Johannesburg was born. And what a bonny, booming baby it was.

It is impossible to appreciate or to understand the happenings on and around the goldfields of the Witwatersrand during the latter half of the 19th century without appreciating the historical context within which they took place. Was the discovery a blessing or a curse? It would appear that it was both. It would make the Rand, as the gold mining area soon became known, the economic heart of the whole sub-continent. It would shift the economic balance inland and it would create a dilemma of epic proportions for the Dutch settlers living there. They could not survive without the Rand, but they could not live in peace with it either.

This book is devoted to describing, from the earliest events onward, how people and circumstances developed to the point where war was seen by the two major protagonists as their preferred next step. How did it happen that the Dutch-speaking Transvaalers, who called themselves Boers, found that they could not tolerate the British, the British colonials, and the other Europeans and Americans who streamed to the Rand, although these people were the economic saviours of their indigent little republic? How did two academically brilliant scholars – Sir Alfred Milner, a Balliol scholar from Oxford and Jan Christiaan Smuts, a double first from Cambridge – come to oppose each other from such very divergent perspectives? And how did an enigmatic anachronism such as Paul Kruger come to play the central role in South African politics and to dominate its history to the end of the 19th century? This is the fascinating story of this book. But it also depicts the drama of the role of South Africa's gold in fuelling the British Empire and paving the road to the South African war.

From the context of the pre-history, discussed in the first part of the book, the chain of events that prepared the stage for later developments is followed. One might well ask why the discovery of such vast wealth was accompanied by so much distress and so little general prosperity, especially among the local black population. How was the stage set before the first white Dutch immigrant farmers arrived and how did the arrival of the settlers affect the lives of the settled population? All these matters impacted on the events that led to the final denouement. There are many perspectives on the questions raised by these events. They have been researched and discussed by scholars from the disciplines of history, philosophy, sociology, economics, finance and mining, each adding an insight illuminating an aspect of the whole. Authors have ranged from Liberals to Marxists, from serious academics to political apologists to outright proselytizers and the Afrikaner myth engineers.

In Part Two, the story is related of the South African Republic, an amalgam of four miniscule republics originally founded by the immigrant Boers. Their political action stemmed from, and created, certain imperatives that were later developed into policies and actions by the Transvaal polity that carried the germ of their own destruction. Gold, first discovered in the eastern region of the Transvaal, had manifold influences and repercussions for the peoples of that region, but failed to make much impact on the Transvaal polity as a whole. It also represents the first influx of the bane of the Transvaal Boers – the *Uitlanders*. They followed their own imperatives in exploiting the alluvial riches of the area.

Parts Three and Four deal with the turbulent, challenging and boisterous years of the discovery of gold on the Witwatersrand: how the conflicting imperatives of the parties continually threatened to, and on a few occasions did, escalate into violence. There was rampant capitalism, opportunism, great entrepreneurship and cynical exploitation. There was intrigue and backstabbing, but most of all there was the brooding presence of the old President of the Transvaal – Paul Kruger. These entropic elements, stirred together, became a powder keg that eventually exploded in 1899. The particular perspective of this narrative is to follow the role that gold, entrepreneurs, empire builders and the promise of wealth beyond avarice played in this process.

The imperatives to find and exploit the Transvaal gold were as manifold and as divergent as were the parties involved. Apart from the indigenous population and the Boer colonists, adventurers and fortune-seekers arrived from all over the world, as well as highly schooled tradesmen and professionals. Members of virtually every nation on earth made valuable contributions to the eventual success of the enterprise. There was adventure, courage and determination on all sides. This is thus not only a story of South Africans, nor even a story only of South Africa, it is a story of humankind, of humans working, striving and intriguing against the odds and each other – competing but also cooperating.

It all took place long, long ago in a land far, far away ...

Part One

Irreconcilable expectations

~~~❦~~~

CHAPTER ONE

SETTING THE STAGE

Europe, gold and Africa

*E*x *Africa semper aliquid novo* – loosely translates as 'out of Africa there is always something new'. This was the Roman view of the continent and they were very well acquainted with it. Indeed, their empire included the whole of the north coast of the continent and it was a prized possession. In order for the young Roman Republic to become a major European power in the first place, she had successfully to meet the challenge from Africa: the Phoenicians of Carthage. Carthage was already a great Mediterranean military and trading power when the Roman Republic was still in her infancy.

But the deep interior of the continent always remained a mystery to the Romans. Unlike the Egyptians and the Phoenicians, the Romans never ventured much beyond the Pillars of Hercules into the Atlantic Ocean, or down the east coast of Africa via the Red Sea. Herodotus, however, recounts that Pharaoh Necho (610–595 BC) wished to determine whether Africa was circumnavigable. Accordingly, he commissioned a number of ships manned by Phoenicians to undertake the voyage. This fleet sailed via the Red Sea into the Indian Ocean and down the east coast of Africa.

Every year they built a temporary settlement further along the African coast in order to plant a crop. After they had harvested it, they would continue on their journey along the coast. In the third year of their journey, they sailed through the Pillars of Hercules from the Atlantic side and returned to Egypt. They reported that they had 'rowed until the sun rose over their right shoulders'. Herodotus seems sceptical, but since we now know Africa to be circumnavigable, the story gains credibility.

Herodotus also mentions a Carthaginian called Sataspes, who, because he had used violence against a maiden, was given a choice by the Great King Xerxes of being impaled on a stake or of sailing around Africa. That was not a difficult choice. He elected to attempt the circumnavigation but after many months at sea, he lost heart. He returned to 'civilization' and reported that 'at the farthest point he had reached, the coast was occupied by a dwarfish race' and 'whenever he landed, they left their towns and fled to the mountains; but his men did them no wrong, only entering into their cities and taking some of their cattle'.[1]

What is certain, however, is that Europeans did not always harbour such a favourable impression of Africa as the Romans did. Until they had developed sea-going craft and navigational equipment that allowed them to travel down the Atlantic west coast of Africa, the interior remained impenetrable. Between Europe and the interior of Africa, there is the vast and impassable wasteland of the Sahara Desert, severely discouraging overland exploration. The rest of the continent was consequently screened from the European view and Africa was generally perceived as the 'Dark Continent'. But a Dark Continent could hold many dark, but exciting secrets. Thus, to the European mind it was surrounded with an aura of mystery.

It is interesting to look at some of the ideas and events that shaped the European perception of Africa – it was after all with these perceptions and ideas in mind that they eventually set out to discover and explore the continent. Africa was the fabled land of the golden city of Ophir; it was where the fabulously rich gold mines of King Solomon lay, waiting for rediscovery. The Queen of Sheba was also out of Africa and of her beauty and wealth the Old Testament of the Christian Bible is unstinting in its praise. However, in the mediaeval European mind, somewhere, deep within the vast unexplored and unknown continent, also lay the amazing kingdom of Prester John. His was a much more immediate reality for them. He was supposed to be a descendant of the Magi and possessed great wealth.

During the 1130s, Turkish power threatened the Crusader kingdoms in the Holy Land. These kingdoms urgently sought aid from Christian Western Europe. Around 1145, Hugh, Bishop of Jabala, met Pope Eugenius to ask for help. Otto von Freisingen, Bishop of Freising, recorded in his *Historia de Duobus Civitatibus* (1158) that Hugh told the Pope about Prester John, a Christian priest and king whose kingdom was in the extreme Orient. The point Hugh made to the Pope was that they (the Crusader kingdoms) could not expect help from Prester John because he was cut off from them by the River Tigris.[2]

In 1165 the Emperor Manuel Comenius of Byzantium received a (forged) letter allegedly from Prester John. The forgery was quite clever, obviously being based on Otto von Freisingen's report. It played on the hopes and fears of the Europeans for deliverance from the Turks by this, reputedly the mightiest of all Christian Kings.

In part, the letter read:

I am a zealous Christian and universally protect the Christians of our empire, supporting them by our alms. We have determined to visit the sepulchre of our Lord with a very large army, in accordance with the glory of our majesty to humble and chastise the enemies of the cross of Christ and to exalt his blessed name.

For gold, silver, precious stones, animals of every kind and the number of our people, we believe there is not our equal under heaven.

The letter caused a sensation. Not only were copies circulated widely, but excerpts were even made into song. The official response to the letter was from Pope Alexander III, who sent a Papal emissary in 1177 with a letter for Prester John, carried by his physician, Magister Philippos. Nothing further was ever heard of the letter, the physician, or of Prester John.

Prester John was originally thought to rule in Asia, but as trade increased European familiarity with that continent, it became apparent that the priest king was not there. By the 14th century, all searches for Prester John and his kingdom in Asia had proved fruitless. Rather than give up on this hopeful and glamorous legend, however, Europeans decided that they must have been looking on the wrong continent. Where better to seek this mysterious kingdom, then, than on the continent of mystery itself? They turned their eyes towards the interior of Africa. Always associated with fabulous riches, Africa could easily harbour the most fabulously rich and powerful king in all Christianity.

There was an actual Christian kingdom there, the Nestorian kingdom of Abyssinia, latterly known as Ethiopia. East Africa was sometimes conflated in European thinking with the 'Indies', and so here, they thought, must be that great Christian King in the East. It remains a striking phenomenon of the European psyche that, centuries after the fall of the Crusader countries, when European exploration of the coastal waters of Africa began, they were still on the lookout for signs or tidings of the kingdom of the mighty Prester John.

The Portuguese sent several expeditions to make contact with Prester John's kingdom and the reports that came back confirmed the belief that he had finally been found. Thus, it came about that it was in Africa that Prester John's kingdom was thought to lie when the earliest printed maps of Africa first appeared. The legend eventually passed from common belief, but not before leaving a number of maps illustrating this wonderful myth. As far as Europeans were concerned therefore, thoughts of Africa constantly intermingled fact with fiction and legend, but, somehow, Africa was always associated with visions of gold and fabulous wealth.

The Arabs and the Chinese enjoyed much more early success in trading with Africa. Their trading relations with African coastal communities thus date from far earlier. They concentrated on relations with the African east coast and colonized it right down to the spice island of Zanzibar. The Mediterranean galley ships of the Europeans were unsuited to navigating the waters along the African coast, but the ships used in the North Sea offered greater promise. It is from the latter that the successful Portuguese caravels were later developed.

When the Portuguese Prince Henry the Navigator set out with his new ships and navigational technology, it was to the African coast that he turned in the hope of finding gold and wealth.[3] The indigenous black people of Africa had of course been known to

Europeans for centuries. They were always highly regarded for their physical strength, superior endurance and ability to perform hard labour. When Prince Henry did not find much gold on these travels, he quite contentedly settled for the black variety – slaves. Slaves were already being traded by the local kings and chieftains with Arab traders, as they had been doing for centuries. Some evidence suggests that these West African societies had been involved in trade with Western Europe, through various intermediaries, from as early as 7000 BC. However, their first direct contact with Europeans actually occurred only during the 15th century.

It is remarkable that the slave trade never really reached southern Africa.[4] Whereas black slaves were obtained in great numbers from both the east and the west coasts of Africa, where poor, luckless individuals were provided in greater numbers by local rulers than by direct Portuguese slave hunts, slaves never were taken from the south to the same extent. The geography of Southern Africa largely isolated the region, thus protecting its people from these ravages.

After leaving Luanda in Portuguese Angola on the west coast of central Africa, a ship could not find a safe harbour along the dangerous African shore until it reached the southern part of Mozambique on the African east coast. There were harbourages available at and around the Cape of course, but the coast is swept by dangerous currents, hidden rocks closer inshore, extreme winds and massive waves, known as Cape rollers. The whole region was thus best avoided.

Added to these navigational obstacles is the fact that on the western shore, south of the mouth of the Congo, there are no navigable rivers giving access to the southern African hinterland. The habitable interior is also separated from the west coast by the oldest and most formidable desert in the world – the Namib. Beyond that, lies still more desert. Although not quite as barren as the Namib, the Kalahari stretches up to the Vaal River, while the semi-desert of the Great Karroo stretches down almost to Cape Town. The lush Mediterranean-like beauty of the Cape of Good Hope is a veritable oasis in the arid surrounding landscape, which continues north for hundreds of miles along the west coast.

The difficulty of access exists only from the west coast, but matters were different on the east coast. There the interior of the southern sub-continent was accessible and the slave trade would thrive from Delagoa Bay in the 18th century. The indigenous inhabitants of Southern Africa were thus not completely isolated from the rest of the world, nor were they spared the ravages of the slave trade. When the first white settlers met up with the black peoples of the interior, they were already raising white corn as their staple food. To this day South Africa is one of the largest producers and consumers of white corn, due to the native people's traditional preference for this product against the yellow variety. Exactly how corn reached these tribes from Mexico is unknown, but the most reasonable assumption would be that it was introduced by Arab traders. Arab traders had been trading up and down the African east coast for centuries.

Similarly, it appears that the locally grown marijuana (known locally as *dagga*) is not indigenous either. Although it has been traditionally used by most of the native inhabitants, including the insular and shy San (Bushmen) for as long as anybody can remember, the local product is apparently of Chinese origin.

It is unlikely that these tribes traded directly with either the Arabs or the Chinese. However, the well-known international trade network in which the impressive Limpopo Valley settlements played a vital part, even before Great Zimbabwe became the most important link, would have been readily accessible to most Southern African tribes south of the Limpopo.[5]

In 1815, Britain recognized the right of the Portuguese to take captives between Cape Delgado and Delagoa Bay in Mozambique. The export of slaves from northern Mozambique rose from 47,000 during the first decade of the 19th Century to 129,000 during the decade from 1820 to 1829. Some evidence suggests that this increase, and especially the low price paid for slaves, is probably the single most important event that gave rise to 'the time of troubles'. These terrible times in South Africa have a direct bearing on the later events described in this book. It set the scene that confronted the Dutch settlers and the gold diggers when they penetrated the region.

The people of South Africa

When referring to the indigenous peoples of Southern Africa, one must tread warily. Whether or not Africa, and more specifically perhaps, the western part of the promontory known as the Witwatersrand, is the cradle of humankind is moot. It is, however, a matter of archaeological record that the interior of South Africa, and particularly the area later known as the Transvaal, have been inhabited by humans and their anthropological forebears for hundreds of thousands of years.

Who these original people were cannot be established with any degree of certainty – in fact, not even with uncertainty. In this respect, Southern Africa is obviously not unique. The identity of prehistorically indigenous peoples is enigmatic all over the world. However, these people would be the only ones who truly qualify to be called indigenous. All others migrated at one time or another into the areas they now occupy.

Almost invariably, the approach relating to the indigenous peoples of southern Africa has been Euro-centric. It was largely the white man's delusion, perhaps honestly, but certainly conveniently, held that the black tribes of South Africa were migrating south into the empty interior just about the same time as the white settlers were busy migrating northwards into the same empty space.

Nothing could be further from the truth. The archaeological record (as well as extensive linguistic and other studies) shows that the interior of the country had been populated for many thousands of years. It appears that the inhabitants of longest standing are the San and Khoi. They were widely dispersed in population groups throughout the sub-continent. In the interior, over centuries, black peoples moving down from the north were displacing the lighter-skinned Khoi and San groups.

Although Early Iron Age occupation of the Transvaal is certain, it has not delivered the overwhelmingly rich evidence of its activities that the Late Iron Age has, especially from about AD 1400 and later. The southern highveld was the focus of extensive human occupation and during the same period, numerous settlements arose on the eastern Transvaal escarpment as well. In whatever way these societies developed, the evidence is clear that the Early and Late Iron Age inhabitants of the Transvaal were Bantu-speaking peoples. They were black people, as opposed to the San and Khoi peoples who also inhabited the area and who were hunter-gatherers, speaking an unrelated language and not practising metallurgy.

Among the Bantu speakers living south of the Limpopo, four broadly defined groups are usually distinguished. They are the two large linguistic groups of the Tswana-Sotho and Nguni speakers, followed by the smaller Venda-Lemba and Tsonga groups. These distinctions are essentially linguistic ones. For the sake of clarity, the later geopolitical appellations of Transvaal, Free State, Natal and the Cape Colony will be used throughout.

Broadly speaking, and with only minor exceptions, the Nguni-speaking people reside on the coastal and inland regions of Natal and in the eastern coastal parts of the Cape Colony. They count among them probably the three best-known black nations of South Africa: the Swazi, the Zulu of Natal and the Xhosa of the Eastern Cape. There are many clans within each of these broad groupings. For example, there is the Thembu, a Xhosa clan with its own identifiable culture and distinct history. Ex-President Nelson Mandela is a Thembu hereditary chief, recognized as an aristocrat among all the Xhosa.

The Tswana-Sotho speakers generally occupy the Transvaal, the Free State and the adjacent western regions that include the vast and beautiful country of Botswana. The Venda-Lemba is a relatively small group that lives exclusively in the north-eastern, Soutpansberg area, of the Transvaal.

Among the Tswana-Sotho-speaking people, there was very little development in the way of state formation. The absence of true state formation among the Tswana has been attributed to fissiparous tendencies within their chiefdoms. The social and political structure of both the Sotho and Tswana, before the 'time of troubles' is striking for its fragmentary nature. This great weakness made these communities very vulnerable when they came under pressure during the Difaqane, as the 'time of troubles' is more properly known.

All Tswana ruling lineages can be traced to one of three founding ancestors, called Morolong, Masilo and Mokgatla. Morolong appears to have lived in the western Witwatersrand around the 13–14th centuries; Masilo appears to have lived in the northern Witwatersrand area around the 14–15th centuries; Mokgatla appears to have lived in the north-eastern Witwatersrand area around the 15–16th centuries.

The Witwatersrand therefore appears to be the heartland of the Tswana speakers, but when the first Dutch settlers arrived, the Witwatersrand appears to have been wholly depopulated. The later history of these Tswana ruling lineages is marked by fission and division into more and more chiefdoms. Eventually the Tswana inhabited the whole of the Transvaal as well as areas to the west and northwest.[6]

In the northeastern Transvaal, the Pedi formed what could be described as a state in a loosely organized 'federation'. It was the only state formation among the Tswana and is discussed here in some detail, as the Pedi play an important role in the history of gold and war in the Transvaal.

A Tswana chiefdom is really a 'tribal estate' with the chief as estate manager; it is an integrated unit made up of three separate delineated areas, each area set aside for a specific purpose. There was a residential section which was large enough to be termed a village or even a town. In the western Transvaal, some towns were surrounded by sturdy stone walls. The towns, called *metse*, were closely settled and accommodated perhaps some 25,000 people. Next, there was arable land that the chief, who possessed supreme executive, legislative and judicial power, allocated among family households. A family household was the smallest component of a chiefdom. Finally, there was land designated for grazing, access to which was also controlled by the chief.

As will be seen in later chapters, the efficiency of this socio-economic political system was generally capable of, and did deliver, substantial economic surpluses. It was on this ability that the labour policy of the gold mines relied for the efficacy and cheapness of the migratory labour system.

The Pedi, situated in the lush eastern Transvaal, is a Tswana chiefdom that is different from the others. It can be argued that the higher rainfall area that they inhabited condensed the area required by the population for economic exploitation. This smaller, more densely populated area thus allowed the Pedi chief to amalgamate a number of separate 'tribal estates'.

This structure led to the Pedi to adopt a hierarchical social structure, headed by a royal lineage (*bakgomana*), although he was really a paramount chief. The system was flexible in that aliens were readily incorporated and accepted among the commoners. Slaves or captives were the lowest levels in their hierarchy.

The Pedi polity, however, can be described neither as a state, nor as a nation. Rather, it is a federation of chiefdoms built by force and marriage. The Pedi rulers were able to maintain their rule from the Soutpansberg Mountains in the north, to as far south as the Vaal River. Although the rule was initially established by force of arms, it was maintained by the giving of royal wives to subordinate chiefs and the recognition of local autonomy.[7]

Sekhukhune, a Pedi paramount chief, was destined to play a terminal role in the fortunes of the first Boer Republic in the Transvaal.

The Difaqane

The 'time of troubles' is known by various names among the people of South Africa, but most often it is called the 'Difaqane'. The word conveys the idea of a forced removal and therefore emphasizes the uprooting of settled communities that took place because of the prevalent violence. The Xhosa use the word *Mfecane*, which might be derived from the word *ukufaca* meaning to be weak and emaciated from hunger.[8]

The importance of the events during this period can hardly be overemphasized. The present demographic structure of South Africa owes much to the events that occurred during the two crucial decades between 1820 and 1840.[9] It is not surprising that the causes and effects of such cataclysmic events have been a subject of contention between historians for many years past. Although much of what happened will forever remain hidden by the smoke of chaos, modern research and discovery have resulted in a much clearer picture, slaying many myths in the process. The overall impact of the Difaqane was also varied: some societies were severely devastated; some were forced to migrate and establish themselves in other parts of Africa; others withstood the traumas and even consolidated their position.[10]

We now know that the disturbances began in about 1817. Fundamentally, the cause was a struggle that developed between certain Nguni tribes (clans) to gain access to trading with the Portuguese through Delagoa Bay. This is modern-day Maputo, formerly Lourenço Marques and the capital of the ex-Portuguese colony of Mozambique. Dingiswayo was a powerful chief of one of the clans, the Mthethwa. He had long dreamt of gaining access to trading via this bay. However, other tribes who inhabited the southern, western and northern approaches, jealously guarded access to the bay. Dingiswayo apparently did not take any aggressive action to realize his dream, but another clan, the Mabudu, struggled continuously and eventually gained access to the southern shore of the Bay. They then entered into an alliance with Dingiswayo, fulfilling the latter's dream of direct access to the Bay.

Zwide was another powerful chief in the area. He and his tribe lived inland and to the west of the bay. This new alliance now cut off his access to the Delagoa Bay trading area and this is what probably drove him to attack the two allies in 1817. He won the fight, killing Dingiswayo in the process but in so doing, he unwittingly initiated the great Difaqane that would engulf the whole sub-continent.

Shaka, the man who would become the great warrior king of the Zulu, was then only a young commander in Dingiswayo's army. The Zulu were at that time only one of the Nguni clans, and one of the smaller ones at that. Shaka found himself in Dingiswayo's army because the Zulu owed allegiance to Dingiswayo. But Shaka was a military genius. He vowed to take revenge for the defeat suffered by Dingiswayo's forces. He was such an impressive warrior and military strategist that he was soon given command of the whole army and within two years, he was ready to do battle with Zwide.

Shaka's defeat of Zwide was so thorough that Zwide's people and their remaining leaders fled in all directions. One of those leaders,

Soshangane, fled northwards to the Delagoa Bay area where he entered into violent conflict with the people living along his escape route, but he also entered into trading arrangements with the Portuguese 'for the supply of ivory, slaves and other wares'.[11] Large-scale anarchy then ensued, spreading out in an ever-widening circle, the epicentre of which was in the hinterland of Delagoa Bay.

Later events, including two years of massive drought and failed crops, sent further shock waves of refugees south over the Kei River and into the eastern Cape. Other groups fled west over the Drakensberg, killing and pillaging as they went, thereby destabilizing the Cape Xhosa and the Sotho communities in the Free State. The refugees plunged into, raided and drove settled communities from their homes, who, in turn, did the same to communities along the path of their flight with the effect of falling dominos. The fragmented Sotho and Tswana communities could not hold their own in the ensuing chaos. The whole of the eastern part of the South African sub-continent was thus thrown into a state of violent turmoil.

Fortunately, there were also stabilizing forces at work. Moshweshwe, a chief with a south Sotho power base in the mountain stronghold of Thaba Bosiu, and chief Sekwati of the Pedi tried with some success to halt the chaos. Moshweshwe's efforts would result in the modern state of Lesotho, but the Pedi would eventually be emasculated as a political and military power by the British. But at the time of the Difaqane, these two chiefs set up new centres of power and order in their respective strongholds. They became safe havens for people fleeing from the murder and mayhem of the Difaqane and afforded them an opportunity to start rebuilding their lives under the auspices of these powerful chiefs.

The Difaqane had a devastating impact on the Tswana-Sotho speakers. Apart from the Pedi, many of their chiefdoms had been severely disrupted, dislocated and the communities scattered. The fact of their fragmentary settlements had made them vulnerable in the first place. After the dispersion of the Difaqane, they were even more vulnerable.

Even the Pedi were severely tried. They were almost the first victims of the fleeing Zwide, who nearly destroyed their economic power base by his incessant cattle raids. This was followed by

invasion in 1822, again from Zululand, by Mzilikazi and his followers who had decided to break away from Shaka. Mzilikazi was one of Shaka's outstanding young generals and Shaka apparently had a special affection for him. He regarded Mzilikazi as his protégé. Mzilikazi was actually Zwide's son-in-law, who, together with his followers, had changed sides from Zwide to Shaka.

Mzilikazi's break with Shaka was a result of a sharing of the spoils of war. After a successful military campaign in which many cattle were captured, Mzilikazi disagreed with Shaka on the portion due to the latter. Because he expected severe punishment at the hands of Shaka, Mzilikazi led his followers, mainly from the Khumalo clan, across the Drakensberg and into the eastern Transvaal.

Although Mzilikazi beat the Pedi in battle, he had by no means conquered them. He tried to set up a new territorial base in that eastern area, but continued conflict with the Pedi eventually convinced him to seek safer pastures. Accordingly, Mzilikazi and his followers, who would later become known as the Matabele nation, moved westwards. They established themselves in a safer territorial base in the area of the Marico River, in the Western Transvaal. This was where they were based when the Dutch emigrant farmers first came into the Transvaal.

This, then, was how the stage was set in the interior of the sub-continent when what would later become known as the Great Trek started. Apart from the strong and still cohesive Xhosa nation in the eastern Cape, Moshweshwe had established, and was building, a strong, settled and prosperous nation in his mountain stronghold that bordered the eastern Cape, Natal in the east and the Free State in the west. The open veldt of the Free State had not yet returned to normal and the Tswana-Sotho-speaking communities were still recovering from the devastation of the Difaqane. Under the tyrannous rule of Shaka, a strong Zulu kingdom had developed north of the Tugela River in Natal. But the whole area south of the Tugela, up to the Pondoland border, and bordered in the west by the Drakensberg Mountains and the Indian Ocean in the east, was in chaos. This chaotic area would be the basis of the later colony of Natal.

To the north and west of the Zulu, the Swazi were solidly strengthening and maintaining their territory; north of the Swazi border, the Pedi were consolidating their position in the eastern Transvaal. The southern border of Pedi territory was Swaziland, while it shared part of its southeastern border with the Zulu. Its eastern border, however, was demarcated by the low range of mountains called the Lebombo Mountains, to the east of which lay Portuguese territory. The Lebombo Mountains still form the eastern border of South Africa with the modern state of Mozambique.

To the west of the territory of the Pedi, chaos still reigned in the Transvaal interior, with unsettled communities struggling to survive and many hiding in mountains and forests. Mzilikazi and his Matabele had settled in the western Transvaal on the Marico River, from where they were systematically building a polity by subjugating surrounding tribes and exacting tribute from them.

When the Dutch colonists started immigrating into the interior of the Free State, the Transvaal and Natal from 1836 onwards, it was in this cauldron of bubbling violence that they found themselves. While they might have thought that they were moving into empty land, they in fact became full-scale participants in the Difaqane. Wittingly, or unwittingly, they were another destabilizing force in an already destabilized situation.

To them, it was an opportunity, but fraught with danger. According to their understanding, if they could prevail, nirvana was theirs. How they handled the challenge would make the difference between success and failure in the long term. But much of the story still has to be told before it reaches the stage where the Dutch emigrant farmers arrived on the South African highveld to colonize it.

CHAPTER TWO

BRITISH EXPECTATIONS AT THE CAPE

Prelude to annexation

What was Britain's business at the southern tip of the African continent? Why did it go to so much trouble and expense over so many years to maintain a presence in a part of the world that showed so little promise? These are the fundamental questions. Initially, none of the European powers thought they had any business in that part of the world.

Despite the long-standing European fascination with Africa and things African, nobody seriously seemed to want to colonize the continent – at least not initially. The Portuguese happily traded slaves and other items with the east coast communities, as did other European nations – but nobody planted a colony.

Exploration of the African coast in a southerly direction was merely undertaken to discover a sea route to the east, where true European trading interests lay. Africa was merely a continent lying in the way of a viable trade route to the east. The overland route was arduous, not under European control and thus always subject to interruption, high tariffs and arbitrary duties. The cost of camel caravans was also extremely high. As against that cost, a small caravel with a twenty-man crew could carry the same payload as a thousand camels.[1] After Bartolemeu Diaz circumnavigated the Cape of Good Hope at the end of the 15th century, the sea route was open.

The route was, however, such a long one that, from the start, it appeared necessary to establish halfway stations to revictual ships on their way to and from the east. Without such stations, ships were forced to carry all the crew's food for each leg of the journey from the start of that leg. This restricted the amount of cargo that could be carried, and additionally, because of the lack of technology to keep food fresh for long periods, the danger to health was real.

Because of the navigational hazards, however, the first attempts to build a victualling station on the long and arduous sea journey was not on the southern shores of the continent, but was built by the Dutch East India Company on the island of St. Helena. This island lies somewhat west, off the coast of Africa and to the north of Cape Town. Proceeding to safe harbour on this island was an easier and safer course than approaching the treacherous Southern African coast.

During the 17th century, the East India Companies of the English, Dutch and French all considered the establishment of a base along the route. From the 1590s, the Khoikhoi had already supplied Dutch and English crews with fresh meat in return for tobacco, copper and iron. Everybody was thus aware that Table Bay was a viable site for a victualling station and as navigators became more familiar with Cape waters, the safe harbour of Table Bay became more attractive.

Only the Dutch company took action and on April 6, 1652, Jan van Riebeeck stepped ashore in Table Bay. At the base of Table Mountain, a cliff-faced mesa rising precipitously 3,000 feet out of the Atlantic Ocean, he and his men landed on the northern shore of the 'fairest cape in all the circumference of the world' as Sir Francis Drake so aptly described it. There the Dutch built the first European structure on the southern subcontinent of Africa, a wooden fort.

Van Riebeeck had instructions to establish a vegetable garden, a hospital and facilities to allow ships to take on fresh water and meat. Meat was obtained by trade with the Khoikhoi, who were, initially at least, happy to barter cattle at the wooden fort built by van Riebeeck. Later, relations between the Dutch and the Khoi soured, then deteriorated. Some 200 years or so later, the Khoi had virtually vanished as a separate people, but not without a trace. Their genes live in all Africans, from the Xhosa to the Afrikaners – in all who inhabit the land.

Even long after the founding of the station at the Cape, the journey to the East was still a grave risk and obviously a strenuous trial for seamen. The Cape Journal of the Vereenigde Oostindische Compagnie (V.O.C.) indicates that the sickness and mortality rates among the sailors were very high. Three vessels which arrived on 18 February 1726 had lost between them 251 men out of a total of 557 on board; another two which arrived on 15 February 1732 had lost 370 out of 439; in 1771, twelve ships lost between them 1,034 men – approximately half their crews – chiefly from scurvy.[2]

The facilities of the Cape station were never exclusively used by the Dutch. The British and French merchantmen that plied the route to India and the East routinely docked and victualled at the Cape. Ships had to pay for whatever produce they acquired, so the cost of maintaining the station was partly defrayed by trade with the visiting merchantmen. Indeed, the visit by a whole fleet could bring sudden prosperity to the Cape community, as happened when a French fleet visited the Cape during the American War of Independence.

It was never the intention of the V.O.C. to establish a colony. The station at the Cape was a necessary facility and was supported only as far as it was strictly required for that purpose. In 1657, however, the company revised its stance on colonization. The change of policy was not due to any real change in intention. It was thought at the time that to allow nine company servants to establish their own farms would facilitate the station's effectiveness in supplying the ships. However, events are often wont to take their own course, quite beyond what their initiators might have intended.

The upshot of the matter was that the settler community in the colony grew, albeit slowly. The company changed its policy regarding colonization a few times during its tenure at the Cape, so that the colony did not grow consistently. Even when the company decided to encourage settlers from Europe, the Cape attracted far fewer settlers than, for example, the colonies in North America. By

1795, when the British first annexed the Cape, the free burghers in the colony numbered a mere 15,000.

Its growth as a cultural community cannot be compared to that of the North American colonies either. Probably due to the company's pusillanimous approach to settlement, the colony lacked many of the facilities of a sophisticated European cultural outpost. Because the settlement remained so small for such a long time, and given the humble origins of most of the settlers, education was never a high priority. The three Rs and church catechism were all that was available at several primary schools during the company period. The schools were attended by white and black (slave) children in the settlement.[3]

Although an attempt was made to provide secondary education in 1714, nothing came to fruition until two colonists, Serrurier and Fleck, launched a successful campaign in 1790, 138 years after the founding of the Cape settlement. This lack of a culture of education was to have important repercussions in the history of the Afrikaner and consequently the whole subcontinent.

Another far-reaching development during the V.O.C. years was the importation of slaves. As with the lack of the establishment of education among the settlers, so the establishment of a culture of dependence on slave labour was to have far-reaching implications for the later history of the subcontinent. The first slave shipment arrived in 1658 and another in 1659. The importation of slaves also continued apace under British administration.

Slaves owned by the company never exceeded 600, but by 1795, privately owned slaves numbered 16,839, slightly more than the free burghers in the colony. Due to the lack of plantations at the Cape, it was long thought that Cape slavery was essentially more 'benign' than in comparable slave-owning societies. Based on all the evidence, recent research has come to the conclusion that in the 18th century the Cape was 'one of the most closed and rigid slave societies so far analysed by historians'.[4]

As far as the Cape being a halfway station to the Indies is concerned, it clearly served its purpose well, especially as the settlement grew in its ability to produce food. The trade with the East would have been virtually impossible for the Europeans without this essential facility. This became increasingly apparent, as European interests in India and the East grew more extensive and lucrative. This happy situation was set to continue and probably would have, but for the advent in Europe of Napoleon Bonaparte.

The Cape changes hands

In 1794, the French Revolution gave birth to the rule of Napoleon and the period of the Napoleonic wars followed. During this Europe-wide contretemps, the Netherlands was invaded and occupied by the French. The Patriots came to power in The Hague and forced William, the Prince of Orange, to flee in exile to England. There then arose two governments of the Netherlands: the government in exile, operating from London, and claiming the allegiance of the Dutch, and the government in The Hague, who contested this claim. The government of the Netherlands was, of course, subject to such constraints as were placed upon them from time to time by the occupying French.

By this time, British influence had largely supplanted that of the Dutch in the East Indies. The Cape sea route had also by then become a more important lifeline to trade for them than for any other European power. They were rightly concerned that their sea lines to the east could be cut by denying them access to the Cape. Therefore, Henry Dundas, then Secretary of War in Britain, obtained authorization from the exiled Prince of Orange to send an expedition to take possession of the Cape. The understanding was that any Dutch territory taken by the British would be returned when a general peace was signed.

Sir James Craig, armed with a letter from the Prince of Orange requiring the Commissioner General of the Cape to hand over the government of the colony, was given charge of a small expeditionary force to take over the Cape, with or without the consent of Sluysken, the Dutch Governor. After some local resistance, the task was successfully completed on 16 September,

1795 when the colony surrendered with very few casualties on either side.

The *modus operandi* of the administration would be dictated by the purpose of the takeover. The sole intention of taking possession was to secure the trading route to the Indies for British shipping. In this respect, the British occupation of the Cape differed not one iota from that of the V.O.C. Neither colonial acquisition for its own sake nor colonization were even remotely within British contemplation at that time. Craig, quite correctly, saw his administration as a temporary one and he made as few changes as possible. The legal system would be maintained intact, while Roman-Dutch law would remain the common law of the colony. Local laws would also remain in effect. Local affairs were left to the burgher councillors of Cape Town.

Nevertheless, Craig immediately made one change that signified, more than anything else, what would be the root problem, then and later on, between the British and the burghers of the colony: he required humane treatment for all people in the colony. He immediately outlawed all judicial torture and the more bizarre forms of execution that were regularly carried out in public. Humane treatment of black slaves was totally anathema to the locals. The Cape Court of Justice immediately protested in a letter to Craig, contending that 'cold and rude' slaves 'would hardly consider the privation of life as a punishment, unless accompanied by such cruel circumstances as greatly aggravate their bodily suffering'.[5]

Given this background, it is no wonder that Craig developed a low opinion of the local burghers. He was astounded by

the ignorance, the credulity, and the stupid pride of the people, particularly the Boers. The most absurd ideas as to their strength and importance are prevalent among them, nor indeed is there any opinion on any subject too ridiculous ... not to be adopted by them.[6]

Although the frontier people thus remained somewhat restive, and despite an inconsequential rebellion led by one Marthinus Prinsloo, the British occupation and administration of the Cape continued without any serious challenge until 1803.

The Batavian interlude

By 1803, the erstwhile United Netherlands had become the Batavian Republic. In terms of the Treaty of Amiens, signed in February 1803, the Cape was returned to the Batavian Republic as heir to the V.O.C. The British withdrawal was soon followed by the appointment of Governor Janssens and J. A. de Mist as Commissioner General.

Before the return of the Cape, a debate had been going on in Britain concerning its future. The considered opinion of some very influential people, including the Admiral of the Fleet, Lord Nelson, was that the Cape was not of much use. Since the running of the colony had been very expensive, the government of Henry Addington was glad to be rid of it.

The British were not alone in their misgivings. Whilst the Batavians set out to stay at the Cape they also had substantial reservations about its long-term value as a colony. However, their stay was destined to be short-lived. In 1805, Napoleon resumed hostilities in Europe, the Treaty of Amiens was in tatters and the Cape was again a hostage to fate.

Although the Batavians had very little time to bring about change, they put into effect sound administrative structures and procedures. Nevertheless, what they put in place alienated Cape opinion. The problem was not that the Batavians could not govern or that they were seen as intruders, because they were not. The real problem between them and the burghers stemmed from the same source as between the British and the burghers: it was their ideology. In the view of the burghers, the Batavians were guilty of supreme blasphemy in their tolerant view of creeds other than the Reformed Church and in their willingness to secularize marriage and public education, as well as their liberal humanitarianism. These were innovators of a kind the colonials had been taught to view with extreme suspicion.[7]

The importance of the Batavian interlude is the light that it sheds on the cultural chasm that had developed between the Cape burghers and their European roots. Many later historians, especially Afrikaners, tend to stress the difference in philosophy between the Boers and the British. The truth is that the Boers would have suffered exactly the same frustrations with an administration by any other Western nation. Indeed, had they enjoyed longer tenure at the Cape, the idealistic Batavians, filled with the milk of human kindness, would probably have offended the sensibilities of the Cape colonists much more, and much sooner than the more pragmatic British did.

The basic problem was that the perceptions and value systems of the Western world had moved on, but the Enlightenment had passed the Cape burghers by. The burghers entertained cardinal misperceptions of the principles of the Enlightenment.[8] The appreciation of the philosophical chasm that had developed between the colonists and their own cultural heritage is fundamental to the understanding of later events in the Transvaal and indeed, in 20th-century South Africa.

Britain comes to stay

In Britain, meanwhile, Addington's administration, manned by carefully selected mediocrities, had been caught off-guard by Napoleon's resumption of hostilities in May 1803. Under Addington's administration, the armed forces had atrophied, even the navy had lost half of its effective fighting complement.

With the resumption of hostilities, Napoleon's express aim was to crush the British. He required the facilities of the Batavians to do so. They had no choice in the matter, but were ordered by the French to shut up and put up – which they did. It was thus inevitable that the British would return to the Cape. However, due to the depleted state of the British military, no early action could be taken and the problem of securing the Cape route to the east had to be postponed for more than two years.

In January 1806, a British force of 6,700 troops landed on Bloubergstrand in Table Bay. Governor Janssens had sent a small force to oppose them that was quickly defeated. The Governor surrendered 10 days later after he had initially retreated into the

Hottentots Holland Mountains that majestically screen the Cape peninsula from the interior.

The Napoleonic wars were to last for another nine years, but the British were in the Cape to stay indefinitely. Their aim, like the first time round, was unchanged. The trade route to the Indies around the Cape of Good Hope had to be protected at all costs. The fact that there was a sizeable and territorially ever-expanding colony attached to the Cape was an unfortunate happenstance that would be dealt with on an *ad hoc* basis. But there was a difference in the occupational intent of the British as compared to that of the Batavians. The British had come 'to occupy a fortress', unlike the Batavians, who had come 'to inaugurate a social revolution'.[9]

At the end of the Napoleonic wars in 1815, there was a general pacification among the countries of Europe. Britain returned to the Netherlands all its former colonies that it had taken possession of, except Guinea and the Cape. A treaty between Britain and the Netherlands transferred the Cape Colony to Britain in return for British acceptance of responsibility for the Netherlands' financial commitments of £6 million owed to other European powers during the wars.[10]

Empire and a special colony

With possession of the Cape came responsibility for some 80,000 people spread over some 90,000 square miles. At the Cape lived approximately 25,000 burghers who were the most prosperous members of the colony. The white burghers were of Dutch, German and French origin, although they all spoke a Dutch dialect, which was later to develop into the cultural language of Afrikaans. The slave population accounted for another 30,000 souls, thus giving a total population of around 55,000 people living under settled circumstances.

Du Pré Alexander, the Earl of Caledon, was appointed the first British governor of the Cape. In terms of his instructions, he ruled autocratically – by proclamation, being responsible only to the

Secretary for War and the Colonies in London. For the next 30 years, consecutive British governments viewed the Cape primarily as a military outpost with the result that the first governors were all military men. In September 1811, the Earl of Caledon was succeeded by Sir John Cradock, later Lord Harden. He was again succeeded by Lord Charles Somerset in April 1814. The first governors immediately set about making the British presence permanent and as economically viable as possible.

The single most important principle of British colonial policy, as is to be expected, was that a colony should not be a liability to the mother country. Under the circumstances, it could hardly avoid being a financial liability, but the intention was to keep the burden as light as possible. After all, the whole purpose of obtaining colonies must be to gain an advantage rather than a burden. That is undoubtedly all colonial policy's bottom line, because no country would reasonably consider colonizing a territory unless it at least expected some positive, preferably economic, benefit. This is also the gravamen of Marcello de Cecco's authoritative thesis. His analysis concludes that British Imperial policies, *inter alia*, demanded the following:

1. Britain's role was as a long-term investor in the new countries; and
2. The new countries, including those within the Empire, had to transform British investment into demand for British exports.[11]

The case of the Cape was, however, a special one. The benefit that Britain expected was twofold: in the long term, it expected the Cape to protect the very lucrative trade route to the Indies and in the short term, it was to secure the island of St. Helena, where Napoleon was being held prisoner. The Cape was not seen as a promising 'investment' colony in the mould suggested by de Cecco's analysis. The somewhat restricted imperial expectation of Cape occupation is demonstrated by the manner in which this acquisition's running costs were accounted for in Britain. The Cape administration's accounts were not published with those of Britain's other colonies, but were reported as part of general government expenditure.

The aim was thus to produce the expected benefits of occupation at the lowest possible cost, rather than as an investment that was expected to deliver a profit at some stage, preferably in the not too distant future. Realizing this expectation would prove to be Britain's greatest challenge and probably its greatest failure.

Its greatest dilemma was that for military and naval purposes, only the Cape Peninsula and False Bay were needed. But with these two strategic landmarks came 'a too extensive colony' sparsely populated by a few unruly Dutch herdsmen, with a formidable black nation pressing on its borders and with demoralized Khoikhoi and Bushman scattered about. Only around the Cape were any of the amenities of civilization, or settled forms of administration, to be found.[12]

Nevertheless, the Governors resolutely shouldered the burden and tried to make the best of matters. There was never a consistent British policy at the Cape. It could hardly be expected. Policies must inevitably change as governments in London change and as the personalities and personal agendas of those placed in charge of the colony change. Nevertheless, in the broadest possible sense there was complete consistency in the aims of the policy. Whatever the policy details, the merits or demerits of policies adopted from time to time by Governors, High Commissioners and governments might be, in essence they all strove to achieve the expectation of effective protection of the sea route around the Cape at minimum cost to the exchequer.

When diamonds were first discovered at Kimberley in 1867, the first thoughts of the British officials were that the by then vastly bigger colony would, at last, become economically self-supporting.[13]

The exigencies of British expectations thus demanded policies that would achieve at least the following:

1. Ensure that the settled population of the colony would be peaceful and loyal subjects of the Crown.

2. Establish and maintain an effective agricultural community that would not only sustain the colony itself, but would also be able to generate sufficient surplus to sustain a resident British garrison, victual ships and export produce.

3. Promote a just and equitable administration of law according to the precepts of generally accepted civilized norms of justice within the colony.

4. Stabilize the colony's borders along defensible frontiers.

5. Establish and ensure lasting peace with the peoples neighbouring the colony's frontiers.

Although the British administration at the Cape was largely successful in achieving the first three policy aims, they only achieved them against bitter opposition from the Dutch inhabitants, especially those on the eastern frontier. The last two aims were not to be. Due to various circumstances, the British presence in South Africa grew greater and increasingly expensive. J.S. Galbraith tracks this process admirably and terms it a process of 'reluctant acquisition'.[14]

How these policies influenced the actions and opinions of the Dutch frontiersmen will be told in the following chapter.

CHAPTER THREE

EXPECTATIONS ON THE EASTERN FRONTIER

People's expectations are a function of their background, experience and attitudes. The expectations of the Boers on the eastern borders of the Cape can thus only be understood within the context of their particular history and circumstances.

The term 'Boer' is adopted here with some caution. As so often in South African history, names are loaded with special meanings and one man's pride is another's pejorative. The Dutch word 'boer' merely means farmer, without any special connotations, which meaning it retains in modern Afrikaans. The word, when spelt with a capital 'B' as in 'Boer', strictly indicates a 'white', Dutch-speaking inhabitant of the later Boer Republics, whether he is a farmer or not. The Dutch-speaking colonials of the Cape were termed 'boere' only if they were farmers. The plural form 'Boers' is an Anglicism and is only found in English writing. Both in Dutch and in Afrikaans the plural is 'boere', whether spelt with a lower or an uppercase 'b'.

That the Dutch-speakers of the eastern Cape border area adopted the term 'Boer' as an identity demonstrates the extent to which these 'sons of the soil' saw themselves one-dimensionally as agriculturalists. When what is after all only an economic activity becomes one's total identity, virtually all other human endeavours are placed beyond reach and aspiration. There would be a heavy price to pay for this restrictive mindset, as will appear from later chapters.

But this is not yet the end of possible confusion, because the Dutch speakers at the Cape later came to identify themselves as 'Afrikaners' and never as 'Boere'. Already in 1707, one Hendrik

Bibault described himself as an 'Africaander'. The term served as recognition by them of their 'Africanness' and expressed their permanent adoption of Africa as their home. By necessary implication, it also acknowledged the fact that they were no longer 'European'.

Another element needs to be pointed out. Those who regarded themselves as 'white' and were accepted as 'white' by others who regarded themselves as 'white', adopted the epithet 'Afrikaner'. As later scientific studies have shown, when it comes to being white or not, perception is often reality. Thus, not all who spoke the same language were accepted as Afrikaners.

During the latter half of the 19th century, many Afrikaners came to appreciate that the language they were speaking was no longer proper Dutch. It had in fact developed into a separate language from a Dutch patois, which had itself been the linguistic result of the melting pot of peoples, cultures and languages at the Cape. The language came to be called Afrikaans by its speakers, who included many who were not accepted as Afrikaners.

Later, the term Boere and Afrikaners, both epithets indicating self-perceived white people, became interchangeable. The interchangeability only developed late in the life of the Transvaal republic and gained growing acceptance after the South African War, when Boers wished to identify with the aspirations of the Afrikaners at the Cape. Before that cataclysmic event, they never thought of or referred to themselves as Afrikaners or to the language they spoke as anything but Dutch.

Of course, the Boers of the later Republics and the Afrikaners at the Cape were related by blood and they thus easily identified with each other. The Boers merely represented those Dutch-speaking people, mostly white, but including many of mixed descent, who had moved further away from the Cape through the Trekboer phenomenon and later the Great Trek. However, the Dutch at the Cape and the Boers were eventually sufficiently separated by time and historical experience to allow a significant cultural gap between them to develop. Furthermore, during the time of the Boer Republic's relations with the Cape Dutch were not always equally cordial, nor would their interests always coincide.

Keeping the above in mind and for the purpose of greater clarity, the Cape Dutch will henceforth be referred to as Afrikaners while the eastern Cape Dutch farmers, including those who later removed themselves to the interior will be referred to as Boers.

The Cape melting pot

The melting pot from which came the Boers and the Afrikaners was an interesting mix of European and African people. The grant of farms to free burghers by the V.O.C. encouraged the immigration of women to the colony, but for many decades, men would substantially outnumber women in the settlement. Simon van der Stel, himself born in Mauritius of mixed European and Indian descent, saw, amongst others, to the settlement of 180 French Huguenot refugees, who had fled from religious persecution in France.

Van der Stel settled them along the Berg River among Dutch settlers. He required them as far as possible to learn, worship and communicate with the authorities in Dutch. The normally fiercely parochial French acquiesced, probably because they felt abandoned by their mother country through their late persecution and bolstered by the certainty that they had left it forever. The descendants of the Huguenots would later form a core element of the Afrikaners and the Boers.

The V.O.C. had the whole of continental Europe to draw on for its servants and seamen and did so. Seamen were rarely the best potential settlers and the history of settlement at the Cape bears rich testimony to that fact. They were often some of the roughest and even the most criminally inclined members of European society. Nevertheless, the settlement grew.

After 1750 the directors of the V.O.C. tried to encourage settlement; they succeeded in drawing substantially more German speakers than Dutch speakers. However, the German language never flourished at the Cape mainly because these settlers included more males than females. These men married Dutch women, as well as some free black women, and their children were brought up to speak High Dutch. Notwithstanding the diversity of their backgrounds, the European population at the Cape thus became more culturally uniform, speaking Dutch and practising the religion of the Dutch Reformed Church.[1]

To this European mix must be added the influence of the indigenous Khoikhoi and slaves imported from various parts of Africa and the East. Many slaves were imported from Dutch Malaysia and they enriched the local culture not only with the admixture of their own culture, but also with their rich and spicy cuisine. Added to the French love of good food and wine, a unique, flavourful Cape Malay cuisine of great variety and sophistication was created.

A substantial amount of intermarriage and 'crossbreeding' between all these groups took place. Some of the offspring were accepted into 'white' society, while others, especially those of the Muslim religion, remained outside the enclave of privilege. This development resulted in the gradual development of a free, but subservient, Dutch-speaking 'Cape Coloured' community. The community developed from Malay, Free Blacks, Khoikhoi and 'mixed race' people, living side-by-side with the European community at the Cape. Their numbers greatly increased when the British between 1838–40 finally emancipated all slaves.

The fact remains, however, that within a few decades the European community had become the dominant group. All others had been relegated to a position of legal and political inferiority. This was not only the situation in fact, but its existence came to be accepted as God-ordained and any question as to its correctness regarded as sacrilege. Raising this perception of inequality to the status of divine revelation put it beyond rational debate for more than three centuries, at least as far as the *ingenui* Europeans were concerned.

The reasons for this development have been shown to be quite straightforward. Simply put, European dominance had been part and parcel of V.O.C. policy. They had, after all, both the economic and the military power to dictate the terms of the settlement at the Cape. The factual situation and its concomitant race attitudes came about, specifically because only Company (V.O.C.) servants and freeburghers could hold land or gain political power in the official hierarchy of the colony. But since the Company recruited its servants and free immigrants in Europe and brought few Asian or Eurasian employees and settlers to the Cape, it created the precedent of a political and economic élite, which was almost exclusively European.

By importing slaves, none of whom were European, it intensified the correlation between legal status and race. And by regarding Khoikhoi initially as aliens and later as subjects who were not freeburghers, it effectively precluded them from political and economic advancement in colonial society.[2]

On the other hand, the race attitudes found at the Cape were not unique among settlers from Europe. The same attitudes are found in other parts of the world where Europeans settled. The colonies in North and South America, for example, also developed ideas on race similar to those at the Cape. But then it also has to be remarked that the colonization policies that were followed in those regions were very similar to the policies followed by the V.O.C. at the Cape. In those colonies too, colonial policy resulted in European ownership of the land and political and economic privilege contrasted with Black servility and powerlessness. It is thus not surprising that similar attitudes to race arose in geographically separated colonies.

In as much as the term 'imperialism' is widely accepted to describe 'the expansion of all technologically advanced peoples at the expense of the technologically backward',[3] it is fair to say that South African white and more particularly, Afrikaner race attitudes owe and trace their origins to Dutch imperialism in the 17th and 18th centuries. Many later Afrikaner academics and politicians have laid claim to an Afrikaner history of stoic opposition to imperialism. Afrikaners or Boers, they are far from being imperialism's antagonists. Indeed, they are its children.

Pack your things and trek

The Boers living on the eastern border of the Cape colony at the time when the British finally annexed it in 1806 had arrived there by a process of incessant outward movement from the original Cape settlement. The movement had been continuous virtually from the outset, but had greatly increased in speed and in volume after 1700. The Great Trek, which eventually gave rise to Boer settlements in the Transvaal, was to take place by these people.

It must be kept in mind that it was as little the wish of the V.O.C. as it would later be of the British to create an extensive colony. The main object of the V.O.C., as a trading company, was to profit from trading, specifically in the East. The initial and later attempts at settling 'free burghers' at the Cape had been undertaken with the aim of allowing them to grow food at minimal expense and effort to the company. It was, in a sense, a form of risk management. The free burghers would grow wheat, tobacco and vegetables, make wine and herd cattle at their own cost and risk, the produce of which enterprises, if successful, would then be available to the company to sell to visiting ships. The company always retained for itself the right of first access to visiting ships, while it commandeered produce from the settlers at prices fixed by it.

The V.O.C. indeed tried its best to govern the Cape responsibly. It tried to control the excesses of its appointed officials; it ruled subject peoples, such as the Khoikhoi eventually became, through their chiefs and most importantly, they discouraged the uncontrolled expansion of the settlement. In this latter enterprise, they had more hope than success.

Conditions for the free burghers at the Cape were indeed not particularly difficult. At the beginning of the 18th century, it was still possible for the small farmer to realize 20 per cent per annum on his capital.[4] This situation soon changed and gave rise to the emergence of the 'Trekboer', a term which might loosely be translated as 'itinerant farmer'.

Freebooting colonists

Simon van der Stel, and later his son Willem Adriaan, both V.O.C. governors at the Cape, gave impetus to crop farming, especially vines, in order to meet a real demand. Soon, however, the company was unable to provide sufficient markets for the increased production. By 1705 the crop farmers were experiencing economic difficulties. They lacked sufficient capital and labour to continue successfully. At the same time the Trekboers, being exclusively stock farmers, started to emerge as the most important element in Cape expansion.

There has been much debate about the motivation and reasons for this development. It seems reasonably certain that it was not significantly motivated by business principles. Although the Trekboers required certain supplies from civilization, especially guns and gunpowder, they became substantially self-sufficient. A Trekboer 'used the fat tail of his Hottentot sheep for candle and soap making; he shot game for his meals and used the skin to make *karosses* (blankets) to preserve his own livestock'.[5] Indeed, at the time of the Great Trek in 1835, a man's clothes, from his shoes and trousers to his shirt and hat, were mostly D.I.Y. from game skin.

Although the Trekboers periodically returned to the Cape to sell their hides, ostrich eggs, carcasses and other surplus products, this was not business — it was subsistence. Poor to non-existent roads and extremely long distances made such journeys decidedly uneconomical were they to be undertaken for profit.

There was indeed very little that the authorities in Europe, be they Dutch or British, could do to contain the size of the colony. The free burghers simply freebooted into new territory, but as already noted, without completely severing their ties with the Cape, tenuous as they were. The Cape authorities really had no option but to recognize the *de facto* growth of the land area of the colony. This they did by the establishment of administrative centres further and further away from the government hub at the Cape.

In an attempt to exert some control over the moving frontier, *Drostdye* (magistracies) were set up in Swellendam in 1743, at Graaff-Reinet in 1785 and at Uitenhage in 1803. These wandering farmers were, after all, Cape colonial citizens and to a greater or lesser extent they, the authorities at the Cape, were obliged to accept responsibility for them and their actions.

Landdrosten (magistrates) and *Heemraden* were appointed by the company to represent the Cape administration on the frontier and at least to see some system of justice exist on the ever-expanding frontier. *Veldcornetten*, known as the farmer's friend, were local burghers appointed with some policing and judicial authority and were specifically empowered to call up commandos and keep records of able-bodied male citizens who were liable for military service. All actions against indigenous peoples in which groups of Boers participated as organized commandos, were viewed as 'military' operations.

Of course, the Trekboers were not unopposed in their outward movement because the San and the Khoikhoi generally inhabited the interior of the country. Generally, the Trekboers were able to elbow them out of the way by forcing them to retreat or to remain as labourers. To the north and northeast, however, San hunters of a different mettle confronted them. The Trekboers suffered real anguish at the hands of these people who steadfastly and effectively protected their hunting fields. Even full-scale commando raids, undertaken to wipe out the San people permanently, were singularly unsuccessful in attaining that result. Appeals to the authorities in the Cape also had mixed results. Gradually, however, the San were pushed back and they retreated further inland or accepted incorporation as labourers for the Boers.

There was less serious opposition to the trek in an eastward direction until the Boers came face to face with the first Black nation in the shape and form of the Nguni-speaking Xhosa. The Xhosa were eventually to prove an insurmountable obstacle to the Boers who, by then, had an insatiable appetite for more land.

The ability of the Cape settlement to spread rapidly was the result of a number of factors. Most important among these were 'the quest for water and pasture and the ease with which the indigenous inhabitants could be forced to retreat or to enter service with their stock'.[6] The rapid expansion of the Cape Colony up to 1806 was thus not a function of European expansionism, much less European imperialism. As a first cause, the spreading European colonization was undeniably the result of the settlement of Europeans at the Cape. The racial attitudes of the colonists were also a product of V.O.C. policy, but neither European politics nor European economics drove the colonial expansion. The dynamics and imperatives of the expansion were entirely home grown by what could be termed the de-tribalized* Europeans of the Cape.

Missionaries – the bane of the Boers

The Boers were not the only ones trekking north and east from the Cape. The missionaries soon joined them. The work of Christian missionaries among the indigenous population must be noted since in many respects, they had a substantial influence on events.

Shortly after the first arrival of the British in 1795, the first Christian Protestant missionaries also arrived. Their mission was to send 'the Glorious Gospel of the Blessed God to the Heathen'.[7] To a large extent this theology was anathema to the Dutch Reformed Church of the Boers, although they later relented, but only somewhat. They were never enthusiastic missionaries under the V.O.C. in any part of the world and no more so than at the Cape, where they tended to an even stricter interpretation of Calvinism than either the Netherlands or the Scottish Presbyterians.

The missionary invasion started with the arrival of the first missionaries from the London Missionary Society in 1799 led by Dr. Theodorus van der Kemp, followed by the founding of the South African Missionary Society. Then missionary zeal, in quick

---

*The term 'de-tribalized' is a very useful one, but dates from the late 20th century. Coined by apartheid apologists to describe black people who had all but cut their ties with their traditional areas, but had also not become fully westernized, it is descriptive of any people who are in a transitory stage of cultural and economic development. These 'de-tribalized' black people were indeed developing a modern African culture based on a marriage of many traditions, but adapted to the urbanized, industrialized experience of South Africa. The situation created special problems for the purveyors of inequality as their doctrines were predicated on the existence of rigid separate nationalisms, which had each to be accommodated in a separate, designated 'homeland'. Such ideologues are usually only confused by the facts and therefore tend either to ignore them or to falsify them.

succession, brought the Anglican Church Missionary Society, The Basle Society (Swiss Calvinists), the Paris Society (French followers of Robert Haldane, a Scottish Calvinist) and the American Missionary Society to the shores of South and Southern Africa.

There was very little local missionary enthusiasm at the Cape. Dominee M. C. Vos, the Dutch Reformed Predikant (Minister) of Tulbagh, who was himself of part-slave descent, founded the Society for the Expansion of Christ's Kingdom and in 1824 the Dutch Reformed Church established missions among the Cape Coloured Community, rather than attempting the conversion of 'Kaffirs'.* These were modest attempts in concept, but to its eternal embarrassment, the Dutch Reformed mission was successful and over the next two centuries built up a substantial following under the Cape Coloured population.[†]

It must be obvious that the Boers and missionaries would inevitably be on a collision course. As already indicated, the Boers' *Weltanschauung* diverged to such an extent from that of the rest of the civilized world, especially from that of dedicated missionaries, that they would be predictably incompatible. Janssens, the Batavian Governor, had previously pointed out that the Boers habitually referred to the Khoikhoi as creatures (*schepsels*) rather than as people (*menschen*).[8] It must be pointed out, however, that the word *schepsels* does not have all the negative connotations that the word 'creature' can have in English. It merely means something that has

---

* The word is derived from the Arabic K'fir, meaning heathen. This word was hauled into the Dutch and Afrikaans languages to describe all black people who were heathens in the sense that they were not Christians – at least not initially. The irony is that in Arabic, the word designates any non-Muslim. In its proper sense then, the Boers as well as the blacks, were all equally Kaffirs.

† At that time, the embarrassment did not arise to the same extent as it did later. It arose latterly from the Dutch Reformed Church's unstinting support for apartheid, which included a legal prohibition on 'mixed' worship. Imagine selling the love and charity of Christ to people while telling them that they are unfit to worship in the same church with you. Not surprisingly, this congregation became a hotbed of anti-apartheid agitation and spawned some of its most active and widely recognized opponents, such as Dr. Allan Boesak.

been created, in the sense that 'we are all God's creatures'. It therefore does not deny their humanity *per se*.

The usage quoted by Janssens was not limited to references to the Khoikhoi. All black people were afforded the same treatment and also referred to as 'black things' (*swart goed*), thus denying them human status. Unfortunately, this usage is prevalent among a certain proportion of Afrikaners to this day, although definitely no longer by a majority of them. As will also be shown in later chapters, the denial of human status to people of colour, although pervasive, was certainly never universal among Afrikaners or Boers, even in the heyday of their Republics.

British policy and Afrikaner myths

In trying to achieve their own expectations in annexing the Cape, as discussed in the previous chapter, the British adopted policies that they hoped would achieve those ends, but the impression thereby made on the settled population was not always favourable. The further away from the Cape settlement the Trekboers were, the less amenable they were to the new administration. A number of central events during British administration before 1835 gave rise to some of the building blocks of Afrikaner myths that were later, at the time just before and after the South African War and into the mid-20th century, to be used very effectively to gain and maintain Afrikaner political power.

It cannot be said that the previous relations of the Cape colonials, and the Trekboers, with the V.O.C. and later Batavian administration, were especially cordial. They were not. But the take-over by Britain was even less welcome, although, with minor exceptions, it was accepted in a spirit of mild resignation. To soften the blow, the British decided to keep things pretty much as they were, except for such matters as were incompatible with their moral and ethical standards, especially torture and slavery. Most civil servants were kept in the posts they had occupied under the Batavians. They reported to the Batavians one day and to the British the next.

Law at the Cape

The British deliberately retained the Roman-Dutch legal system as the common law of the Cape colony. Roman-Dutch Law had been the common law of the Netherlands until the Napoleonic wars and had been practised as the common law of the Cape since its founding.

Roman-Dutch Law could be left unchanged because, despite differences of detail, it and English common law, both being based on Roman law, were entirely compatible in their precepts and attitudes to justice and fairness. Both systems were accusatorial in procedure as opposed to the less compatible inquisitorial systems of France and other Continental countries.

Nevertheless, because of the English training that legal practitioners and judges would receive, many English law principles were gradually introduced into Roman-Dutch law at the Cape. This infusion greatly contributed to the further evolution and development of Roman-Dutch law into the common law system that applies in South Africa to this day. This gives South Africa, together with another ex-Dutch colony, modern Sri Lanka, a unique legal system. With the rest of Western Europe, the Netherlands adopted the Code Napoleon as the basis of its legal system, but South Africa escaped that development solely due to the British annexation of the Cape in the course of the Napoleonic wars.

Notwithstanding the good intentions of the British in not replacing the Cape's system of common law, it was British administration of law that would give rise to two seminal incidents in Afrikaner mythology: the so-called 'Black Circuit' of 1812 and the Slagtersnek Rebellion of 1815. The Slagtersnek Rebellion had a direct causal link with the 'Black Circuit'.

The normally high principles of justice demanded by Roman-Dutch law had in practice been severely compromised at the Cape and even more so on the frontier. People of colour received greatly more severe sentences than Europeans did for the same crime. The evidence of white people was always accepted over the evidence of any Khoikhoi witness or witnesses from any other indigenous people. It appears also that no criminal or civil complaints by people of colour against their masters would even be entertained.

Circuit courts established

In order to bring the advantages of impartial justice to the frontiers of the colony, Lord Caledon requested permission from London to establish circuit courts along the lines of the English courts, where High Court Judges made regular tours of country areas.

The more immediate trigger for this request was the constant stream of complaints being received at the Cape against the Boers' treatment of indigenous people, particularly from the Bethelsdorp mission of Van der Kemp and Read. Van der Kemp was a character of epic proportions, but a totally dedicated missionary and protector of his Khoikhoi neophytes. His battle against attempts to stop labour-hungry Boers from indenturing his charges had already commenced under the Batavians. It continued under the British.

The local British officer, Colonel Collins, who had previously been appointed Commissioner for the Eastern Districts, was not sympathetic to the missionary's claims and protestations. He investigated the station, opined that it was of no benefit and recommended its closure, a course of action that would have released the Khoikhoi at the mission for labour to the Boers. James Read then took up the cause of a number of Coloured servants who had claimed to have suffered maltreatment by their employers. The stream of complaints became a flood, some of which found their way to the highest quarters in London.[9]

Lord Caledon quite properly decided that the best course of action would be to allow this flood of allegations to be tested in a court of law. His application to London for authority to institute circuit courts was one of Lord Caledon's first acts, but permission was only received in 1811, when he was about to leave the Cape. Caledon proclaimed the court on 16 May, establishing a quorum of two Justices of the Supreme Court with power to review the decisions of the *Landdrosten* and to try the more serious cases itself. The judges were former V.O.C. and Batavian legal officers van Ryneveld and Truter, the latter being the former's successor as chairman.[10]

The Black Circuit

The first circuit court of 1811 went about its duties without incident. The frontier Boers were not against the exercise of the judicial function at all. Indeed, they were a litigious lot who were fond of nurturing lawsuits. The problem was not law itself; the real problem lay in the concept of equality before the law.

The second circuit of 1812 became infamous among the Boers, who dubbed it the 'Black Circuit' (*De Swarte Omgang*). As Lord Caledon had intended, the circuit court was to be the opportunity and proper forum to sort the chaff from the wheat as far as complaints against the Boers were concerned. With typical missionary zeal, Read and van der Kemp had encouraged their flock to place every possible complaint that they could think of before the court. In the final result the tally came to over 100 murders allegedly having been committed, with some individual Boers standing trial on some 8 or 9 counts.

The judges were, if anything, probably inclined to attach less weight to purely Khoikhoi evidence and even less biased courts would have dismissed most of the cases. It thus happened that the vast majority of cases were in fact dismissed and the accused found not guilty. Nevertheless, there were some convictions; enough to infuriate the Boers.

One would reasonably expect that the Boers would have felt largely vindicated by the proceedings. In any normal society, the opportunity to clear one's name of frivolous accusations in an impartial court of law would be welcomed. Indeed, it would also serve as a lesson to those who too easily make wild accusations that under the rule of law such action serves no purpose, unless some credible evidence backs it up. It was thus a salutary lesson in law to all concerned.

Not so for the Boers. It became a black day in their history, not because they alleged that the judges were incompetent or biased against them, or that unjust procedures were followed, or that the convictions were clearly wrong, or any other criticism of a substantial nature.

Their only complaint was that people whom they regarded as their inferiors had accused them at all. It was a supreme injustice for them to have to face trial in a court of law on the complaint of a party who was not white. Thus, implicit in their attitude is that such 'lowly' beings as Khoikhoi and Blacks had no right to be heard in a court of law, certainly not to complain against their 'betters'.

Given this attitude, there was no possible compromise that a civilized administration could make to mollify them. Sir John Cradock, Lord Caledon's successor, to his credit, did not even try. In fact he was as committed to equality before the law as Caledon had been.

The Slagtersnek Rebellion

It thus happened that in 1815, complaints of maltreatment were laid against one Freek Bezuidenhout, prominent among the 'vagabond' farmers in the wild country over the hills in Graaff-Reinet.[11] Johannes Auret was the *Veldcornet* in charge; he was despatched with some support troops to summon Bezuidenhout to court. Bezuidenhout was in an ugly mood, probably having in mind a repeat of the Black Circuit; he started firing on Auret and his support party. Freek Bezuidenhout was killed in the ensuing shoot-out.

Freek had a brother Hans Jan Bezuidenhout, who swore vengeance. He persuaded some farmers to join him in an armed defiance of the authorities. He also tried to persuade the soldier burghers to join him, but they refused. He then tried to enlist the support of the Xhosa chief Ngcika, but with the same result.

The *Landdrost* of the district, Jacob Cuyler, then acted against the rebels. Cuyler, a hard and unyielding man, was an American loyalist who had come over to the Cape with Baird's troops. He was one of the first 'foreigners' to be appointed to such a position. He managed to persuade the majority of the rebels to surrender and they were pardoned. The hard core who persisted in the insurrection were beaten into surrender by Khoikhoi troops. The latter were a permanent mounted force in smart green uniforms, very effectively used on the eastern frontier. In the skirmishes that followed, Hans Jan Bezuidenhout and one soldier were killed.

After trial in the circuit court, five of the ringleaders were sentenced to death by hanging. Execution by hanging was, in those days, still a public spectacle. The five men were thus brought for hanging to a place called Slagtersnek. When the first of the five men was hanged, the rope broke. The other four were then forced to wait for a couple of hours before a new rope could be procured, while the public grew more agitated by the minute. The hanging then continued and the four others duly met their fate.

'Slagtersnek Rebellion' is clearly a misnomer. It was hardly a rebellion and it did not take place at Slagtersnek. Nevertheless the place made an impression on the spectating public because of the undoubted strain on the nerves caused by the delay in the execution. Consequently, this inglorious episode of lawlessness made it into Afrikaner mythology as proof of the unrelenting persecution of Boers by the British.

Anglicization

Another important element in Boer persecution mythology, and one of the reasons later advanced by Piet Retief in his explanatory *Manifesto of the Great Trek*, was the policy of Anglicization, followed by Lord Charles Somerset from April 1814 onwards. Lord Charles agreed with Bathurst, the Colonial Secretary in London at the time, that the Cape Dutch must realize that they lived in a British Colony, with British institutions, and accept the official use of English.

Consequently, he sought to replace Dutch by English in all spheres of public life. In due course, English became the sole language of the Cape legislature, although all laws and regulations were also promulgated in Dutch.

This policy was by no means revolutionary, as it was the same policy that was previously followed by the V.O.C. to cement the polyglot European settlers into one Dutch-speaking community. In 1822 Somerset caused a proclamation to be issued that declared English to be the exclusive language of the courts, after an inaugural period of five years. This would not preclude an accused or a witness from using Dutch or whatever other language was preferred, but it would entail making use of an interpreter.

In the schools, special incentives were given to teachers who taught through the medium of English. It is clear that Dutch education suffered in the process, in both the short and the long term. In the country areas especially, English was hardly ever heard or spoken. Thus, school became an ordeal for children who could hardly communicate with their teachers. Coming so soon after the Batavian regime had taken the trouble to place education on a sound footing, it caused widespread resentment.[12]

It appears that the Anglicization policy was successful in education, since even in later times education (in the Cape) was consistently through the medium of English. Except for some 11.2 percent of schools, Dutch was not even taught as a subject. In the case of the 11.2 percent of schools teaching Dutch, tuition was only given for four hours per week. Remarkably enough, even institutions founded and run by the Dutch Church were in essence English.

For this state of affairs the laxity of local authorities should be blamed, not British policy. Local authorities' power resided in the fact that they were responsible for defraying a substantial part of the costs of schooling in their areas. Consequently, they had sufficient power to demand more Dutch in those schools, if they so chose.[13]

As far as the Boers on the eastern border were concerned, however, education policy had very little effect on them. The main reasons were that they had never had regular schooling facilities in the first place and, second, as a consequence, they had not developed a culture wherein schooling and education were highly valued.[14]

Even in the Dutch Reformed Church there were many empty pulpits. After a number of vain attempts to recruit Dutch Ministers to fill them, Somerset managed to secure the services of a team of Scots clergy. In all fairness, this action did not engender any ill feelings. The Scotsmen all learnt to speak Dutch before they came out to the Cape and they eventually integrated into Afrikaner society quite seamlessly – even introducing haggis into South African culinary tradition. In time they and their descendants became leading members of Afrikaner society.

Except to the extent already mentioned in the schooling system, the policy of Anglicization was not a success. Although a similar policy had worked for the V.O.C., Dutch was too ingrained in the general population by the time of the second British occupation. In fact, Cape Dutch had already developed to a stage where it was on the verge of becoming a distinct and separate language.

However, by no means did all Afrikaners embrace the idea that Cape Dutch should be the official language or that it was good for anything other than communicating with servants who, by that time, had accepted it as their only language. In addition, the speakers of many other languages were being incorporated into the colony as its borders expanded. To think that such a polyglot community could be coaxed into a monoglottic whole was a pipe dream.

Although the Anglicization policy did not have much of an impact on the Boers on the Eastern frontier, the policy was still perceived as part of the whole process of relentless British persecution. It was a perception that would also be used effectively in the Afrikaner's self-perception as a victim of British persecution.

The Albany settlement

There was a long history of violent clashes all along the colony's eastern frontier. The purpose is not to recount them here, but mention must be made of Colonel John Graham's war of 1811–12. It started with the murder of *Landdrost* Stockenström the elder in December 1811. Graham, the newly appointed eastern commissioner, ruthlessly took revenge for this. At the head of a mixed force of Boers, regulars and the then newly formed Khoikhoi Cape regiment, he cleared the area known as the Suurveld of its indigenous inhabitants, destroyed the crops and burnt the kraals.

London was not happy. The Governor's job was to protect the sea route from the French, not conduct frontier wars and expand the colony. Cradock's successor received specific instructions to settle disputes more diplomatically. On his arrival as governor it was thus abundantly clear to Somerset that peace and stability would never be realized on the colony's borders as long as land-hungry Boers were pushing against the fiercely resisting Xhosa. As a result, cross-border raids were constant threats, followed by reprisals and counter-reprisals.

He therefore decided to annex the recently cleared Suurveld under the name of the district of Albany. The district came up to the line of the Fish River and he envisaged the settlement of less itinerantly inclined British people in this area. His idea was that the line of Block Houses that had been built along the frontier would be supported by scattered villages of settlers, who would act as a buffer between the Boers and the Xhosa. The Colonial Office was slow to react, but during the first half of 1820, some 4,000 settlers arrived from Britain.

Some came in organized parties with wealthy leaders, who received special privileges for recruiting ten or more adult males. Most males were either farmers or tradesmen and included a sprinkling of soldiers, teachers and clergy. The community was a literate one, but none of them were known to have owned land in Britain.

The settlement was a huge success, although not for the purposes of establishing peace on the border or for containing the growth of the colony. Clashes with the Xhosa were to continue for almost another 50 years and the territory further to the east was to be added to the Cape in a piecemeal fashion until it met the Natal border.

Relations between the British settlers and the Boers were cordial and remained so up to the time most of the Boers left on their trek to the interior and Natal. The new community quickly acclimatized to their new surroundings and developed the toughness of character and harsher racial attitudes common to inhabitants of turbulent frontier areas throughout the world. Nevertheless, they did act to an extent to bridge the gap between colonial and African society, through trade, missionary work and the employment of black people as labourers within the colony.

The Albany settlement must be seen as a serious attempt by Britain to stabilize the eastern border. In essence, it was an attempt to stem the ever-outward movement of the Boers. As previously explained, the land hunger of the Boers had become a way of life. The acquisition of more and more land was necessitated in the first instance by the large families the Boers tended to have. Families of ten or more children were not uncommon, sometimes reaching twenty. Farms were usually divided between the sons, but that meant that farms tended to become smaller. With open borders, the father's farm usually devolved upon the eldest son and the others had to look for farms for themselves. By that time every Boer regarded a 7,000 acre farm as his birthright. Farms were not bought and paid for as long as there was 'free' land to be occupied. Since men came of age at 16 and girls often married as young as 13, vast stretches of land would be occupied within a generation or two.

The socio-economic condition of the frontier Boers

As previously explained, the trekking background of the Boers, to which can be added the exigencies of frontier existence, gave rise to a particular set of socio-economic conditions. These conditions are formative of the Boers' outlook and expectations. They are therefore central to an understanding of their attitudes and actions when later they settled parts of what first became known as the Transvaal and which they, the Boers, would later ambitiously style the South African Republic.*

In the previous chapter it was mentioned that the philosophical Enlightenment movement of the 18th century had passed by the Cape Afrikaner, but especially the Boer. Even more importantly however, the Industrial Revolution had also done so and would carry on doing so until the end of the 19th century. What can safely be said is that by 1900 the Boer population had not been

---

* De Zuid-Afrikaansche Republiek or Z.A.R., was neither South African, since it did not encompass the subcontinent, nor was it properly called a republic, for reasons that will be discussed later.

significantly influenced by the great changes that the Industrial Revolution had wrought in Europe during the 19th century.[15] Of course, by the time of the start of the Great Trek in 1835, only the first industrial revolution was in progress. The second revolution, in which Britain would lose her prime position as an industrial power to the United States and Germany, was still in the future. Nevertheless, taking all the circumstances into consideration, it is not surprising that the second one would also not ruffle the lives of the Boers. The Industrial Revolution, like all great changes in society, was really an urban process. At the very heart of everything that the Boer lacked was the lack of urbanization.

The de-urbanization of the Boers as they were known at the time, can be laid at the door of the mercantilistic policies followed by the V.O.C. at the Cape. It is arguable that its policies prohibited the Boers, later calling themselves Afrikaners, from maintaining contact with a possible urban society.[16] First, the company discouraged the establishment of industries at the Cape. This, in turn precluded an important driving force of urban development. The Afrikaner was thus denied the opportunity of qualifying himself as a schooled labourer. The lack of natural resources such as minerals and forests was an additional factor that militated against the Cape being drawn into international trade.

Second, the fact that farmers were not allowed to sell their produce at the most advantageous prices discouraged commercial production and encouraged them to produce only for their own consumption. This was not quite true of wine production, but the ability to produce wine was limited by climate and the expertise of the erstwhile French Huguenots.

Third, the low profit margin of crop farmers encouraged the conversion to animal husbandry. The physical mobility of the herdsman quickly removed him from civilization's hub. Usually, when pioneers moved away from civilization, their isolation was only temporary and contact with other people would speedily be re-established. In the case of the Cape Boers, however, isolation was mostly permanent.

In the context of the broad development of civilization, man-kind developed from hunter-gatherers via a pastoral lifestyle to an agricultural existence. In the case of the Cape herdsman pioneers, however, the process was practically reversed. 'Farming less and hunting more, bartering more and buying less, the standard of living of the Cape frontiersman soon sank to the level of the thirsty land upon which he lived.'[17]

Instead of the city attracting the farmer, the city dweller was attracted to the self-sufficient life in the interior. As the herdsman moved into the interior, he largely abandoned the European lifestyle and economic institutions of his ancestors. On their large farms they lived far apart with the result that community life was only loosely organized. The only times that their isolation was somewhat lifted was when commandos were organized, when supplies were bought or at the celebration of the quarterly *Nagmaal.** They had virtually no educational facilities and hardly any reading matter was available, except for the Bible in High Dutch, which only a few of them were able to read and even fewer could understand.

The self-sufficiency of life in the interior, the total absence of industry and ready availability of Khoikhoi or other of the indigenous people as labourers, resulted in very little attention being devoted to developing schooled labour among the Boers. Since coloured people exclusively did manual labour, the Boer soon developed an attitude that manual labour was beneath his status. Upon reaching adulthood, young Boers started looking out for farms, not trades or professions. Thus, while in Europe and North America a white proletariat was developing, the white wage labourer totally disappeared in South Africa.

By contrast, the agriculturalists at the Cape and its immediate environs enjoyed a relatively sumptuous lifestyle. They lived in good homes, had fine furniture and enjoyed a full community life. In addition, they enjoyed the advantage of regular educational facilities, albeit only at an uncomplicated, primary level. In these developments also lie the seed of the later differences between the Cape Afrikaners and the Boers. It would be from the Western Cape

---

* Unlike most Christian traditions, the Dutch Reformed Church only celebrates the Lord's Supper once every three months.

farming community that more prosperous Afrikaner entrepreneurs would later move to the Witwatersrand.

Boer expectations

What then can be said of the expectations of the Boers of the eastern border area? It seems quite clear that they did not have the expectation of wealth, nor did they really demand better educational or economic opportunities. They only required more land and more servile labour. They wanted continuously open horizons and from government they primarily demanded help in driving off those that stood in their way and protection from those whom they had displaced, whenever such assistance was required. They did require judicial services, especially to enforce labour laws, but also to decide issues between the burghers themselves, but it seems that for many, if not for most of them, it was a strict requirement that justice be partial to them.

They also demanded the labour of such people as they saw as their inferiors. They expected a legal system that recognized their peculiar perception of master and servant in perpetuity. This demanded that black people must be servile and could not question or bring a master to book in a court of law.[18] By necessary implication it also meant that servants had the duty to serve, but no concomitant rights against the master. Likewise, masters had an enforceable right to demand service, but no enforceable duties to the servant.

They wanted a socio-political system that would ensure that they would live as masters of all they surveyed and coveted, be it land or black people. Their lifestyles had largely become reclusive, ignorant and culturally impoverished. This situation was cherished by most of them as an 'identity' and a 'way of life' that required protection. Such values as these could only be protected by large measure of isolation from the rest of the civilized world and the ideas of the Enlightenment.

Again, it cannot be stated that every individual Boer held these views and expectations; that would hardly be a fair judgement.

Nevertheless, it must have been the view and perspective of a substantial majority, given that later Afrikaner commentators and historians made such villains of those who sought impartial justice and lionized those who opposed them.

This view is largely vindicated by, for example, General J.C. Kemp, who, in a remarkable piece of semi-literate historiography, accurately describes the attitude of probably the vast majority of Boers. He writes that the real trouble between Boer and Brit was to be found in the British belief that white and black, both in heaven and on earth were equal in all respects. He suggests that it was precisely the British attempts to put this theoretical equality into practice that, from the very beginning, caused the problems between them. This was because such a policy was directly opposed to that of the colonists. The colonists had learnt, he added, through the experience of one-and-a-half centuries to regard and treat the native as underprivileged on the intellectual/spiritual level and as inferior on the social level.[19] He then goes on to extol the aristocratic nature of the Boers, summarizing in one sentence the history of the Cape Coloured people as being mainly due to people who tried to practise typical English politics. He then deals with the Slagtersnek rebellion, correctly identifying it as a result of the clash in value systems. He quotes at length from Boer War propaganda wherein those executions are described as a heinous murder.[20]

It is not difficult to see that, given British expectations and sensibilities, they and the Boers would constantly be at odds. Added to this great disparity in expectations and value systems, the inconsistencies of British policy must also be mentioned. Over the years the officials in charge saw their duties differently. Some sympathized with the Boers and their aspirations more than others did.

Thus, the Boers were often frustrated with the vacillations and inconsistencies of British policies as well as the perceived influence of missionaries. J.S. Galbraith sees the hand of the British Treasury in much of this vacillation. Be that as it may, by 1835 all these problems resulted in a great number of Boers moving away from the eastern Cape frontier in a concerted and organized manner, to seek their fortunes elsewhere.

The number of Boers that left the frontier was so substantial that the movement became known as the Great Trek. The great drive to colonize the interior of the subcontinent had begun.

CHAPTER FOUR

THE PARTING OF
THE WAYS

The fundamental difference between the British insight and expectations and those of the Boers had now reached a critical point. The British did not want to grow the colony. It was enough trouble and expense already. But these considerations meant nothing to the Boers. The Great Trek can be seen as the result of the successful containment of the growth of the Cape colony, at least at that point in time. It is thus clear that the urge to settle new areas, to expand European settlement and to colonize the subcontinent further, sprang from the imperatives driving the Dutch farmers, not from the imperatives of British imperialism. In fact, British imperialism and Boer expansionism were at such cross-purposes that these became major factors in the ever-growing animosity between the two groups.

Many volumes have been written on the reasons for the Great Trek. The important matter to note here is that it happened. The Great Trek was not a single movement at a single time. It consisted of numbers of people who grouped themselves together under leaders and trekked out of the colony in groups, taking all their earthly belongings with them in their tented ox wagons. Of course, they would not be Boers if they did not take along such slaves as they had (not many), but also as many servants and labourers as were willing to accompany them – and many were. These stoic pioneers were, after all, going out to tame new territory, implying hard, backbreaking toil – how were they to do it if there were not many servants and labourers in tow?

There exist long litanies of complaints and problems that caused and influenced the Great Trek, but the immediate trigger was the invasion of the colony by 10,000 Xhosa warriors, who crossed the Keiskamma River at Christmas 1834. These terrifying warriors, standing over seven feet tall in their magnificent white plumes, destroyed farms, cut men to pieces, took cattle by the tens of thousands, but did not harm any woman, child or missionary. Terrified families fled to the comparative safety of Grahamstown and Colonel Harry Smith[1] quickly assembled a force to deal with the invasion. The force consisted of a few hundred regulars, reinforced by Boer commandos and the Khoikhoi regiment known as the Cape Mounted Riflemen.

After four months, this force prevailed. Sir Benjamin D'Urban, the then Cape Governor together with Colonel Harry Smith, misunderstanding the powers of a Xhosa paramount chief, forced an agreement on to the Xhosa Chief Hintsa that he never had a hope of getting his people to adhere to. Lasting peace was out of the question under the circumstances and D'Urban's actions, as well as his suggestion to annex more Xhosa territory 'as compensation', were ill received in London.

Lord Glenelg, the Colonial Secretary at that time, fired off a despatch in response to Sir Benjamin D'Urban's suggestion of annexation, claiming that he had totally failed to understand British policy. He fumed that as 'to the assumption ... that an enlargement of the British dominion in Southern Africa is a national advantage, I find myself unable to assent'.[2] Lord Glenelg did not only have a problem with colonization in principle, it was also just too dammed expensive.

Clearly, extensive colonies were not favoured by the men of Whitehall, especially those in the Colonial Office. Colonies were expensive and very often embarrassing. Some of the worst of these problems often originated in South Africa, and the war of 1834–35 was at that time the best example of both elements.

Frustration and resolve

Although the war had been concluded successfully for the colonists, many had had enough. The vacillation of British policy on the eastern frontier and the incompetence of many of the officers, servants and agents placed there created general dissatisfaction among the Boer and British settler population alike, but most of the Boer colonists came to the conclusion that they would be better off on their own. This conclusion was strengthened by the appointment of Andries Stockenström, a staunch advocate of black people's rights, to the post of Lieutenant Governor of the eastern districts of the colony.

He had long been against the acquisition of more land and had indeed advocated the return of land that had already been incorporated into the colony to the Xhosa. This frustrated one of the most important expectations of the Boer colonists, namely that of open frontiers and unlimited expansion onto new land. They realized that with this appointment, the British government had set its face against any support for, or tolerance of, further advances onto Xhosa land.

For the Boers, the Xhosa nation had become an insurmountable obstacle in their expansionist way of life. They had to try to move around that obstacle, as the obstacle had obviously no desire to move itself out of the way. Modern historians agree that the decision to trek away from British ruled territory was the 'best solution' to a set of problems that faced the eastern border Boers. It is significant, given later Afrikaner historiography of persecution, that the trek took place from a point furthest removed from the seat of government at Cape Town. The Afrikaners of the Western Cape did not move, yet the oppressiveness of the regime, if it were so, would have been most acutely felt and strictly administered there. *Au contraire*, many Afrikaner families were prospering under the British administration at the Cape.

The trek did not take place into an unknown wilderness. The Boers already knew the areas to which they intended to move reasonably well, numerous hunting parties over many years having traversed the territory quite thoroughly. In addition, they had planned the mass exodus at least eighteen months in advance. In September 1834, the *kommissie-trek* (commission trek) under Piet Uys set off to investigate the settlement possibilities at Port Natal, the present site of the city of Durban, while other smaller parties explored the Soutpansberg area in the Transvaal and still others the area known today as Namibia.

The trekkers did not all leave the colony at the same time. Although certain groups were large, such as those under A.H. Potgieter who left in late 1835 or early 1836 and Gerrit Maritz and Piet Retief who left in 1837, many smaller groups also left from time to time during the period. Some estimates[3] conclude that between 1835 and 1840 some 15,000 people left the eastern frontier to settle in areas outside British control.

First, however, they all headed for Thaba'Nchu, bordering on Moshweshwe's stronghold of Basutuland. Thaba'Nchu is today part of the Free State Province, but at that time, it was the staging area for the voyage to the Promised Land – if only they could decide where that was.

Thaba'Nchu, Moshweshwe and the Sotho

Thaba'Nchu was the site of a Methodist mission station and the capital of Moroka, the chief of the Rolong tribe of Sotho speakers. In many ways the area west of the Drakensberg and North of the Orange River, which was occupied by the Southern Sotho, bore the brunt of the disruptions and dislocations of the Difaqane. In the eye of the storm was the fortress of Thaba Bosiu, the stronghold of one of the ablest of the great chieftains, Moshweshwe.

During the Difaqane, Moshweshwe was able to consolidate his people around him and to provide a haven for those who had fled, all of whom he welcomed. He offered them protection because he foresaw that their presence also made his position more secure. There was, after all, safety in numbers. Although the initial impact of the Difaqane came from the east, it spread inland, past Moshweshwe's kingdom. Thus, eventually, the Difaqane threw more and more people into Moshweshwe's sphere of influence from the west.

It is estimated that approximately 12,000 people, not counting the Voortrekkers, migrated into his region during the years 1833 and 1834.[4] These were mostly uprooted Tswana, but they included

Kora, Griqua and Basters (people of mixed white and Khoikhoi race). A particularly large group of about 7,000 of the Rolong Tswana tribe, under the chieftainship of Moroka, was established at Thaba'Nchu. Moshweshwe welcomed them as he had the others. They were his clients, being under his protection, but he regarded them as a buffer between the inner core of his state and possible aggressors from the land beyond.

The Boers chose Thaba'Nchu as their staging area because it allowed them to skirt the settled Griqua communities and it had ample grazing for their cattle while they waited for all to assemble there. It had the further advantage of being within a well-travelled area where the local chiefs were known to be friendly.

Since the beginning of the 1830s Cape traders had come to this area to buy grain, cattle, wool and hides from the Southern Sotho, while selling them commodities such as clothing, obsolete and inferior firearms, horses and liquor. However, there were other considerations that were just as important. The area had virtually become the granary of the highveld. Despite the disruption of the Difaqane the Southern Sotho had by 1837 enough grain stored to last between four to eight years.

Both Moroka and Moshweshwe were also well acquainted with the Boers, long before they decided to use Thaba'Nchu as a staging area for the Great Trek. Since the 1820s, Trekboers had started arriving in the area of the Orange River, pushing across it to the north for grazing. With the mass migration of Boers that started in 1834, there was a trekker community of more than 5,000 at Thaba'Nchu by 1837. Local chiefs regarded the trekkers as temporary sojourners, which indeed, most of them were. Relations were therefore cordial and the Boer trekkers were granted grazing rights and a staging area. Shrewdly, Moshweshwe also regarded the trekker presence as a further line of defence against the Ndebele or any other groups with hostile intent.

Unfortunately the cordial relations did not last. Not all the Boer immigrants eventually left for Natal or the Transvaal. Those remaining behind soon made clear their intent to remain permanently. They began claiming permanent title to land to which Moshweshwe and other chiefs had only granted temporary access. Soon the wrangle for land started and in 1843 Moshweshwe signed a treaty of friendship with Sir George Napier, the Governor of the Cape. The treaty defined Moshweshwe's territory as between him and the Cape colony, but it did not settle disputes with the Boers, which only escalated.

By 1844, long after the Great Trek had come and gone, Moshweshwe declared all land exchanges between his people and the Boers null and void. This started a long period of land disputes, including wars and skirmishes in which, from time to time, the British would become embroiled to a greater or lesser extent. Eventually Moshweshwe's kingdom was saved when he requested British protection and it became a British protectorate.

Moshweshwe's canny diplomacy, sound political insight and military prowess did, in the end, keep his kingdom standing against Boer expansionism, although he was forced off much of the best land originally occupied by his people. Thus, his leadership allowed his people to escape being sucked into the quagmire of the later apartheid state, although they would not be completely protected from its ravages. One of the kingdom's largest exports would always be the labour of its people. The tiny kingdom's mighty neighbour always did, and always will, have a great influence on its fortunes.

One polity of trekkers

But these developments still lay far in the future. Notwithstanding the staggered nature of the trekker movement and the multiplicity of leaders, the trekkers regarded themselves as one polity. At Thaba'Nchu every group who came from the colony would first 'join the community' in a sense, before moving further either on their own or in cooperation with other groups of trekkers. They set out to explore the country further in the hunt for the perfect place to enjoy the much-anticipated idyll, before returning to Thaba'Nchu.

Such was the case with Hendrik Potgieter, who had scouted across the Vaal River, but found himself attacked by Mzilikazi and his Matabele warriors. He returned to Thaba'Nchu, having been semi-successful against Mzilikazi, since he had managed to hold out against them in a pitched battle, but had lost all his party's cattle in the process. These losses were made good by Moroka in a chiefly gesture, demonstrating his alliance with the Boers.

After the return of Potgieter from his excursion across the Vaal, Gerrit Maritz, leading a large party of trekkers, arrived at Thaba'Nchu. The leaders decided to hold an open meeting of all trekkers on 2 December 1836. They chose a Citizens' Council (*Burgerraad*) of seven with Maritz as president and Potgieter as commander of the army. Hardly had this step been taken, when fiery dissension broke out and split the *Burgerraad* right down the middle.

There were numerous arguments, not only resulting from policy disagreements, but also from personality clashes between Maritz and the authoritarian Potgieter. The single most important disagreement was the question of where the trekkers should head next. The one polity could not decide on one destination. They knew they wanted to settle in virgin territory, but that was virtually the only point of agreement.

Potgieter was in favour of heading for the highveld across the Vaal River. He was convinced that they would be able to drive off Mzilikazi with the help of some of the other black tribes. He was convinced that gaining access to the sea from the highveld through the Portuguese territory of Mozambique was the proper strategy for the Boer trekkers to follow. Maritz and his supporters, on the other hand, saw Natal as the Promised Land.

For all his irascibility, Potgieter's insight was accurate. He argued that there were already British subjects settled in Port Natal where Shaka had allowed them to settle. And where British citizens lived, he argued, the British flag would soon follow. This proved to be an accurate assessment of the situation, for it was exactly what was to happen to the first Boer Republic of Natalia – it would be annexed by Britain and thereafter remained a British colony until 1910.

The second Citizens' Council

In April 1837, a new election was held for the *Burgerraad*, since the first one had been emasculated by disagreement and dissension.

The result was a blow to any hope of Voortrekker unity because Potgieter did not even gain a seat on the council. However, on the 6th June 1837 the new council, sitting at Winburg, a nascent Voortrekker town that had meanwhile arisen near Thaba'Nchu, did manage to adopt Nine Articles of Association as the constitution of the 'Free Province of New Holland in South East Africa'. A 'state' without even a putative territory. It must be seen, however, more as the fundamental document of a society, a company, rather than as the constitution of a state.

In this, the second *Burgerraad*, Piet Retief was elected Governor (*Goeverneur*) and Maritz 'Judge President of the Council of Policy' together with a string of other imposing titles. Retief also took over the job of commander of the army from Potgieter. They appointed Jan Bantjes, a man of mixed blood, as their official secretary.

Retief laid down some remarkably 'liberal' guidelines in July, when he issued 'Instructions to Commandants and Field Cornets' (*Veldcornetten*). *Veldcornetten* were entrusted with the task, *inter alia*, of bringing to trial before *Landdrosten* and *Heemraden* people accused of maltreating servants, as well as those who 'booked in' the children of Bushmen or other aboriginals for service.

'Booking in' of aboriginal children was a system of slavery where a supposedly orphaned child was indentured into service with a family, but was automatically free upon reaching maturity. The system was recognized under the British administration at the Cape and many Boers enthusiastically availed themselves of this 'facility', both before and after Retief's instructions. It is an open question as to what extent such 'booked in' children were informed of their emancipation upon reaching maturity.

A remarkable inclusion in Retief's instructions was his making *Veldcornetten* responsible for, among other things, the supervision of subject people.[5] From this instruction, the only reasonable inference is that it was the Boers', as well as Retief's, own intention from the beginning to move into new territory and there to subject to Boer authority such people as might be found *in situ*. This is a clear colonizing and imperialist intent that gainsays Retief's 'Manifesto' of February 1837, published by him in Grahamstown before he and his followers left the colony. Therein he declared:

> we quit this colony with a desire to lead a more quiet life ... *We will not molest any people, or deprive them of the smallest property*; but if attacked, we shall consider ourselves fully justified in defending our persons and effects, to the utmost of our ability, against every enemy. (my italics)[6]

Like so many political manifestos, Retief's was all preaching and no practice; long on piousness, but short on serious intent.

Further dissension

In the midst of the existing tension between the trekkers at Thaba'Nchu, and within days of the adoption of the Nine Articles, Piet Uys and his party arrived. Although an affable man who had bred and raced horses in the Albany district, Uys and his followers dissociated themselves completely from the Nine Articles and the regulations of Retief. Potgieter had at last found an ally against Maritz and Retief. Hard words fell, men flourished their guns, but Retief's diplomacy prevailed.

They patched up their differences sufficiently to mount a joint expedition against Mzilikazi in September. The purpose of this expedition was to remove the powerful presence of the Ndebele from the area across the Vaal River into which Potgieter wanted to move. The offer of assistance by the other trekkers to drive off Mzilikazi and his people must have been a powerful factor in mollifying the disgruntled Potgieter. Nothing could unite the Boers more than the prospect of fighting black people, especially if it had the added bonus of making more land available for them.

The view from Cape Town and London

The emigrant farmers enjoyed greater sympathy for their emigration from the British settlers on the frontier than from many of their kinsmen in Cape Town and the environs. There was no sympathetic move of Afrikaners from the Western Cape, with the result that the Trekkers were denied the services of professional people such as doctors, lawyers and even ministers. Afrikaner families were themselves divided on the issue. Some remained while others emigrated.

The absence of ministers was due particularly to the opposition to the emigration by the Dutch Reformed Church in the Cape. The minister of the Stellenbosch congregation, Tobias Herold, condemned the whole idea in a strongly worded article. The absence of ordained ministers was a great trial for the emigrating Boers and was to give cause for much dissension later in the trek.

The opposition of the Cape Church would eventually lead to the splintering of Dutch (later Afrikaans) churches in South Africa and great political animosity in the Boer Republics. The breaches have not been healed to this day, although the main historical reasons have been subsumed under variously contrived disputes. The so-called three Afrikaner 'sister Churches' exist and operate separately from one another in modern South Africa. Despite the lack of any substantial theological differences, very little sororial love is lost between them.

In contrast to this opposition, there was some understanding for the trekkers from the British settlers on the eastern frontier. In July 1836, the *Graham's Town Journal* commented that 'the circumstances of the frontier farmers require the most attentive and humane consideration on the part of the government; hitherto they have been treated without the slightest regard to their personal feelings or their prejudices'.

The trek caused some anger and resentment in the British administration. On the one hand, the colony had lost probably its most intractable opponents of British administration, but at the same time, it had lost a substantial number of those subjects who could be relied on for commando duty and to help protect the eastern border of the colony. In British eyes, and in the international law of the time, the emigrating Boers were still British subjects. Trouble caused by them might eventually require intervention by Britain and even war, with exasperating expenses for the British.

Quite justifiably, it was feared that the Boers would come into violent conflict with the blacks. In addition, the Boers' proclivity for treating indigenous people very harshly, including heartless physical abuse and enslavement, did not augur well for any lasting peace and calm in the region, apart from the moral reprehensibility of such conduct. In London, Lord Glenelg, upon receiving the news of Retief's death at the hand of the Zulu King Dingane, commented: 'Much as I lament the fate of these misguided men, it was not to be expected that the natives of the countries adjacent to the Colony would suffer themselves to be overrun by those invaders.'[7]

Sir George Napier, the Governor of the Cape at that time, rather saw the absurdity of continuing to maintain that the emigrating farmers were British subjects while making no attempt to control them. Legally, whatever territory was occupied and controlled by a country's subjects was occupied and controlled by that country. Hence, any territory that the Boers might come to control would legally be controlled by Britain. This placed a responsibility on the authority's shoulders that they did not wish to assume, but that they could not easily escape either.

One of the results was the enactment by Lord Melbourne's Government of the Cape of Good Hope Punishment Act of 1836. This Act declared British jurisdiction (not sovereignty) in Southern Africa up to the 25th southern parallel, and outlawed the Voortrekkers. The jurisdiction included all the territory between Cape Agulhas, the southernmost point on the African continent, to a line some 50 miles north of Pretoria.

Such a vast tract of land was not controlled by Britain at that time and with a police force of some 2,000 at its disposal, it could never control it. Claiming jurisdiction was therefore nothing more than a legal fiction and a desperate gesture which would prove to be to no avail. The proclamation did not deter the Voortrekkers. It was never invoked in a court of law and was not given any force or effect, except to the extent that it allowed Sir George Napier to appoint a magistrate at Port Natal in 1842. Technically, every Voortrekker was an outlaw and therefore risked arrest, should they enter an area where British jurisdiction might be enforced.

In October 1838, Napier already foresaw that the annexation of Boer-occupied territory would be the only practical solution. He summarized the British point of view neatly when he wrote that 'the British nation will never consent either to allow the emigrants to perish from want or the sword, or to permit them to attack and slaughter the natives of the countries they invaded'.[8]

Although the British were unable to execute and maintain a policy in accordance with Napier's sentiments, and despite numerous changes of course, it would underlie much of the British policy toward the Boers followed in later years. It particularly presaged the first annexation of the Transvaal by Shepstone in 1877.

While the British anticipated with trepidation the further European settlement of the interior and correctly gauged that it would result only in multiple further complications, the trekkers regarded their adventure quite differently. At last, they would be able to come and go as they pleased. They would no longer be constrained by officials pontificating in faraway places. They would be able to deal with the natives as they pleased, without any outside sanction. Most of all, they could enjoy an easy-going, unconcerned, trouble-free way of life, where even the nearest neighbours were never within sight or even shouting distance.

Or so they thought …

CHAPTER FIVE

THE TRANSVAAL UNSETTLED

The relatively flat terrain of the highveld does not offer the natural strongholds that are available in the Drakensberg Mountains at the edge of the escarpment on the eastern seaboard. This range of rugged mountains defines the central plateau of the subcontinent from where it descends majestically down to the coastal plains. It runs from south to north, parallel with the east coast of South Africa, but on average a 100 or so miles inland. Just south of Delagoa Bay it turns northwest and continues into the interior towards the modern-day Polokwane, previously known as Pietersburg.

It is therefore not surprising that the two strongest and most enduring indigenous states, Lesotho and Swaziland, are both located in the Drakensberg. The Pedi and the Venda also inhabited parts of the Drakensberg and although they eventually lost their independence under the onslaught of Boer expansionism, ably assisted by British militarism, they were able to hold out virtually to the end of the 19th century.

The other Tswana and Northern Sotho speakers were not so fortunate. They inhabited the relatively flat terrain of the highveld which, apart from the Magaliesberg, offered very little assistance in military defence. The Tswana of the Transvaal highveld were thus exposed and vulnerable to the marauding Mzilikazi. But Mzilikazi was not the only destabilizing force in the Transvaal during the Difaqane. Other tribes also trekked through the region, spreading death and destruction as they went.

The Tswana had limited options in response to these disruptions. Some, like the followers of chief Mogale, dispersed and hid in the Magaliesberg – hence the name (Mogale's Mountain). Other chiefdoms resisted the attacks as best they could, while yet others temporarily accepted Matabele overlordship. Then came Andries Hendrik Potgieter and his followers.

Driving off Mzilikazi

After their first encounter with Mzilikazi, the Voortrekkers knew that they could never live across the Vaal River with Mzilikazi and his followers on the loose. A joint force of Voortrekkers thus left the Thaba'Nchu camp with the intent of driving off Mzilikazi to make the Transvaal available for Boer settlement, at least so in their own judgement.

The united Voortrekker commando moved north from Thaba'Nchu with their numbers augmented by a group of Moroka's Rolong warriors to help them against Mzilikazi. When they crossed the Vaal River, they recruited the assistance of a number of Tswana chiefdoms to assist in expelling the Matabele. The Tswana were naturally pleased to help in driving those off who had so recently invaded their territory and disrupted their lives. Pretorius' commando group was thus enthusiastically joined by groups from the Hurutshe and Ngwaketse tribes.

Together they set out and fought a pitched battle against the Matabele. The battle lasted nine days and in the process the Matabele suffered thousands of casualties. They were driven far north, across the Limpopo River. Mzilikazi eventually settled there in what is today known as Matebeleland in modern Zimbabwe. In so doing, he overpowered and subjugated the Shona, who were already settled in the area that Mzilikazi now invaded. Thus, the Shona became clients of Mzilikazi, much against their will.

The Voortrekker expedition returned to Thaba'Nchu with enormous booty. There the Boers fiercely fell out among themselves in deciding on the distribution of the spoils. They eventually parted the worst of friends, each going their own way. Retief and Maritz, later to be joined by Andries Pretorius and his followers, set off for Natal, but Potgieter remained for the moment at Winburg, the surrounding territory of which he summarily laid claim to.

After November 1838, Potgieter thus ruled two Voortrekker communities, in which task he was assisted by a Council of War (*Krygsraad*). Despite his later disastrous foray against Dingane in Natal, after the murder of Retief, in which foray Piet Uys and his son Dirkie were killed, the dictatorial Potgieter rather fancied himself as a military man and was not in favour of highly democratic institutions. For that reason he governed through a Council of War, rather than an elected Council of Representatives.

The two Voortrekker settlements governed by Potgieter were one around the town of Winburg in the modern Free State and the other north of the Vaal River, situated on the banks of the Mooi River, where the town of Potchefstroom would later be built. The settlement on the banks of the Mooi River was founded after the expulsion of Mzilikazi to beyond the Limpopo, but Winburg had been claimed by Potgieter while the other trekkers were still encamped at Thaba'Nchu. The latter two areas were adjacent, but there was a lot of open, yet unclaimed territory between Winburg and Potchefstroom.

The retreat of the Matabeles allowed many Tswana chiefdoms to rebuild. Mogale's people came out of their mountain redoubts and settled on the fertile plains again. Initially the Tswana welcomed the Boer presence on the Mooi River as protection against the Matabele, but this congenial state of affairs was not destined to last overly long.

The first Voortrekker state

Although Potgieter did not join the other trekkers in Natal, the idea of one Voortrekker polity remained. Founded by the Natal Voortrekkers in March 1839, the Republic of Natalia, with its legislature situated in the town of Pietermaritzburg in Natal, admitted to its *Volksraad* (Peoples' Council) representatives of the Winburg and Potchefstroom communities. It was a representative democracy in form, but not in substance. It was racially and denominationally exclusive – only white, Calvinist, Dutch Reformed Church members could be citizens. It explicitly contemplated rule over subject people and was thus never, not even in principle, anything but an instrument of oppressive colonization. This would be a feature of all later Boer and Afrikaner constitutions.

In order to give effect to the inclusion of the highveld communities, an *Adjunkt Raad* (a sub-council of the Peoples' Council) was set up at Potchefstroom in 1841. It was to operate as a committee of the full Raad in Pietermaritzburg and to report to that Raad twice annually. There is, however, no evidence that it ever reported to the Volksraad in Pietermaritzburg, or that it regarded itself as a subordinate of the Volksraad.

The Republic of Natalia was the first Voortrekker attempt at state formation, claiming the area bordered by the Drakensberg in the east, the Black Umfolozi in the north, the Umzimvubu River in the south and the Indian Ocean in the west. This was a wild and ridiculously ambitious claim. The area claimed would entail sovereignty over a substantial part of the Zulu nation and over the long-established 'white' settlement of Port Natal. The whole area was populated by a large mass of people, black and white, who were, by definition, excluded from citizenship of the new 'State'. They knew nothing of it and would vehemently object to its claimed jurisdiction over them.

Not by any stretch of the imagination, or of public international law for that matter, could this fledgling state pretend to that territory. The claim was not only devoid of all merit, it was devoid of all substance. The significance of the claim is, however, that it gave clear notice of Boer intent to take possession of that whole area, with or without the cooperation or consent of the inhabitants. It serves as further confirmation, if any were needed, of the oppressive, colonizing nature of the Voortrekker movement, both in its intent and in its execution.

Polities proliferate across the Vaal

Due to historical developments that fall outside the scope of the present discussion, the Volksraad of the Republic of Natalia capitulated to British annexation on 15 July 1842. The annexation scuttled Boer colonial ambitions in the area of Natal, but their land hunger would not be satiated. This would prove a constant source of trouble for a vacillating British administration.

The Volksraad at Pietermaritzburg continued to exist until October 1845, but the Potchefstroom *Adjunkt Raad* severed its ties with it on 7 August 1843, directly because of the Volksraad's capitulation to the British. By adopting a set of Thirty-Three Articles, apparently to be read in conjunction with the constitution of the Natal Volksraad, a new Voortrekker Republic was thus founded north of the Vaal River.

It differed from the Natal constitution inasmuch as it did not define any territory for the state. It is therefore to be questioned whether the Thirty-Three Articles really qualifies as a founding document of a state as such. Similar to the constitution of Thaba'Nchu, it has much more of the character of the articles of association of a company than of the constitution of a state. This does not mean that Boer ambitions were less grandiose north of the Vaal, merely that they were still in the process of creating a territorial government.

Between 1845–48 Potgieter decided to move to the eastern Transvaal, because he wished to be closer to Delagoa Bay, which he still perceived to be the Boers' natural trade route to the sea. His move was also motivated by the Cape of Good Hope Punishment Act. He wished to live north of the 25th southern parallel. He moved to a place he named Andries Ohrigstad, after the Dutch trader who would meet him there to establish trading relations.

Andries Ohrig never showed up and that particular enterprise turned out to be a dismal failure. The establishment of the route was also opposed by both the Pedi and the Portuguese. The tsetse fly brought disease to humans and animals resulting in a very discouraged mood among the people of Ohrigstad. Meanwhile, some Natalians, disaffected with the takeover of Natal by the British, had also moved to Ohrigstad. They had trekked once again to remove themselves from British governance.

Potgieter fell out with the Natalian Boers over his autocratic style of government, which they would not accept, but not before a constitution had been drawn up by the Ohrigstad Volksraad in 1846. Since the trading venture had failed, Potgieter thereafter removed himself and his supporters to an area in the Soutpansberg, a mountain range further north, where he once again founded a separate polity on the military lines that he favoured. The Ohrigstad people also removed themselves to the present site of Lydenburg, which they found more endurable than the malaria-infested area of Ohrigstad.

Without much fanfare, another group of Voortrekkers had previously established themselves near the Marico River, close to the site of the recently departed Mzilikazi's old headquarters. By 1849, the area north of the Vaal thus already contained four separate, mutually isolated and far-flung Boer communities, namely Potchefstroom, Lydenburg, Soutpansberg and Marico, each with its own independent political structure.

With Potgieter now removed to the far northern reaches of the Transvaal, Pretorius came back into political ascendancy. He returned from Natal, where he had been quietly living under British rule, and tried to assist the trekker community at Winburg, still nominally part of Potgieter's fiefdom, to oppose the annexation of Trans-Oragnia (the area between the Orange and Vaal Rivers). Sir Harry Smith's impetuous decision to annex the territory had taken everybody by surprise, although, given the sentiments expressed earlier by Napier, such a move was to be expected at some time or other. Harry Smith gave Pretorius and the Winburg trekkers short shrift at the battle of Boomplaats. The annexation of the area was thus a *fait accompli*, although it was never formalized by promulgation in Letters Patent.

The road to the Sand River Convention

After the defeat at Boomplaats, Pretorius wound his way to Potchefstroom in search of more promising political pastures. This, in the permanent absence of Potgieter, he found there. The first job at hand was to unite the four disunited trekker communities into one body politic. This was ostensibly achieved at a meeting in Hekpoort, close to the modern-day town of Krugersdorp, on 9 February 1849, when the Potchefstroom and Potgieter's Soutpansberg communities decided to establish a United Volksraad.

The Voortrekker communities were so fissiparous that they could not agree on a head of state, although they did agree that 'Head of State' should be a military post. Potgieter's influence was clear in this decision. In January 1851, at a meeting of the United Volksraad at Derde Poort, near the present-day Pretoria, they decided to have four Commandants General, one for each of the four communities. Pretorius was appointed for Potchefstroom and Magaliesberg. Such unity was more apparent than real and would not last long after the death of Pretorius.

Since the United Volksraad had decided in January to meet three times per year, Pretorius tried to convene meetings in September and December of 1851, but could not achieve a quorum on either occasion. He thus had to rely on the cooperation of his Potchefstroom Krygsraad for authority when he negotiated the Sand River Convention with representatives of the British Government in January 1852.

The Sand River Convention

The Sand River is a generally dry, sandy riverbed that fills with water only during the rainy season between September and March. It meanders along the Southern Free State until it joins up with the Gariep (Orange) River. With the proclivity for violent thunderstorms in the catchment area the river is given to dangerous flash floods during these periods. Nevertheless, for reasons not specifically recorded but probably due to its proximity to Winburg, it was the chosen site for an important meeting.

On the banks of this dry river, Messrs. Hogge and Owen, representing the British Government, met with Andries Pretorius, ostensibly representing the Boer settlers north of the Vaal River. It was the middle of January 1852. Of course, Pretorius did not represent all the Transvaal settlers, simply because he could not arrange a meeting to obtain their authority to do so. However, he assumed, probably correctly, that they would not have opposed this move on his part. The purpose of the meeting was to discuss matters arising from the settlement of Voortrekkers north of the Vaal River.

Pretorius' outlaw status had to be revoked in order for him to be able to enter the British territory of the Orange River Sovereignty safely. Pretorius had cleverly threatened to side with Moshweshwe against the Orange River Sovereignty, unless the independence of the Boers north of the Vaal River was recognized. By September 1851, Hogge and Owen had virtually persuaded Earl Grey, the Secretary of State for the Colonies and his Prime Minister, Lord John Russell, to abandon the Orange River Sovereignty. They were thus receptive to the idea of recognizing the independence of the Boers north of the Vaal, on condition they desisted from enslaving the local population.

Essentially, this is what is provided in the Sand River Convention. The settlers north of the Vaal would have the fullest right to manage their own affairs and to govern themselves according to their own laws, without any interference from the British Government. The Boers undertook to refrain from all forms of slavery; they were guaranteed access to guns and ammunition, while both parties undertook to refrain from arming black people. The British Government disclaimed any alliances or agreements with any of the black nations north of the Vaal.

In its preamble, the Convention declares itself to be a minute of a meeting between her Majesty's Commissioners who had been appointed to settle the affairs of the east and north-east boundaries of the Cape Colony, on the one hand; and the deputies of the emigrant Boers, living north of the Vaal River, on the other hand. However, it is questionable whether the commissioners ever had the authority to enter into this agreement, since the Vaal River did not then or at any other time form any of the boundaries of the Cape Colony. The Cape's northernmost boundary since 1847 was the Gariep (Orange) River. On the face of it, it thus appears that Her Majesty's Commissioners were exceeding their authority.

It is not really a treaty, nor can it properly be regarded to fall within the ambit of public international law, since it is not an agreement between sovereign states. It is certainly not the recognition of a state north of the Vaal River, since no borders, other than the Vaal River, are recognized or contemplated. Indeed, no territory is at issue. The convention really purports only to regularize the status of the people who settled north of the Vaal and to create mutual rights and obligations.

The problem with the agreement is its vagueness. It appears to be an executive act that contradicts at least the Cape of Good Hope Punishment Act, which was still in force at the time. Although, as previously mentioned, that Act was virtually worthless in practice, it was nevertheless an Act of Parliament as far as British law was concerned. It could therefore not be validly negated by an executive act, such as the Convention. Thus, as far as it contradicts an Act of Parliament, the agreement would be null and void in British law. This appears to be the likely legal scenario.

Thus, as a document recognizing the independence of the Transvaal as a state, the Convention must fail: it simply did not even purport to do so. The independence of a new state north of the Vaal could strictly speaking only be recognized once such a state, displaying at least some semblance of the statehood requirements of public international law, had come into existence. This the settlers beyond the Vaal had not yet achieved.

Notwithstanding all questions regarding the legalities and technicalities, Pretorius went on his way, believing that he had a binding agreement. The British Government did not concern themselves with the legalities too much either, as they were relieved to have found a cheap way of avoiding further responsibilities beyond the Vaal.

The British only wished to rid themselves of responsibility north of the Orange River. This was achieved by the Bloemfontein Convention of February 1854. Economic reasons were the driving force for the abandonment of British rule north of the Orange. The decision to upset Sir Harry Smith's impetuous act had in fact already been taken by the Cabinet two years earlier, in March 1853. Quite simply, informal empire had become a better proposition than formal rule.[1] But the Cape of Good Hope Punishment Act was only repealed in 1863.

The Transvalers now had their open borders across the Vaal in search of which they had trekked from the eastern frontier of the Cape Colony. The challenge now would be to actually create a viable state out of the raw bush, the craggy mountains and the scattered population groups living across the river. It needs more than guns and gunpowder to fashion a state. But this was a lesson the Boers still had to learn.

Part Two

Open borders across the Vaal

CHAPTER SIX

FOUNDATION AND COLONIZATION

State formation in the Transvaal, unlike its sister republic in the Free State, would always prove to be problematic. The local black tribes remained largely outside the Boer Republic, except as farm labourers. Boer constitutions always specifically excluded black and coloured people from having any land or civil rights within the Republic, notwithstanding that hundreds of thousands of black people lived within the boundaries of the territory they claimed.

The local black communities remained loosely organized under different chiefs, each trying to protect only their own interests. They were thus never able to unite and face the immigrant Boers as a united body. Indeed, the Boers often used local rivalries to their advantage, playing one tribe off against another. The only meaningful exception was the Pedi in the eastern Transvaal. The time would come when they would shake the struggling Boer Republic to its foundations.

The efforts of the Transvaal Boers to bring about a viable polity were hampered by the fact that neither the leaders, nor their followers, had any clear idea of what was required to forge a viable state. The result was that Transvaal constitutions, even the much later one of the South African Republic, would always remain a hodgepodge affair with vague and often impractical provisions that continuously threatened to ignite into fully fledged constitutional crises; a serious crisis would, however, only occur towards the end of the 19th century. But even more serious was their inability to establish a viable economy in the territory. Nevertheless, they soldiered on as best they could.

On 15 March 1852, Pretorius and Potgieter met at the town of Rustenburg where, for the first time in their lives, they appeared to reach some unanimity. Unfortunately for the Transvalers what they reached unanimity on was disastrous. They agreed to remain dual Commandants-General and, amazingly enough for ostensible republicans, they agreed that their heirs would jointly succeed to these ranks in perpetuity. Worst of all, the Volksraad appears to have accepted this decision.

Having thus agreed, Potgieter returned to his home in the Soutpansberg, where he died on 16 December 1852. Pretorius, although much younger than Potgieter, was not to survive him by long. He died seven months later, leaving the nascent state with his son, M.W. Pretorius as an able, but inexperienced leader.

The nascent state

Boer society mainly required two things – land and labour. Both needs could be met by colonizing as much land as hands could be laid upon and then forcing the local population in one way or another to labour on the newly created farms. Thus, immediately after the Convention and now facing open borders, the Boers started their expansionist and colonizing activities in earnest. Additional land was obtained by simple expropriation or, if this was not feasible, loose tenancy arrangements were entered into with local chiefs. These tenancy arrangements would then later be arbitrarily converted to outright ownership.

Their methods of labour recruitment were equally predatory. In the western Transvaal, somewhat later in 1852, a Boer commando attacked the Kwena town of Dimawe. They trampled the tribe's fields and drove off the defenders. They captured more than 200 women and children to be 'booked in' as 'apprentices' to labour on Boer farms. David Livingstone's home mission at Kolobeng was attacked and ransacked in the same raid.[1]

The Transvalers were never able to fully assert their authority over all the Tswana living between the Vaal and Limpopo Rivers. They imposed a 'hut tax' and sought to extract labour through 'agreements' with chiefs. They had only limited success in these ventures, often committing gross atrocities in attempting to enforce these taxes and ostensible agreements.

The imperatives of land and labour would remain the main driving forces for Boer expansionism until after the South African war at the turn of the 19th century. The unfettered satisfaction of these demands formed an important element of the Boer striving for independence. Much resentment was caused by the alleged 'hemming in' of the Transvaal by the British. Such allegations, supported by substantially flawed academic studies, were effectively used during the 20th century to promote Afrikaner Nationalism.[2]

High expectations and poor prospects

With the Great Trek, the socio-economic conditions of the cattle farming pioneers of the eastern Cape border were largely transposed to the area north of the Vaal.[3] Due to what might almost be called a process of natural selection, only the poorest of the trekkers settled themselves in the region across the Vaal River. Consequently, the living conditions of the Boers deteriorated as they moved northwards. Their greatest assets remained land and cattle.

Economically the Transvaal Boers resembled the black communities around them more than they would ever care to admit. They had in fact become a white African tribe. Only their concept of individual property ownership differed from that of the other tribes. However, their economic conditions were inferior to those of the Tswana who were, in addition to being adroit hunters and herdsman, successful crop farmers and metalworkers. A major advantage that the Tswana had, in common with all the subcontinent's indigenous peoples, was that they did not depend on outside labour. The Boers would always be dependent on imports of basic foodstuffs and the availability of black people as labourers, willing or coerced.

On the military side, the Boers had two major advantages over the Tswana – horses and greater access to modern technology in the form of guns and gunpowder. In addition, because of their hunting lifestyle, they developed great horsemanship and sharp-shooting skills. Their development of the latter attributes is comparable to the experience of pioneers in the American West.

These factors allowed them largely to dominate the Tswana whose access to the same technology was not only limited, but also foreign to them and they did not develop their skills early on. It was part of Boer strategy to ensure that such access was denied, in which enterprise they were largely supported by the British. Later, indigenous communities would become threateningly formidable when properly armed, as had the Khoikhoi in the Cape Colony.

In many ways, the Great Trek can be compared with the westward move in the United States of America. The most significant difference between the Great Trek and the westward movement in the US was the lack of any accompanying process of urbanization in the Trek. In South Africa, there was no 'urban frontier' that kept track with the move to the interior. The difference can be laid at the door of America's prodigious natural resources in minerals and navigable rivers that were already known and available at the start of the move. Thus, in America, the physical movement of the population could be accompanied by a process of urbanization from the outset. This process created opportunities for social and economic mobility, which were totally lacking in the circumstances of the Trek.[4]

The Boers were followed into the interior by English speakers, many of them original 1820 settlers from the Albany district on the eastern Cape frontier. The British immigrants had not lost their urbanized culture in the pioneering process. They captured the market as traders and entrepreneurs. English speakers and other aliens had no competition from the agrarian Boers who needed to buy their gunpowder, coffee, flour and other necessities from them.

The traders set themselves up as shopkeepers at the venues where the Boers chose to celebrate their quarterly communion. Thus, towns came into being at these places, but the townspeople were English speakers, and the Dutch, or Afrikaans speakers were poorly represented, if at all.

Towns notwithstanding, there was no process of industrialization, even on a small scale. The English speakers in the towns were traders and the Boers were primarily hunters and then pastoralists. Initially there was plenty of game. For many years, a reasonable living could be made from trading the products of the hunt. By 1860, however, game numbers had been depleted to the extent that more Boers began to concentrate on livestock farming. The growth of livestock farming was such that it became possible to export livestock for slaughter to the Cape.

Crop farming never reached any great heights in the Transvaal. Only very small areas were devoted to it. Mixed farming was more pronounced on farms in the north, while farming in the south was devoted almost exclusively to livestock. Some contemporary visitors to the area saw the introduction of the railway as the answer to the Boers' backward ways. It was thought that

> the railway would bring about a total revolution in the economic life of the Transvaal Republic. It would rouse the Boers from their rest; it would enthuse them with ambition in the struggle for survival. It would transform the South African to equivalence with more developed nations and equip them with entrepreneurial ambition. The old methods of crop and livestock farming, partly natural, partly destructive, will have to make way for culture.[5]

The Transvaal Boers were thus ill equipped to aspire to independent statehood. Apart from their predatory land and labour policies, they were unqualified to establish any economic base for a modern state. They were by force of circumstance Jack-of-all-trades, but master of none. The virtual absence of schools and educational facilities resulted in only one trade being accessible to them – farming. However, even in this trade abject ignorance was not an asset, which explains the poor results they achieved and the fact that their Republic remained an importer of basic foodstuffs up to its demise.

The general application of all trades for subsistence was of course, a necessity, but it did not lead to any great competence in any particular trade.[6] In any event, the Boers could not see the value of being trained in any one trade. There was 'no demand for scientific specialization and [specialization] as such would have very little success in the land'.[7]

It is therefore not to be wondered that their state coffers were perennially empty. They had great expectations of building a railway line to Delagoa Bay in order to be independent of British controlled harbours, but they had very little conception of what it would take to make such a railway economically viable. In any event, Delagoa Bay was in Portuguese territory. The irony was that Portugal had itself been a virtual colony of Britain since 1703.[*][8] The Transvalers, although they were probably blissfully unaware of it, could thus only choose through which British colony they preferred to send their goods. Mozambique was the shorter route, but it lacked proper port facilities. Politically, however, it made no difference which port they chose – Cape Town, Durban or Lourenço Marques. Consequently, the Transvaal would not gain greater political independence by trading through Portuguese territory.

The Delagoa Bay line would, however, have one major advantage. Delagoa Bay was the nearest harbour from the Transvaal, and after the Suez Canal opened on 15 August 1865, it would present the shortest sea trade route to Europe. The Republic lacked only trade goods that could form the basis of such commerce. Live cattle were not a great proposition for export to Europe or the East and a railway could not be made viable on the export of products of the hunt. Without exports, the Republic would not have any foreign exchange to pay for imports. Nevertheless, they would pursue the dream, but it would bear no fruit until the arrival of gold: the gold mines of the Witwatersrand would supply the missing piece of the economic jigsaw puzzle.

The proposed Delagoa Bay line and the resulting 'railway politics' would play an important part in the fortunes and misfortunes of the subcontinent along the road to war.

---

* The British and the Portuguese signed the Treaty of Methuen in 1703. It was an alliance and a trade agreement that allowed Portuguese exports into Britain at preferential rates and bound Portugal to import a wide variety of manufactures from Britain. Portugal sent Brazilian gold by the shipload to Britain to settle the difference in value between the exports and the imports. The alliance and the trade agreement were to last in perpetuity and are still in effect.

The aftermath of the Sand River Convention

As might be imagined, the Boers interpreted the Sand River Convention as recognition of a new state, which it was not. The Convention's silence on the question of borders did not deter them; on the contrary, their ambition knew no bounds. They might well have claimed jurisdiction north of the Vaal as far as Egypt, but contented themselves (for the moment) with the Limpopo River as a northern border – the river beyond which Mzilikazi had been driven.

Just as had happened in Natal, Boer territorial claims became increasingly ambitious. They wrongly regarded the Sand River Convention as having given them undisputed ownership of all territory north of the Vaal River and the right to fix the western boundary to suit themselves. They thus chose the Kalahari as their Western boundary, which was a vague enough description to allow for endless disputation. In the east, they initially claimed the Drakensberg, but the Lydenburg Boers' dealings with the Swazi and Pedi soon resulted in the shifting of that claim eastward, to the Lebombo Mountains.

The Boers also claimed sovereignty over all the Tswana in the Transvaal. They based these claims on the grounds that they had displaced Mzilikazi as the Tswana's overlords. It is extremely doubtful whether such a claim, even if true, would have sustained a valid legal claim even at that time. In this case, it was only a partial truth at best. While some Tswana chiefdoms had been subject to the Matabele, notably the Hurutshe, Rratlou-Rolong and Kgatla, others like the Thlaping, Ngwaketse, Kwena and Ngwato were not and had never been.[9]

In any event, sovereignty is a concept that applies to territory, not to people as such. If a state is sovereign within a specified territory, the people living within that territory are then subjects of that state. By driving off Mzilikazi and his people with the help of some of these 'subject' chiefdoms, the Boers gained sovereignty neither over the territory nor over the people they claimed. Indeed, even the South African Republic never became a sovereign state, but that forms a later part of this narrative.

Nevertheless, the claims clearly indicate that the intention of these Dutch immigrant farmers was never to liberate, but to subjugate. Theirs was nothing other than a policy of oppressive colonization. The strategy is even more pernicious in the light of the agreement at the Sand River to the effect that 'all trade in ammunition with the native tribes is prohibited, both by the British Government and the emigrant farmers on both sides of the Vaal River'. It is a classic case of the expansion of technologically advanced people at the expense of technologically less advanced people.

United in disunity

The dual leadership agreed upon between Potgieter and Pretorius before their deaths immediately gave rise to problems. However, Pretorius' son, M. W. Pretorius, left the northerners alone until he called a conference at Potchefstroom to consider a draft constitution which he had had prepared by a commission. The proposed constitution styled the new republic 'De Zuid Afrikaansche Republiek' (The South African Republic). It provided, *inter alia*, for a single President as head of State, only one church, the Dutch Reformed, no equality between black and white and no property ownership for black people. The constitution was accepted, but in the aftermath, the Potgieter supporters and the Lydenburgers mutinied on the issue of single leadership. The Lydenburgers thereafter operated as 'De Republiek Lydenburg en Zuid Afrika'. They only rejoined the 'South African Republic' three years later, on 3 April 1860.[10]

Although the constitution provided that Potchefstroom would be the capital, Pretorius had a more central site in mind. This was next to the Aapies River (a creek really) and in February 1857, Pretoria was born on the banks of the Aapies. It was first called Pretoriusdorp, and then renamed Pretorium before it finally became Pretoria.

The young Pretorius had great political ambitions, but he was unable to realize most of them. His idealistic adventurism, coupled with a lack of political realism, soon led to chaos, including an armed confrontation with the Free Staters when he suddenly claimed all land north of the Orange River as part of his Republic.

The state he had created north of the Vaal was at best a haphazard affair and with the added burden of weak administration, it soon sank into civil war and anarchy. This period gave impetus to the rising political star of Paul Kruger, who conducted the civil war on behalf of the Potchefstroom faction against Stephanus Schoeman, his opponent from the supporters of Potgieter of the Soutpansberg.

The most important result, however, was that the state became bankrupt. The Republic's finances had never been anything but problematic, but at that stage, not even a financial genius could save it, and Pretorius certainly was not one. It thus happened that after Pretorius and his delegation failed in securing the Transvaal's bid for the newly discovered Kimberley diamond fields, the Volksraad asked Pretorius to resign, which he did in 1871. This development also had the salutary effect of ending the ill-fated principle of hereditary leadership.

Burgers on the cusp

The Volksraad then adopted a rather surprising course of action. Having consulted with President Brand, the then President of the Free State, they invited Thomas François Burgers of the Cape clergy to stand for the now vacant position of President. The reason for this move was that they wished to find a President who was not historically linked to either the Potgieter or the Pretorius factions.

Burgers accepted the nomination and won the presidential election. Given the circumstances in the Transvaal, he was an unlikely candidate for President. He was only 37 years old, well educated, widely travelled and married to a Scotswoman. Despite his lack of experience of government administration, his education, personality and life-experience should have stood the nascent state in good stead. However, these very attributes caused him to be so far removed from the character and background of the people he had to lead, that he might as well have come from a different planet. Catastrophe was virtually guaranteed.

When he was approached to make himself available, he was the minister of the Hanover (a town in the Cape colony) congregation of the Dutch Reformed Church. He had had a disagreement with his Church Council over alleged heresy that had been referred to the Synod, the senior body of the Church, for disciplinary action. The Cape Synod censured him for heresy, but Burgers won the day by taking the matter to the Cape Supreme Court, which overturned the Synod's decision and reinstated him. This action did not endear him to the Church. He was also on friendly and familiar terms with Charles Darwin, a fact apparently not widely known at the time.

Nevertheless, he cherished an ideal of

a coming Dutch African Republic for the whole of South Africa; but his ideas were altogether too visionary and unpractical for the people he had to deal with. A considerable minority were opposed to him from the first on account of his religious views. His determined efforts to infuse some vigour and 'go' into the stolid and ignorant Boers made him still more enemies; and his precipitancy and want of practical knowledge brought about the crash which had long been impending, but which might have been staved off a little longer.[11]

Burgers arrived in Pretoria on 27 June, 1872, to be sworn in as State President. His first task was to try to restore the finances of the Republic. Great must have been his shock upon taking over to find that the Boers were not the most reliable taxpayers. Not only was there no revenue flowing into the state's coffers, but also, even such monies as were available had not been collected. Apparently, the one piece of non-lethal technology that was considerably appreciated by the Boers was the printing press. For every financial need that arose they called on this machine to provide the wherewithal. Unsurprisingly, only the currencies of the Cape Colony and Natal commanded any respect at that time. The South African Republic was undoubtedly bankrupt in 1872.[12]

As a consequence, all civil servants, who lived on a salary paid in Republican currency, were also bankrupt. Inevitably there was a great deal of corruption and petty theft. The fiscal chaos made commerce even more problematic than it would otherwise have been. People paid their debts with Republican currency, but preferred to barter and exchange goods rather than to earn currency, other than 'foreign' currency. The latter, if obtained, would be hung on to for dear life. Merchants issued little cardboard squares known as 'good fors' to avoid using the local currency. A similar 'ticket' system was used for putting in the collection plate at church services.

Unfortunately, there was no Alexander Hamilton to take control of the finances and arrange a sinking fund, as was done in the US when the Federal Government assumed the States' debts after the War of Independence. However, Burgers did the best he knew how and raised, with much difficulty, £66,000 from the Cape Commercial Bank. He used the borrowed money to redeem the Republic's worthless paper money and to pay the arrear salaries of the Hollanders who had been employed as civil servants.

He knew this would not be sufficient. New sources of revenue would have to be found and found soon. He started to make himself very unpopular with his new citizenry by his efforts to bring order to the chaos and to stave off further financial crises. He fired corrupt officials and insisted on proper accounting in all departments of state. Infamously, he tried vigorously to collect all unpaid taxes and to ensure the collection of new ones.

As for possible new sources of revenue, he pinned a lot of hope on the possible discovery of payable gold. Fortunately, his predecessor, M. W. Pretorius, had already convinced the Volksraad to throw the country open for gold prospecting. Before the change in the law by Resolution of the Volksraad on December 21, 1870, prospecting for gold was strictly forbidden, although one P. J. Marais, a Cape Afrikaner with experience in California and Australia, had been allowed to prospect in 1852. However, on that occasion the Potchefstroom Volksraad swore him to secrecy on pain of death, but promised him a reward of £500 should he succeed in his search. Although he found some traces of gold, his expedition was not successful.

Gold finds had been reported almost immediately after the change in the law, but it was to be during Burgers' tenure of the Presidency that the first gold rush in the Transvaal took place. Many burghers (citizens of the Republic) thought this to be the economic miracle they had been waiting for. Unfortunately for them, the discovery was on land in an area that was hotly contested by the Swazi, the Pedi and the Boers of Lydenburg.

CHAPTER SEVEN

GOLD TO THE RESCUE?

There was always talk of gold in the Transvaal. Even before the trekkers arrived, hunting parties across the Vaal had reported gold outcroppings on the Witwatersrand. In 1866, Karl Gottlieb Mauch, a German schoolmaster with an impressive personality and a passion for gold arrived in the territory. He traipsed all over the territory, acting like a badly trained pointer.

He was an extremely energetic explorer, always rushing hither and thither across the whole of the area north and south of the Limpopo River. Always hot on the trail of a fabulous gold strike, he eventually reported a find on the Tati River, north of the Limpopo. He combined evidence of ancient gold workings with the traces of gold he had found in the Tati River to develop a fascinating theory that Africa had once supported a great gold industry.[1] It seems that Mauch honestly believed that the fabled mines of King Solomon would be discovered somewhere in the area that he had prospected. This was just the sort of story out of Africa that would make the pulses race of many people in Europe and America.

Potchefstroom quickly became inundated with strange characters arriving from all points of the compass, seeking directions and guides to the Tati River. All this activity did not leave the Transvalers unmoved. They sent a commando group under Commandant Jan Viljoen to Mzilikazi in an effort to extract mining concessions from him. Whatever Mzilikazi's response might have been, the then president, M. W. Pretorius, was not about to moderate Boer ambitions; in 1868, he summarily claimed the Bubye River, a northern tributary of the Limpopo, as the Transvaal's new northern border. This extended the Republic's claimed northern frontier to include Mauch's gold strike on the Tati and all the land right up to Lake Ngami in Central Africa.

Neither of the two interested European powers, namely Britain and Portugal, did anything about these wild claims. They knew the financial straits that the state was in; despite all its posturing and pretensions, they expected it to fold sooner rather than later. The impact the collapse of the Transvaal would have on the borders of the colony of Natal, Griqua-land West, the newly formed diamond rich territory, and even the Cape colony itself, was potentially very disturbing. Also, in keeping with the spirit of Napier's earlier expressed sentiments, Britain would feel herself obliged to take a hand in these matters before a catastrophe occurred. It was with some trepidation therefore, that British officialdom kept a close watch on developments.

In the process of travelling all over the country, Mauch had pointed in virtually every direction as being the location of a great gold treasure. The Tati 'gold field' proved to be nothing of the kind and left many of the prospectors destitute. Having triggered a rush to the Tati River, Mauch's unceasing energy focused his fossicking attention on the foothills of the Drakensberg beyond Lydenburg. He now pointed in the direction northeast and east of Lydenburg in a general sort of way. This resulted in the only real reward for all his life's labour; they named a range of these foothills the Mauchsberg. In a wry twist of fate, the Mauchsberg looks over the rich alluvial goldfields of the eastern Transvaal – the gold that Mauch had failed to find.

Mauch never managed to discover any specific find of payable gold and he died penniless, as did all those who followed his pointers. Nevertheless, his 1867 reports of gold did start, if not a full-scale gold rush, then at least a steady stream of prospectors and diggers into the Transvaal. Initially, the Transvaal became famous, not as a place where gold might be found *per se*, but as a staging area for prospecting for fabulous riches further north. The initial perception would soon change.

Prospectors and diggers

The first really competent party of prospectors arrived from Natal in 1869. Led by Edward Button, the party included George Parsons and George Sutherland. Another prospector, Tom McLachlan, later joined them. Sutherland was the most experienced prospector in the group, having spent most of his life prospecting for gold on the alluvial diggings of California and Australia. Mauch had also influenced them. The latter's latest comments on the area east of Lydenburg diverted them from travelling to the Tati River and they started panning the streams in the eastern lowveld.

It is probable that this group found gold in the eastern territory of the Transvaal some time before the change in the law that allowed prospecting and therefore kept it quiet. Given the paranoid Transvaal government and their valueless currency, the prospectors probably realized that they would be better served by discretion and selling their gold to the Bank of Natal.[2]

However, as soon as the Transvaal changed its stance on prospecting and actually promised rewards to the finders of payable mineral deposits, Edward Button put in a claim for a strike at 'Eersteling' (first one). Button obtained a concession from the Volksraad and proceeded to London where he founded the Transvaal Gold Mining Company with a capital of £50,000, a greater capital base than that of the state that gave him the mining concession. It was to be the first company to mine gold in South Africa. It immortalized Button, but never showed a profit.

Thomas McLachlan, G.R. Parsons and J.L. Valentine made the strikes that really started the gold rush rolling. They applied to Jansens, the *Landdrost* at Lydenburg, to have their claims registered. Jansens held an inspection *in loco* and reported very positively on the strike to the Volksraad, which was by then already ensconced in Pretoria. He found several people already working there 'and not one has returned home empty handed'. The diggings were proclaimed on 14 May 1873. Thomas François Burgers, the President of the South African Republic, announced in the

Government Gazette that the area of Ohrigstad River, district of Lydenburg, was open for digging.

Because the towns of Lydenburg and Andries Ohrigstad were the easternmost Boer towns, the gold strikes were reported to the outside world as having occurred in the Lydenburg district. This was hardly correct. The first true strikes of payable gold were found very far to the east and south of Lydenburg and Ohrigstad.

The gold was alluvial and was found in virtually every one of the crystal clear streams that run down the valleys and gorges of that verdant, mountainous and magnificently beautiful stretch of countryside. If the real value of gold is to be found in its physical beauty, as the ancient Egyptians maintained, then it could not have been found in a more appropriate natural setting. The area enjoys high rainfall, thus covering the rolling mountain scenery with, for this part of Africa, unaccustomed green and lush vegetation. The deep, wooded valleys are filled with rainforests on their slopes and must have been a proper Eden in those early days of discovery. At that time the whole area was still teeming with game and unspoilt by the hand of man. Even so, it is still awe-inspiringly beautiful today.

However, as will be explained presently, the land was dead-centre in a three-cornered controversy: the Swazi claimed it; the Boers claimed that the Swazi had ceded it to them (for 100 cattle); and the Pedi claimed that it had never been the Swazi's to cede in the first place, as it was ancestrally theirs. This controversy was, in due course, to play a central role in the downfall of the South African Republic.

Prospecting continued and soon McLachlan, that intrepid prospector, made an even richer strike on the plateau above his first strike. Soon that area would be swamped with diggers and a large diggers' camp arose. Diggers streamed into the country at such a rate that Jansens feared that they would all die of hunger. He underestimated these hardy adventurers who were survivors, first and foremost. There was still game in abundance and they traded with the local Pedi inhabitants for their other food requirements.

Some of the diggers had done reasonably well on the Californian and Australian diggings. They generally arrived by ship, disembarked at Cape Town and travelled by ox wagon or carriage to Pretoria and then on to Lydenburg. It was all on foot or horseback from there. Many came via Natal, which was reasonably close by.

Most diggers from overseas were, however, not so fortunate. They took a cheaper route on steamers through to Delagoa Bay. Most of them then walked all the way to the diggings, some 250 kilometres through hot, humid bushveld. The going through the dense, thorny hardwoods of the bushveld was not easy and in addition, the country itself was difficult to navigate in. The coastal plain is quite flat up to the Lebombo Mountains, which look more like low ridges than a mountain range. This flat land is densely covered with thorn trees and bushes, which makes it very difficult to see far ahead. With vision being restricted, it is extremely easy to lose one's direction unless one is very familiar with the terrain. The dim track worn into the veldt by the feet of predecessors was the best guide to the gold fields, but wild animals sometimes necessitated a hasty detour which often left the traveller disoriented, lost and in mortal danger.

But, formidable as they were, even the many dangerous animals such as lion, elephant, leopard, wild dogs, hippo and crocodiles were not these adventurers' most awesome obstacles. It soon became known that one had to reach the diggings within two weeks of landing at Delagoa Bay as the area was infested with malaria and the odds of contracting the disease were about 2 to 1 in the summer months. Malaria has a gestation period of approximately two weeks and therefore, if the traveller did not reach the diggings within two weeks, the fever might get him on the road and that would be the end of the road for that pilgrim, as the diggers liked to refer to themselves.

The first arrivals were fortunate as they all found gold – and plenty of it. They staked their claims but then found no provision for registering them. There were no dispute resolution provisions and basically, no law and order. The only law the Volksraad had deemed necessary, immediately after Buttons' discovery, was to declare all mining rights the property of the state and to make provision for some rewards to be paid to the discoverers. However, nobody ever managed to wrest any reward out of them.

The New Caledonia gold field

Many of the diggers now arriving were from California and Australia. These men were veterans and they knew how a proper gold field was run. Jansens was hovering in the background, representing the government and so they collared him. They told him in no uncertain terms, and in plain English, what they thought of him and his government. Although no verbatim record of this conversation is extant, it must have been pretty tough on poor old Jansens; these hardened diggers were unlikely to have minced their words.

Nevertheless, Jansens apparently kept a cool head and organized a diggers' committee as a sort of legislative assembly, to frame rules and regulations for the diggings. They elected a Major W. MacDonald, an American who looked like a character from a Bret Harte story, as Gold Commissioner. He would be responsible for registering claims, collecting claim fees and settling disputes between the diggers.[3]

Since he was the diggers' own choice and knew how to handle difficult situations, Jansens was happy to agree to his appointment. Jansens would not have had much choice in any event. The government paid Major MacDonald a salary of £29. 3s. 6d. per month and he earned every penny of it. He proved to be an extremely competent official who started with a community of 250 diggers under his supervision that soon grew to over 1,000. He was to maintain law and order in a very tough community, very successfully for many years.

Jansens, who had been forced to think on his feet as the digger population exploded, with the consequent increases in legal complexities and administrative demands, decided it was time to 'call in the cavalry'. Finding himself unable adequately to explain the reality of the situation to Pretoria, he sent a message to Burgers requesting him to visit the diggings. Both Burgers and the Volksraad agreed that that would be a wise course of action.

Goodness knows what the Volksraad expected when they originally began to encourage prospecting for gold and other minerals, but they now began to fear the presence of so many English-speakers. Not only could their presence rend asunder the Boers' isolation, but, which was even worse, experience had taught them that where the English went, the British flag was soon to follow.

The diggers were not too keen on the prospect of Burgers' visit. They would evidently have preferred as little contact with the Republic as possible. Nevertheless, when Burgers arrived, he soon endeared himself to them. He was a brilliant and fluent speaker of English with a sense of humour to boot. Burgers visited MacDonald's 'office' in McLachlan's camp and scanned the list of claim holders. 'Why' he exclaimed while reading it, 'McDonald ... MacDonald ... two MacPhersons ... a MacTavish ... MacAndrew ... it's all Macs. I am going to call this place Mac Mac.'[4] Although the official name of the area in the documents of Pretoria became 'The New Caledonia Gold Field', nobody ever called it anything but the 'Mac Mac Diggings'.

And Mac Mac remains the name of the area to this day. The remains of the Mac Mac Diggings are one of the many attractions on any visit to the magnificent scenery of the eastern Transvaal. The Mac Mac Falls, like so many waterfalls in the region, is a beautiful sight to behold. The Mac Mac Creek plunges precipitously down a straight rock face into a deep, wooded gorge, along the bottom of which the creek gingerly washes its stony way down to the Mac Mac pools. The outlook point, now unfortunately over-commercialized with roadside curio dealers, is situated right next to the road between Sabie and Graskop. It was a compulsory stop for two generations of the Stephens family on every one of their frequent excursions into the eastern Transvaal. The remains of other old digging sites are also ubiquitous throughout the area.

There is another unique feature of this gold rush area of the Transvaal. It is the only place in South Africa where the streams and dry riverbeds are called creeks and gulches. This bears testimony to the many Americans and Australians who came to these diggings and traversed the whole area, naming places and geographic features as they went. They knew a creek when they saw one. If a stream had water it was a creek, if it was dry, it was a gulch.

Back in Pretoria, Burgers tried to allay the fears of the Volksraad by describing Major MacDonald as an American and 'a good Republican'. As he had agreed with the diggers at the meeting, he fixed claim licence fees at 5 shillings per month and trading licences, which would include the right to sell liquor, at £9 per quarter. It was to be MacDonald's job to collect all of these fees and to remit them to Pretoria. He also did his best to arrange for the development of the area by appointing a committee to oversee the transformation of the trail to Delagoa Bay into a wagon road. He followed MacDonald's recommendation to appoint Thomas Searle and Tom McLachlan justices of the peace, together with Herbert Rhodes (the then not yet famous Cecil John's brother) and Captain Dietrich, an ex-officer in the German Army.

Burgers was enthusiastic about his Republic's new prospects. He immediately arranged to purchase the farm Graskop, from Abel Erasmus, a *Veldcornet* in the area. His idea was to found the capital of the goldfields on that farm and indeed, it is the site of the village of Graskop. But events had already overtaken his plans. Before anything could come of the 'capital of the gold fields', the diggings moved away. There was more gold in them thar' hills ...

A pilgrim finds his rest

An old misanthropic digger called Alec Patterson was the first to move away from his claim at Mac Mac. He was actually known as 'Wheelbarrow Alec', since he had arrived on the diggings, from no one knows where for certain, with all his tools and equipment loaded in a wheelbarrow. He and his wheelbarrow were inseparable and when he moved away, the wheelbarrow went with him.

The diggings apparently became too crowded for his liking so, early one fine morning, he lifted his loaded wheelbarrow and with scarcely a word of farewell he quite literally headed for the hills. No one knows what route he followed, but to get to where we find him later in the story, he must have hauled and pushed his wheelbarrow up and over the spur of a mountain that rises some 2,000 feet.

He settled to rest near a clear stream running in a narrow cleft valley on the other side of the spur he had crossed. There his dreams came true. He panned gravel from the stream and found the elusive bright 'tail' of pure gold dust at the bottom. That is the driving force, the vision and the dream of every digger and on that day Patterson was at the end of his rainbow.

Although he realized that he would have to report his find at some time or other to register his claim, he decided to keep the valley to himself for as long as possible, enjoying his solitude. But it was not to be so idyllic for long. Another digger, one William Trafford, also decided to abandon his claim at Mac Mac. Like Patterson, he crossed the same mountain and discovered the same stream. When he panned the stream and struck gold, he was ecstatic. Legend has it that he then shouted to the hills around him 'the pilgrim is at rest!' As the hills answered his shout with rolling echoes, he decided to call the place Pilgrim's Rest.

He immediately left for the office of MacDonald at Mac Mac to register his claim. Thus, although Alec 'Wheelbarrow' Patterson was the first person to find gold in the creek at Pilgrim's Rest, William Trafford filed the first claim and gave the valley its evocative name. The town named Pilgrim's Rest arose in that valley, on the banks of the creek. It might have aspired to the title 'capital of the gold fields', but it never developed past village stage. The old town is still there, now a living museum, preserving for visitors some of the romantic spirit of those turbulent, but wonderful, days of pioneering adventure.

In a great rush, most of the diggers then abandoned their claims at Mac Mac and hastened to stake new claims at Pilgrim's Rest. By the end of 1873, most of the diggers had moved away from Mac Mac. Inevitably, Major MacDonald, the Gold Commissioner also had to move to where the demand for his services were greatest. Therefore, in January 1874 he moved his offices to Pilgrim's Rest where a steady demand for the registration of new claims kept him busy.

Most of the gold found at Mac Mac and Pilgrim's Rest was gold dust, but a number of memorable nuggets were also found. The most famous one unfortunately exists only as a legend. It was allegedly found under a very large boulder in the bed of the creek and, according to the legend, weighed all of 25 lbs! There is, however, no record of such a find.

Nevertheless, another nugget find is authentically documented. It is the 123 oz. nugget found on the claim of 'Count' Alois Nellmapius. The man's title was pure invention on the part of the diggers, but he was accorded the status of 'Count' because he was regarded as the luckiest man on the diggings. This Hungarian adventurer kept the money he made on the diggings and went on to become the Transvaal's first industrialist, courtesy of the Republic's continuing 'concessions' policy.

Two other famously large nuggets were also found. Henry Glynn recorded one at 208 oz. for which his father paid £750. The other is known as the 'Breda' nugget, which weighed in at 214 oz. and was found in Peach Tree Creek. The nuggets found at Pilgrim's Rest were pale yellow, 'ash blonde' really, because of the large percentage of silver present. The nuggets were highly prized and often set in rings. However, although gold nuggets were the stuff of dreams, extracting gold from the gravel of the creek bed made the real money.

As with all such enterprises, not everybody had the same luck and due to a lack of proper records, it is impossible to say what the value of gold was that was recovered. Some calculations indicate that the fields must have produced between £300,000 and £400,000 per year for the community to have existed on the scale it did. It is said that the Australians were the most expert diggers and they set themselves a minimum target of £8. 10s. 0d. per day.[5]

The case of the disappearing gold

Although all the news from the east was positive, the South African Republic was still bankrupt. Everybody had rejoiced at the gold strike in the hope that the country would now begin to resemble an independent polity, but in vain. Very little revenue, if any, was flowing into the coffers of the state. Burgers had borrowed £60,000 from the Cape Commercial Bank to finance the State, and had spent the money on various salutary projects, but there was no prospect of repaying it. The old paper currency had been called in on the strength of the borrowed money, but the new currency proved to be not much more popular than the old one. The problem was still that the state had no real source of revenue, thus fiduciary money lacked all value. This aspect was extremely worrying for the young President.

On his second presidential visit to the gold fields, Burgers accompanied H.W. Struben, who had invited him along on his own trip to the diggings. Struben was to become famous as one of the pioneers of the Witwatersrand gold fields, but on this occasion he was going to the new gold strike to protect his rights as owner of the farm Poniekrantz, on which the latest strike had been made. The second trip followed just after the move by most of the diggers, including MacDonald, to the new site at Pilgrim's Rest.

Burgers had pressing reasons for this second visit. He specifically wanted to determine why Eldorado was not delivering; the gold bonanza was disappearing into the woodwork. Additionally, he had received a despatch from MacDonald, dated 12 January, to the effect that he was experiencing some difficulty with a number of the new arrivals who were not willing to accept discipline. Burgers was also in receipt of petitions by the diggers, forwarded by MacDonald, requesting representation in the Volksraad and nominating Tom McLachlan and F. P. Mansfield as their representatives.

The basic problem of the disappearing gold was of course, that there was exactly zero financial expertise in the whole Republic. The educated Hollanders who had been brought in to man the civil service were not trained in finance. In fact, there were very few burghers who were sufficiently literate to occupy clerical positions in the civil service, hence the importation of a few Cape Afrikaners and educated Hollanders.

Apart from digger's licences, trading licences and a few other odds and ends, they had no idea how the state could or should generate revenue from the diggings. There was no company law in the state, so the flotation of companies could not be coordinated, nor could they be taxed. There was no way in which it could be determined how much gold an individual digger was taking out of his claim, because the government did not act as purchaser of the gold. Thus, there was no way in which they could tax the diggers or derive any further advantage from the gold they recovered.

Looking at the initial prospecting laws, and the later Gold Law of the South African Republic, it is evident that the Volksraad did not have the faintest idea how the state could benefit substantially from the gold bonanza. Amazingly enough, it seems that the matter of raising revenue for the state had not even been given any proper thought by the Volksraad. Licences were the best idea they could come up with and MacDonald's accounts for 1874–75 show a paltry total income to the state, from all licences and fees of £2,200. Against that, there was MacDonald's salary, which had been increased to £450 per year, and a few other expenses amounting to some further £500 for the year. Clearly, the answer to the state's financial problems did not lie in such meagre pickings.

It is clear that the government should have acted as the only purchaser of gold. With a fair buy/sell spread on the price of gold, the state would not only have realized a healthy profit selling the gold in Europe, or even to the banks in the Cape Colony, but it would then also have been in a position to levy a tax on the money earned by the diggers. On Burgers' second visit to the diggings, one T. Perrin, a Swiss national who had come to the diggings as an assayer, presented this solution to the President.

The problem with this course of action was the economic system that had developed on the gold fields. The diggers, quite understandably, had absolutely no faith in the paper currency of the Republic. MacDonald had already pointed out this problem to the government. He had been given £1,000 in paper money from the government to buy gold, but he experienced great difficulty in purchasing any. Consequently, MacDonald had in an earlier report already stressed the need for coins on the diggings.

The digger community lived largely by barter; not that they were averse to currency in principle, only to the Republic's version in particular. They exchanged their gold for food, their tools, their clothing and for large supplies of liquor. Gold was their money and they owed the Republic nothing.

This situation suited the storekeepers. They made a profit on the goods they sold, and they made a profit on the gold they received. The gold itself they sold to banks in Natal, which was close by. The banks, in turn, shipped it through Durban to the European gold markets. Some of the shrewder diggers spent as little of their gold as possible and hoarded the rest for the day when they had made their stash and would leave the diggings forever. Not many realized this dream.

Perrin had been employed by the state mint in Switzerland and was well informed on money matters. During his stay at Pilgrim's Rest, he drafted a remarkable document in his spare time. This document, which is today preserved in the archives of the South African Mint in Pretoria, argued the case for establishing a mint at Pilgrim's Rest. It was the best financial advice the South African Republic would ever receive and it identified the financial problem of the state and its solution precisely:[6]

When the Californian gold diggings were opened, our first French financier, the late Baron Rothschild, sent over to San Francisco a young man and his family, M. Davidson, for the only purpose of buying gold. The richest man in Europe thought it was worth his trouble to monopolize the gold and create a new branch of his immense firm in the young and well promising country. The US Government soon came into competition with the rich banker, but with one more chance of success, viz. the possibility of Coining.

A mint was created and national coin began to abound in America. So did Australia. Both nations understood that it would be folly to forfeit this grand privilege of a government – stamping and issuing coins.

A mint established near the gold diggings could realize a large profit of which a liberal government would let the diggers have their share. Freight, loss of interest during the time of transport, insurance money, commission of the buyer who has to sell again to any European market, all these are as many expenses saved if gold is hic et nunc transformed into coins. Should the Government give to the digger the intermediary

price between the real value of the finds and the amount offered to him by any other purchaser, the bargain would still be a very remunerative one to both contractors. The price of gold increasing would soon prove an encouragement for all hands at work already, an effective allurement for many yet to come.

Perrin went on into much detail, including a costing of the machinery and equipment required for the mint and careful sketches of the building required. His calculations came to £962 for the project. He also dealt with some possible cash flow problems and how they could be overcome. The document came to 11 handwritten pages and he presented it to Burgers upon the latter's arrival in Pilgrim's Rest in February 1874.

The Staatspond Project

Burgers was much impressed with the document Perrin had presented to him. Without delaying until his return to Pretoria, he wrote a letter to J. J. Pratt, the Republic's Consul-General in London, instructing him to make enquiries from the Royal Mint in Britain, or elsewhere in Europe, as to the feasibility of having some gold coins struck from gold. He would remit this Transvaal gold to Pratt upon his return to Pretoria, before May of that year when the next session of the Volksraad was scheduled. Burgers thereupon bought gold at Pilgrim's Rest, the details of which transaction are not known eventually remitting $22\frac{1}{4}$ lbs to Pratt in London.

At a total expense of £90. 0s. 10d., the gold yielded 837 sovereigns, minted by Messrs. Heaton Son, 'moneyers' of Birmingham. The coins had in relief, the head of Burgers on the obverse side and the arms of the Republic on the reverse side of the coin. A break in the dies in the process of coining, not only caused some delay, but also resulted in two distinct versions of the coin – the 'thick bearded Burgers sovereign' and the 'thin bearded Burgers sovereign'.

The coins were unfortunately not ready by May for the Volksraad's scheduled sitting. They were only ready for presentation on

24 September 1874, when Burgers sprung his surprise on them. He was sure that he had found the answer to the state's financial problems and great must have been his anticipation in revealing the first coins struck from South African gold to the Volksraad. So much greater then must his disappointment have been when, instead of joy and praise, his revelation was met with petty criticism and condemnation.

He had committed two cardinal sins in the eyes of the legislature: he had not obtained their permission before he had had the coins struck and most seriously, he had had a 'graven image' of himself made and perpetuated on the coin, thus offending the law of God. After a long and sometimes acrimonious debate, the Volksraad eventually accepted the following motion:

> The Raad resolves to accept the gold pieces which were laid before it by His Honour the State President and declared by His Honour to be of the exact and same value as one English pound sterling, as legal tender in the Republic.

Burgers gratefully received the decision, thanked the members and gave them each one of the coins in payment for a day's attendance, but the chairman received 24 sovereigns. Burgers named the new coin a 'Staatspond' (State pound), since there was no sovereign in the Republic. The Raad passed a further resolution, at the instance of Burgers, that one Staatspond should be sent to the head of each state that had by then recognized the independence of the Republic. It added that one Staatspond should be given to Burgers as well. Apparently the gift of gold coins to the chairman and members of the Raad had had a salutary effect on the said members' disposition.

Nevertheless, nothing came of all the effort. No further Staatspond were ever minted and nothing came of the establishment of a mint at Pilgrim's Rest, or anywhere else for that matter. Like virtually all of Burgers' ideas, it was too progressive for implementation in such a state. Although the Volksraad had passed the resolution accepting the coin as legal tender, the whole tenor of the debate indicated that the members had not the slightest appreciation of what the importance of the idea was for the further existence of their state. After the initial resolution of acceptance, the whole project died a natural death.

There is an ironic sidelight to the whole story. M. Perrin pleaded for 16 years for the establishment of a state mint in the Transvaal. This was eventually achieved after the discovery of gold on the Witwatersrand, but Perrin only became Master of the Mint in 1899. He held that position for a mere 18 months until, during the South African War, the British took Pretoria. Then the mint was no more.

CHAPTER EIGHT

FROM FLAWED
TO FAILED

Despite all the trappings of power of the South African Republic, the appointment of a Gold Commissioner, the passing of a Gold Law, the registration of claims, the issuing of diggers' licences and so forth, the fact remains that the state was flawed. Not only did the state fail to capitalize on its only hope of economic salvation but the land on which the diggings were situated was in dispute between many parties. The history of the dispute is filled with convoluted twists and turns, but essentially, the trouble started during the Difaqane.

The land between the Steelpoort River and the Crocodile River had been part and parcel of the original Pedi kingdom. With the incursions from Zululand and Mzilikazi's defeat of the Pedi, the population of that particular stretch of land were thrown into turmoil. The Pedi moved into their protective defensive positions in the mountains and the Swazi moved into the vacuum. They tried to assert control, but without conspicuous success. After Mzilikazi had been driven away to the west and before the Boers arrived, the Pedi started repopulating the area.

In 1846, prior to the discovery of gold, the anti-Potgieter faction of the Ohrigstad Boers entered into an alliance with Mswati, the young Swazi king. Mswati was at that time not yet well ensconced on the throne, as virtually every brother and half-brother of his was plotting for the crown against him – and each other. In 1847 these Boers helped Mswati to stave off an invasion by the Zulu under their king, Mpande. At that time, the Zulu King was cooperating with Malambule, also a brother of Mswati and pretender to the Swazi throne. Potgieter, because of his difficulties with the more democratically inclined Boers of Ohrigstad, tried to align himself with the Zulu.

In the upshot, the Zulu invasion was averted, but another conspiring half-brother, Somcuba, took refuge with the Ohrigstad Boers. When they moved to Lydenburg, so did he. In 1855, however, Mswati ceded the territory between the Olifants and Crocodile Rivers to the Lydenburg Boers, probably in return for a Boer commitment to eliminate Somcuba.[1]

The problem with this cession was that it was not the Swazi's land to cede. The land was populated by Pedi petty chiefs and claimed by their King Sekhukhune who was busy re-establishing the Pedi polity by winning over more and more chiefs to acknowledge him as their paramount. Sekhukhune had, moreover, proved the Pedi to be probably the most formidable power in the north-eastern Transvaal when, in 1869, he routed a major Swazi attack in a skilful defensive action fought with breech-loading rifles, making good use of natural ground cover.[2]

Sekhukhune was against the activities of missionaries in his lands. He also had many disputes with missionaries such as Hans Merensky and Dr. Nachtigal of the Berlin Missionary Society over land claims; he specifically strongly objected to their preaching against traditional Pedi practices, such as polygamy. More serious were his disputes with the South African Republic. These concerned competing land claims, labour and taxation.

Land, labour and taxes

As far as land claims were concerned, confusion reigned. The Republic had invited its burghers to claim land for farms as many times as they liked in the disputed area, subject only to an annual quitrent of 30 shillings, payable to the state. This resulted in a total confusion of titles among the Boers, as the area had not been properly surveyed and was so vast it would take years to survey in any event.

Most of the land claimed as farms in this way was already occupied by Pedi communities and in many cases the land was claimed precisely because there were black communities already living on it. The reasoning behind this was that the presence of black people indicated labour and water on the land.

Thus as whites from other areas of the Transvaal, Natal and the Cape scrambled for the farm land, the Republic claimed the Pedi as subjects, since as they preferred to see it, the Pedi had been subjects of the Swazi, who had ceded the land to the Lydenburg Boers. They therefore held the Pedi liable for taxation and for labour services.

Obviously, the irreversibly bankrupt Republic would vigorously try to exact taxes from any source, on any pretext, by any means, except from their own burghers, who were, as previously noted, notoriously recalcitrant taxpayers. The Republic, whose authority over the black population relied solely on superior force, having no other claim to legitimacy whatsoever, was having increasing difficulty collecting taxes from its black 'subjects'.

As far as the Boers' labour demands were concerned, these were equally resisted. The Pedi did not supply the Boers with children captured from their neighbours.[3] The Swazi apparently had no problem with this type of trade and readily complied. The Pedi, to an unusual degree, sought to sell their labour far away. They streamed to Port Elizabeth and, on the Kimberley diamond fields, they were the most numerous black group. Thus, on none of the issues of land, labour or taxation did Sekhukhune concede one iota, nor does there seem to have been any cogent reason for him to do so.

All these matters were constantly on the boil while the diggers were doing their own thing in the valleys and streams of Pilgrim's Rest, Graskop, Sabie and latterly even venturing out to an area closer to Swaziland, at Barberton. Indeed, the gold rush in the eastern Transvaal had a substantial impact on the Swazi. Their country did not have its modern borders which are much retraced from where Swazi people lived at that time (and to this day in many cases). During 1866, a year before Mswati's death, the Boers initiated an agreement between them and the Swazi, demarcating a detailed border between the two countries. Even this border still retained for Swaziland a more extensive territory than its modern border does.

Prospectors looking for gold, but more seriously, concession hunters overran their country after 1873. Concessions of every conceivable nature were wheedled out of the Swazi king. These included prospecting, mining, woodcutting, grazing and hunting concessions. The scope and number of concessions would escalate throughout the 19th century, until, by the end of the century, the country's independence was lost. The eventual subjugation of Swaziland in 1895 was not so much the result of direct imperialist aggression, or even annexation, as of the economic emasculation of the state through the granting of concessions.[4]

The 1866 demarcation of agreed borders between it and the Republic did not ease the pressure on Swaziland. In 1875, when gold fever was running high in the area, the Republic sent an expedition into Swaziland that managed to coerce them into a treaty that imposed subject status on Swaziland. It also gave the Transvaal the right to build a railway line right through the country.

The railway dream

A railway to Delagoa Bay had already been Potgieter's dream when he first decided on the Transvaal rather than Natal as his destination. After the discovery of the gold fields the building of a railway line to Delagoa Bay became an obsession with Burgers, as it would later be of Kruger.

Burgers went to Europe in 1875 to try to raise money to build a railway line to the port at Lourenço Marques. Because of the discovery of gold he received a more sympathetic hearing than before, and in a short time his mission proved successful. He managed to raise a loan of some £94,000 for the purposes of building the Delagoa railway line. He thereupon ordered lots of railway building material, including steel rails and rolling stock, to be delivered to Lourenço Marques.

However, his trip to Europe was cut short by serious developments at home. There was news that the diggers were in revolt and that the Pedi and Zulu on the country's borders were restive. The news did not augur well for obtaining further finance for a railway and Burgers decided to return home immediately. The dream had to be postponed, for the realities were catching up with a bankrupt state harbouring colonialist aspirations.

As a result, the railway equipment he had ordered, which included a luxury presidential coach, would lie rusting in Lourenço Marques for many years.

Reality calling

The origin of the trouble with the diggers that eventually played a part in the hasty return of Burgers from Europe was the Transvaal Gold Law. It was in the process of being legislated in the Volksraad. and a number of its provisions caused serious dismay amongst the diggers. They all opposed the doubling of claim licence fees to 10 shillings per year, while on certain of the other issues their opinions were sharply divided. The members of the Volksraad, their antediluvian attitudes unrestrained in the temporary absence of Burgers, had already decided that the 'Engelse' (Englishmen), as they referred to the cosmopolitan digger community, needed to be taught a lesson. They accordingly proceeded to ride roughshod over all their objections. Even the demonstrable fact that unim-aginative measures such as licence fees held absolutely no promise for the state's future financial prosperity in no way deterred them. The Volksraad accepted the new Gold Law virtually without amendment on 21 June 1875.

The new gold law of 1875 caused a row between MacDonald, the Gold Commissioner, some of the diggers and the government officials in Pretoria. The diggers absolutely refused to pay the 10 shillings claim fee and MacDonald was forced to place 110 of them under arrest. After much further argument and correspondence, the Volksraad stepped down. The regulation was reduced to five shillings per year once more.

After all this acrimony, MacDonald decided that he had had enough. He resigned his post as Gold Commissioner. The diggers gave him a farewell banquet and he left for Lourenço Marques, never to be heard of again. Dr. John Scoble succeeded him as Gold Commissioner.

Burgers returned to the Transvaal, but the damage had been done as far as the diggers were concerned. They had trusted Burgers, but the rift between them and the Volksraad was irreparable. Furthermore, a situation of distrust had developed between the diggers and the Volksraad, who were of the opinion that the President had been too 'liberal' with the 'Engelse'. This was another layer of support for the old 'us vs. them' syndrome that the Boers had been nurturing since before the Great Trek. It would receive further support during events soon to follow.

The end in sight

The end of the road for the Republic was now in sight. Although it would last two more years, the gold at Pilgrim's Rest was running out. It would not support such a great digger community for very much longer. The gold bonanza of the eastern Transvaal was fast slipping through the clumsy fingers of the Transvaal government.

The more serious problem was Sekhukhune. It was a problem that had been in the making for some time and it was not merely a result of the aggravation caused by the Boers' demands for land, labour and taxes. The problem must be seen in the context of a shift in power that had taken place in the area.[5] Sekhukhune, the Pedi paramount, had regained a lot of prestige for the paramountcy among the other chiefs through recent victories over the Swazi. Many of the Pedi, who lived in the ill-defined area in which the diggings were also situated, began to feel more secure in asserting their allegiance to the paramount.

These people had fallen loosely under the authority of the South African Republic, but as Boer demands for land, labour and taxes grew harsher and more excessive, the Sekhukhune paramountcy appeared to them a viable alternative to the oppressive situation under the Republic.

For the Republic, this shift in allegiance aggravated the shortage of labour and the difficulty of collecting taxes. It underlined the necessity to destroy the independence of the Pedi. Consequently white fears were nurtured and rumours were rife that a Pedi invasion of the eastern Transvaal was imminent. It was said also that Sekhukhune was at the centre of a pan-African conspiracy against them. All these elements together were calculated to justify an attack on the Pedi.

The immediate and proximate cause of the war was a dispute that arose between the Boers and a petty chief of the Pedi called Johannes. Sekhukhune had driven Johannes out of Pedi territory many years previously because of Johannes' conversion to Christianity. Johannes had then settled in Botsabelo in the Transvaal, which became a flourishing mission station. The bad treatment he received at the hands of the Boers, most likely their aggressive demands for taxes and labour, eventually drove him back to the Steelpoort River area, in Pedi territory, where Sekhukhune received him with open arms. The case of Johannes was not isolated and it is evident that Boer harassment drove Pedi chiefs more and more to seek Sekhukhune's protection.[6]

War against Sekhukhune

Burger's declaration of war on Sekhukhune of 16 May 1876, apparently took the latter by surprise.[7] Paul Kruger had been the Republic's Commandant-General and should have been in command of the operation. He had, however, previously resigned his position and Burgers left the post vacant. Thus, it happened that the Boer forces were under the direct and personal command of Burgers, an unlikely general.

The Republican commandos were sent against the Pedi during August of that year. In addition to the 2,000 burghers in the commandos, the attacking army included 2,400 Swazi warriors and 600 blacks from other tribes in the Transvaal. They attacked in three divisions. The first division stormed a hill which, because of its natural fortifications, was known as the 'Kaffir Gibraltar'. It was the stronghold of a chief called Matebe. The precise outcome of this engagement is not directly recorded, but the engagement appears to have been a success for the Republican forces.[8]

The activities of the second division, which included the large number of Swazi warriors, would have consequences that were more serious. This division attacked Johannes' stronghold with a previously agreed strategy that the Swazi would attack the stronghold from the one side while the Boers would attack from the other. The Swazi attacked as per the arrangement, but the Boers hung back. Some of the Boers wanted to join the fray, but their commandant said it was too dangerous. The Swazi managed to take the stronghold without the aid of the Boers. The carnage among the followers of Johannes was awful, for the enraged Swazi spared neither man, woman, nor child. Johannes, though fatally wounded, escaped. He died two days later, leaving the remnant of his people in the care of his brother.[9]

The Swazi were so disgusted with the cowardice of the Boers that they abandoned the campaign and returned to their territory. The later attack on Sekhukhune's main stronghold, Thaba Mosega, was repulsed. Despite the force of Burgers' persuasive eloquence, some 1,000 Boers decided to turn around and head home. This left Burgers without resources and he returned to Pretoria where he convened a special meeting of the Volksraad.

The citizenry refused to rejoin the fight and instead they elected to continue the war through mercenaries. They accordingly raised a filibustering corps under the leadership of a German officer called Von Schlickmann. This force, called the Lydenburg Volunteers, was sent to the Steelpoort River valley to engage Sekhukhune in a war of attrition. The Volksraad also had a chain of forts built along what they regarded as the defensible border of 'Sekhukhuneland'. In order to defray the costs of these actions, a special 'War Tax' was raised. This tax cost Burgers the last vestiges of his popularity among his burghers. The citizens flatly refused to pay it.

Despite the fact that Von Schlickmann was killed during the ensuing campaign and that the Pedi repeatedly bested the Lydenburg Volunteers, it appears that Sekhukhune was eventually inveigled into signing a peace accord in February 1877, although the details appear open to question. He allegedly offered to pay a fine of 2,000 cattle and to recognize Boer hegemony. Although this is what was reflected as the agreed terms of the peace in a document signed between Sekhukhune and a delegation of over-hasty Boer Commissioners, it appears that Sekhukhune had not been fully acquainted with the meaning of the document at the time.[10]

It was a consistent strategy of the Boers to fraudulently get chiefs to sign agreements (of which they were purposely misled as to its contents) in which the chiefs signed away all sorts of rights in favour of the Boers. It would thus be hardly surprising if they had not followed this tried and trusted ruse in this case.[11] This was to give cause for a later resumption of the war.

The war and the diggers

During the campaign, the diggings came to a virtual standstill. The digger community was left to look after their own protection, since the government was unable to afford any protection whatsoever. The transport service to Lourenço Marques came to an abrupt halt as all the wagons in the Lydenburg district were commandeered for war service.

The community scraped together a self-defence organization while woman and children were required to sleep in a laager at night. The situation caused a lot of resentment among people in the community. They felt that the government had left them in the lurch. Hostilities came close to the diggings, when a brush with the Pedi occurred on the farm of Henry Glynn at Kruger's Post, a mere 10 miles away from Pilgrim's Rest. The diggers now felt that they had previously paid their fees and taxes to the government in good faith and even now were required to pay a war tax, but they were afforded no protection or support in their own defence by the state.

An Irishman, M. V. Phelan, who owned and published the *Gold Fields Mercury*, a Pilgrim's Rest newspaper, declared in an editorial that those of the community who had been for the Republic had turned against it. He added that they could not serve a state, which forced its laws on its subjects.

The same paper reported in its 28 August 1876 edition that a diggers' meeting had been held to discuss possible terms of friendship between Sekhukhune and themselves. The meeting had also decided not to pay any taxes to the government and to support a plan to invite the British Government to intervene in the dispute between the South African Republic and Sekhukhune. They also proposed that the Republic should agree to join a federation of the British colonies of South Africa.

The idea of a federation of South African states and colonies had been on the table for many years and was well known to all in South Africa at the time. It was thus not an idea that originated in the digger community. During the years of Britain's informal paramountcy in South Africa, between 1854 and 1875, both political parties in Britain supported the idea of federation.

The idea was always linked with plans to reduce Britain's military commitments in South Africa by devolving as much responsibility as possible to the Cape Government which had enjoyed representative government after 1853 and had reluctantly accepted full responsible government in 1872. Given the totality of the South African situation, the idea was eminently sensible and would have worked to the advantage of all.

Sekhukhune was not the only danger to the government of the Transvaal at that time. Because of the Boers' insatiable appetite for land and rapacious labour policies, peaceful coexistence with neighbouring tribes was hardly to be expected. Also, on the eastern border of the Transvaal, Cetshwayo, the Zulu King, hovered menacingly. He claimed a large tract of land that he alleged the Boers had wrongfully taken from him. The Swazi were also sulking after their disenchantment with the Boer alliance in the Sekhukhune war.

In the far north, in the Soutpansberg area, the Venda had long ago ensconced themselves in mountain strongholds. Already in 1867, a Boer force led by Paul Kruger was forced to retreat and withdraw from the Soutpansberg. Many Boers then abandoned their settlements to the Venda, who proceeded to destroy Schoemansdal, a town named for Kruger's old adversary. A few Boers remained on their farms and they paid tribute to the Venda chief to ensure their safety.[12]

Although the motivation of Lord Carnarvon, described as the most positive federalist of them all, became the subject of some academic debate, it is clear that the reasons behind the British politicians' support for a federation was to bring about a limitation of imperial involvement, rather than an extension thereof. This is in full accordance with the previously discussed objectives of British colonial policy at the Cape.[13]

The upshot of the meeting of diggers was that a number of letters and petitions were sent to Sir Henry Bulwer, the then Governor of Natal, as well as to Sir Henry Barkly, who was the Governor of the Cape Colony. In the letters and petitions, the community requested protection and suggested that the Transvaal be taken over by Britain. Their entreaties only met with fairly non-committal replies from these worthies, which was only to be expected since the communications were sent by ordinary post. This meant that the communiqués would inevitably have been opened and read by Republican officials. Similar appeals were probably received from some of the leading citizens of Pretoria, but their identities have never been revealed.[14]

What effect, if any, the letters and petitions had on British policy is unclear, but at the end of January 1877, and accompanied by a force of 25 policemen, Sir Theophilus Shepstone, the then Secretary for Native Affairs in Natal, marched into Pretoria with secret orders, dated 5 October 1876, to annex the Republic under specified circumstances.

After three months of investigations and deliberations with Burgers and the Volksraad, Shepstone decided that the circumstances specified in his secret orders actually did exist. He thus gave effect to these orders on Thursday, 12 April 1877 at 11 a.m., by publicly proclaiming in Pretoria that the territory theretofore known as 'The South African Republic' shall thenceforward be British territory.

This annexation proved to be the saving grace for the Republic that would rise again from the ashes of this dismal failure as an exercise in statehood.

CHAPTER NINE

BRITAIN TO THE RESCUE

Theophilus Shepstone had arrived in South Africa at the age of three as part of a family of 1820 settlers. His father was a mason and supervised the erection of a number of buildings for the London Missionary Society.[1] The young Shepstone was to achieve fame, or infamy, depending on one's point of view, as one of the originators of a political policy of geographical segregation in South Africa. As Secretary for Native Affairs in Natal he moved large numbers of Zulu into designated reserves and would also have liked to have removed the bulk of Natal's black population outside the colony's borders, thus relieving the pressure of black settlement on the colony. However, especially in his early years, he respected, protected and wielded great influence over the Zulu.[2] He was chosen to carry out the annexation of the Transvaal by Lord Carnarvon, who regarded Shepstone as 'heaven born' for the job, because he spoke South African Dutch fluently and was largely respected and trusted also by the Boer population.

There are a number of possible reasons why, in September 1876, Lord Carnarvon suddenly decided to annex the Transvaal. It might be that the failure of Carnarvon's efforts at creating a South African federation had a lot to do with it. He might have reasoned that if the British colonies in South Africa could not be cajoled, perhaps the Boer republics could be coerced to join the proposed federation.[3] The problem with that reasoning is that it disregards the indisputable fact that the Transvaal was in a bad way and that the Free State, lying much closer to the Cape colony, was never threatened nor cajoled in any way to join a federation.

In a speech to the House of Lords on 25 March 1879, Lord Carnarvon denied that the annexation was in any way linked to his wish for a confederation of South African states: 'In annexing the Transvaal the question of Confederation never entered my mind'.[4] But it is always difficult to take politicians at their word in such matters, although it is unclear why he would have found it necessary to disguise his true reasons.

Contemporary English-speaking inhabitants of the Transvaal did not regard the reasons for annexation as put forward by Shepstone as spurious at all. Apart from the digger community of Pilgrim's Rest that had already expressed their concern at developments in the Transvaal, others raised exactly the same issues when they protested the retrocession some years later.

The secret commission issued to Shepstone by Lord Carnarvon, dated 5 October 1876 lends substance to the view that the reasons put forward at the time for the annexation *were* the real reasons. The commission directed Shepstone to make full enquiry into the origin, nature, and circumstances of the disturbances which had broken out, 'to the great peril' of Her Majesty's colonies in South Africa; and if the emergency should seem to render such a course necessary, he was authorized to annex any part of the Transvaal to the Queen's dominions, in order to secure the peace and safety of the colonies. The latter course was only to be resorted to if the inhabitants, or a sufficient number of the legislature, desired it.[5]

All other arguments thus rest on pure conjecture and no hard evidence has been produced to gainsay Lord Carnarvon's publicly expressed intentions. He must have been an exceptionally wily politician indeed to leave no trace of his real thoughts, since his secret and public utterances are all consistent.

Shepstone also took his commission seriously. He did not ride cowboy-style into Pretoria and annex the territory. He did as his commission bade and first made a thorough investigation of the circumstances in the state. He held discussions and consultations with Burgers, the Volksraad and various other parties for three months before he took any action. It also appears that he disclosed his 'secret orders' to Burgers on the first possible occasion.[6]

Aside from the Transvaal's dire circumstances, no other considerations were extant to drive Carnarvon to annexation so suddenly at that particular time.[7] There is no evidence to suggest that Carnarvon had prepared any plans for annexing the Transvaal prior to the reverses suffered by its forces in the war against Sekhukhune, nor that annexation had ever been considered as an option in establishing a Southern African confederation. The conclusion that the Transvaal's parlous situation, and the negative implications thereof for the two South African colonies, were Carnarvon's main consideration in annexing the Transvaal, especially at the particular moment he chose to do so, is inescapable.

That such an annexation might work in happy accord with his plans for a confederation of South African states probably influenced his decision strongly, despite his denials, but that fact hardly invalidates the existence of his expressed rationale.

An awkward legacy

Apart from some written protests from Burgers and the Volksraad, the annexation was uncontested by the Transvalers. Shepstone had done as good a job as Lord Carnarvon could have hoped for and he assumed, quite understandably, that the great majority of the citizens were prepared at least to accept the situation, even if they did not actively support it, or sought it. The civil servants who worked for the Republic were all invited to remain in their posts. Most did so and accepted, not only the new government, but also the administration of whatever policies were thereafter decided upon.

Strange as it may seem, the previous executive council of the Volksraad also remained, but as a consultative body to Shepstone. Paul Kruger, who was part of this executive, carried on with his duties under the new administration and accepted £300 per year in emoluments from the British Government.[8] Everything thus appeared to augur well for the plans of the Colonial Secretary.

Notwithstanding the good intentions of Burgers, the state was as bankrupt when Shepstone took over as when Burgers was in charge. The British Government appointed a Special Commissioner, Mr Sargeaunt, to examine the finances of the country. He reported that when the country was taken over by Shepstone, government officials' salaries were in arrears to the extent of £3,512. 16. 8d., postal contracts to the extent of £7,334. 4s. 9d, and not a penny in the treasury. He also calculated that the total government debt was £295,071. Before the end of 1877 however, the new administration repaid £101,350 of the debt from funds received from the imperial treasury, local banks and current revenue.[9]

The Boers' lack of enthusiasm to pay taxes to their own government may also be gleaned from this report. It appears that there was £17,000 in quitrents due from farmers. There was also a poll tax payable by every burgher who did not have a quitrent farm as well as by every native. This tax yielded only £1,000 per year, with the result, the Commissioner reports, that he can only come to the conclusion that the late government did not attempt to collect tax from any of the strong and powerful tribes.[10]

Indeed, the Burgers administration had been a failure in virtually every aspect of government. Burgers failed to repair (actually to establish) the credit of the state and he had tried, and failed, to create an economy for the country out of the gold bonanza. The novelist, Anthony Trollope, who travelled widely in South Africa at that time, remarked that after Burgers' reforms in education, there were a mere five pupils in the new High School, only 300 more in all the Republic's junior schools, and the total annual expenditure on education was less than £5,000.[11]

It would be grossly unfair to lay all the failures at the door of Thomas Burgers. The situation he had inherited should be taken into account, plus the fact that he had been elected President of a country that was a state in name only. It did not, at the time of his taking office, or at any later stage, even approach the minimum conditions required by international law for statehood. He was merely the elected chief of a loosely organized, ignorant and awkward band of interlopers in a region where the power of technology and a people sufficiently united to oppose them, were sadly lacking.*

It must also be remembered that it was not his ineptitude causing a deterioration of the country – it had never been any better. His failure was merely in not making a country out of the shambles he had found. Ultimately, the failure of the Transvaal was not his failure, but the failure of the Dutch emigrant farmer community as a whole to create a viable polity.

Shepstone at the helm

In his annexation proclamation and his later address, Shepstone did make a number of specific promises and gave certain undertakings. Numbered among these was an express promise that the Transvaal would have a separate, representative responsible government. He had added that generally 'all the change you will feel will be in the direction of increased security and new-born prosperity'.

The Shepstone administration inherited all the problems of the Burgers administration. It is often thought that, as an administrator, he was not a great improvement over Burgers. This opinion probably

---

*Upon reading the wealth of material in reports describing how the Boers generally went about inveigling local chiefs to gain access to their land, later only to appropriate it for themselves; how they plundered and killed to obtain 'orphans' and women for labour, one is inevitably driven to concur with the view taken of them by the Rev. Daniel Lindley, the Presbyterian minister from the American Board of Commissioners for Foreign Missions, when he said in 1837: 'As a body they are ignorant and wicked. Without schools, without teachers, without minister, what will become of them?' Significantly, George Champion, Lindley's colleague, added that when the Boers had finished being the 'scourges of the natives ... perhaps they will be mutual scourges of each other' (*Letters of the American Missionaries 1835–1838*, edited by D. J. Kotze). Lindley joined the Voortrekkers in Natal because he saw that the Boers were in as great a need of missionary work as the Zulu. Although they mistrusted missionaries, they accepted Lindley. He was a born and bred Westerner; he could shoot and ride with them any day.

originated from Henry Rider Haggard, later to write the perennial bestseller *King Solomon's Mines*. He served as a young clerk on Shepstone's staff and reported his personal experience both of Shepstone's charisma and his incompetence. However, from a much more detailed study of Shepstone's administration, it can be concluded that the expenditure by Shepstone's administration was not so reckless as was generally given out.[12]

Sir Bartle Frere had in the meantime arrived in South Africa as the new Governor succeeding Sir Henry Barkly, only to learn of Shepstone's annexation of the Transvaal within a few days of his arrival. Although he had probably been apprised of the impending annexation, he only became Governor-in-Chief of the Northern possessions in mid-1878, in anticipation of the coming federation of South Africa.

Despite the Transvaal Volksraad, the O.F.S. Volksraad and the Cape Parliament having already roundly rejected the federation proposal, Frere still believed that he and the new Cape Premier, J.G. Sprigg, working together, could make the idea acceptable, at least in the Cape Colony. This hope would soon prove to be in vain.

Meanwhile, Shepstone soldiered on in the Transvaal. Assisted only by a small staff contingent, including E. J. P. Jorissen and the 27-year-old Chief and only Justice, John Gilbert Kotzé they tried to give some effect to the promises made during the annexation. The administration received grant-in-aid from the British Parliament of a paltry £100,000 with which Shepstone was supposed to sort out the financial problems of the government. Nevertheless, it did stabilize the country's finances to a large degree and got the Cape Bank off their backs.

Nevertheless, it is generally agreed that the first few months of Shepstone's administration were a disappointing let down. Of the 'new-born prosperity' no evidence presented itself and on the score of representative government, nothing developed, although Shepstone did make immediate work of drafting constitutions for debate.

In the matter of subjugating Sekhukhune and Cetshwayo, however, matters were developing much faster.

Subjugating the Pedi and the Zulu

Sekhukhune had by now rejected the terms of the peace settlement and to all intents and purposes the Pedi still enjoyed their independence. As augured by the terms of the annexation and the following address by Shepstone, Pedi independence would be as objectionable to him as it had been to the South African Republic. Notwithstanding Sekhukhune's rejection of the peace treaty, Shepstone demanded the 2,000 cattle ostensibly promised therein and tried to assert British hegemony.

Sekhukhune did not accede, but he did send 200 cattle in order to keep the peace. Shepstone did not accept this 'deposit' and insisted upon the full number. It was probably impossible for Sekhukhune to accede to the request in any event. The Pedi were at that moment trading cattle for grain as their crops had been devastated by severe drought. In addition, Sekhukhune was defending his paramountcy and striving to reassert his authority over subservient chiefdoms, which had previously detached themselves from the Pedi polity. Cattle and wives played a major role in his ability to do so.

It is unlikely that Cetshwayo was conspiring with Sekhukhune at this stage, as Shepstone feared. However, in response to the still rampant white fears of Pedi aggression and supported by the weighty authority of Dr. Nachtigal's opinion, an imperial force set out for the Pedi capital in October 1878. However, due to the drought conditions and the African blight of horse sickness, the expedition was forced to return even before it reached Sekhukhune's capital.

Before the annexation of the Transvaal, Shepstone seemed to have some sympathy for Cetshwayo's claims against the Boers. Now, however, as the incumbent ruler of the Transvaal, Shepstone adopted the previous government's position on the land question against Cetshwayo. Soon after the failed expedition against the Pedi, in January 1879, the Anglo-Zulu war broke out, fomented by Frere, aided and abetted by Shepstone and ending in the eventual defeat of the Zulu.

The formidable military machine of the Zulu, the creation of Shaka's organizational genius, had been broken up. Cetshwayo was imprisoned in the Castle in Cape Town. However, the war had depleted the funds of the exchequer in Britain to such an extent that its sinking fund had to be suspended in order to avoid a tax on tea.[13]

The British authorities hoped that the defeat of the Zulu would bring Sekhukhune to change his mind and accept imperial subjugation. Sekhukhune was, however, not having any of it. Sir Garnet Wolseley had by then taken over from Frere as High Commissioner for South East Africa. Thus, another imperial expedition under Sir Garnet was sent against the Pedi in November 1879. This was a massive force of more than 14,000 men, which included 8,000 Swazi warriors and 3,000 other Transvaal blacks.

The Pedi, probably in anticipation of just such an attack, had abandoned their previous stronghold of Thaba Mosega for what they regarded to be a more defensible hill called Tsate. Sekhukhune was unable to withstand such might, although he held out until December. In the end he suffered a decisive defeat in which three of his brothers and nine of his sons were killed. The major assault was again left to the Swazi, who lost between 500 to 600 men, while only 13 white soldiers fell.

Sekhukhune at first escaped, but was later captured and taken prisoner. He was jailed in Pretoria while the British appointed his old rival, Mampuru, as chief over the subjugated people. So ended Pedi independence.

Creating an economy

On the economic front, Shepstone had no more success than Burgers. It was still a fact that there was nothing to create a modern commercial and industrial economy with. The vast majority of the Boer population were still engaged in hunting and keeping herds of cattle. Cattle were being sent to market in Cape Town, as had been the practice since the mid-1860s. Although that kept some sort of trade going, it could hardly be considered as commerce.

There were still no Boer tradespeople, traders or shopkeepers. Nor was there yet any demand for training in any trade. Commerce and industry did not even attract their attention. The English and other foreign traders provided the only commerce. The English speakers formed virtually a separate community in the towns. As the number of school-going children suggests, the Boers' total devotion to ignorance was as unfaltering as ever. An amusing passage appears from a letter written and published in the *Cape Argus* by a resident of the Transvaal in 1879:

> Those of us who knew the country [the Transvaal] when it was under the direction of the men who addressed the High Commissioner the other day [a reference to Paul Kruger and a deputation requesting the setting aside of the annexation] are not likely to forget the quality of their rule ... It was not simply education and administrative ability that were wanting – there was the narrow-mindedness which elevated ignorance into a virtue, and the low cunning which knew how to turn peace and power into occasions for personal aggrandizement, and which filled subordinate offices with men who would yield themselves as tools to prejudice and dishonour for their own advantage.[14]

Whatever the merits were of the complaints of the clearly offended correspondent above at that time, every one of these complaints would be fully substantiated, liberally repeated and well documented in future Boer administrations.

The Boers now discovered a new excuse for not paying taxes: they did not recognize the new authority in control after annexation. There was very little chance of ever collecting much in the line of taxes from these people. Shepstone seemed not to have tried very hard. It appears therefore that the exploitation of minerals remained the only possible basis for establishing an economy.

Shepstone did not set too much store by the promise of Pilgrim's Rest. Like many people, he was aware that the gold was giving out. He did not take any further action to augment the state's coffers from this source or to take the plans for a state mint any further. Nevertheless he did visit the gold fields, although he only got round to that in 1879.

On this visit he informed them that the Delagoa railway line would not be built and basically, that they would have to fend for themselves. He originally intended to stay the night in Pilgrim's Rest, but he was disgusted with the diggers who had plied his guard with so much liquor that they were all sodden. He thus had his inebriated troop load up and they retired in disarray, out of town for the night. Shepstone never returned.

The diggers drifted away from the gold fields area. There was no longer enough gold for everybody, although some claims were still productive. The men who had succeeded in pegging the 'leaders' were actually still making money hand-over-fist. Still, none of the bounty managed to reach the coffers of the Transvaal government. But it was not yet the last of the gold bonanza in the eastern Transvaal – the best was yet to come.

The Boer protest movement

Although the annexation was peaceful and uncontested, it did not proceed without protest. The initial protests were lame and almost apologetic, but a deputation, consisting of Paul Kruger, Dr. E.J.P. Jorissen and W.E. Bok, acting as secretary, left for London on 9 May 1877. It was a strange deputation, inasmuch as both Jorissen and Kruger were paid officials of the government whose possession they set off to protest. Although Kruger was not a civil servant, Jorissen was Attorney-General of the Transvaal and had to obtain leave from Shepstone in order to accompany the delegation. The leave was duly granted with full salary.

Although the delegation was heartily received by Carnarvon in London, it returned to Pretoria without any success. There their return was greeted by a large contingent of armed Boers who demanded a report back from Kruger. The atmosphere was electric and rife with all sorts of rumours, but nothing untoward eventuated. However, it did throw a scare into the administration. Kruger was later informed that armed burghers would not again be allowed into Pretoria.

A second deputation seeking to have the annexation set aside was again sent on its way to London in June 1878. This time there were only two deputies and the ever-useful Edward Bok acting as secretary. Accompanying Kruger was a new face, that of Piet Joubert, who had played a prominent role in Boer politics since the early 1860s. Carnarvon, his policies having been thoroughly discredited in Britain, had in the meantime been replaced by Hicks Beach as Colonial Secretary. The change notwithstanding, the second deputation had no greater success than the first.

Upon the return of the second deputation the Boers became more restive. Much of what had been promised by Shepstone at the time of annexation had not happened. There were armed meetings and a further discussion with Frere ensued. Although Frere temporarily managed to assuage Boer feelings, all was undone when he was recalled and succeeded by Sir Garnet Wolseley. This gentleman had less diplomatic skills and in December 1879 insisted that 'as long as the sun shines, the Transvaal will remain British territory'.[15]

Back in Britain, Disraeli's Tory government lost the election of 1880, making way for Gladstone. This development at first delayed further action by the growing number of disgruntled Boers as Gladstone had, in his Midlothian speeches during the election campaign, thoroughly disapproved of the previous government's annexation of the Transvaal. The Transvalers thus fully expected redress when Gladstone took over the reigns of government.

The new Liberal government was formed on 23 April 1880 and on 10 May Paul Kruger wrote to Gladstone, reminding him of his promise. Gladstone admitted in a letter to Lord Kimberley that he was at a loss as how to answer it. On 12 May the cabinet decided to renege on its previous position and decided not to reverse the annexation. Gladstone lamely explained to Kruger on 15 June that annexation would not be reversed because the future of the country lay in a confederation.

The now virtually uncontrollable Transvalers' resentment peaked. At a meeting spot called Paardekraal, just outside the modern town of Krugersdorp, a large gathering of burghers took place in December 1880. Kruger, Joubert and old M. W. Pretorius, who had been resurrected from political death for the purpose of unity, addressed them. They erected a cairn and swore allegiance to God. They accepted the proclamation of the Volksraad that Kruger had assembled on 10 December which called for the annexation to be reversed or armed action to be resorted to. They appointed the triumvirate of Kruger, Joubert and Pretorius as an executive to give effect to the proclamation.

The 'war' that followed was not really a war in the proper sense of the word. It was no more than an ambush and a couple of skirmishes, but it rocked Britain and caught the attention of the world.[16] By that time, Wolseley had in turn been succeeded as High Commissioner in South Africa by General Sir George Colley, a learned, but theoretical tactician with virtually no field experience. He took personal charge of his troops and suffered ignominious defeat and a fatal bullet through the head in the third of the skirmishes, which took place at Majuba Hill.

The whole episode could have been avoided had Colley not acted impatiently, with unwarranted bravado and erred grossly in underestimating the skill of the Boer militia. Colley had also not been informed that Lord Kimberley and Kruger had, 11 days prior to the battle of Majuba, already agreed to a ceasefire and the appointment of a Royal Commission to adjudicate the future of the Transvaal.

The shock of these defeats allowed the moderates in Gladstone's Cabinet to come to the fore. The Boers were amenable to allowing President Brand of the Free State to act as mediator and the Gladstone Cabinet agreed. Negotiations were dragged out for a couple of months, but the Convention of Pretoria was eventually signed on 3 August 1881. This Convention recognized the Transvaal's 'complete right to self-government' and described its borders in detail. The Transvaal would be independent, subject to Her Majesty's suzerainty.

Many of the Boers were extremely unhappy with the specific terms of the agreement, especially Piet Joubert, but the Volksraad nevertheless ratified it on 13 October 1881. This Convention was succeeded by the London Convention of February 1884, which defined the western border of the Transvaal more clearly, did away with suzerainty, but circumscribed the power of the Transvaal to exclude the right to conduct an independent foreign policy. Independence in terms of the London Convention still fell substantially short of recognition of the Transvaal as a sovereign state.

However, the Transvaal now again belonged to the Boers, but there were no more open borders. The country was hemmed in by the agreed borders, which did not include an outlet to the sea. The Boers would have to try to come to terms with living permanently in a territory with a finite land area.

The law of unintended consequences

The chapter started with a discussion of the real intentions of Lord Carnarvon and Shepstone in annexing the Transvaal. Whatever their real intentions might have been, the law of unintended consequences played havoc with them.

Virtually all the problems of the old South African Republic had been solved by the annexation. The much-vaunted dangers of the land dispute with the Zulu had been resolved in the Republic's favour by the hideously expensive, but ultimately successful, war conducted by Britain against Cetshwayo. The difficulties with the Pedi had been resolved when the imperial expedition finally subjugated Sekhukhune so thoroughly that, as an independent polity, the Pedi ceased forever to exist.

Although the economic conundrum remained, the debts of the Republic had been settled and its financial affairs brought into better order. Whether it was calculated, or merely opportune, the rising of the Boers, who had originally meekly submitted to annexation, took place at the first opportunity of reviving the Republic with some hope of permanence. Whereas Shepstone annexed a territory that was a state in name only, the Boers received back a polity with much greater authority over its inhabitants, internal cohesion and consequent credibility as a state. It was also in a position to exercise much greater *de facto* control over the territory it claimed, although it certainly did not control all the land up to the Limpopo. The Venda would only by subjugated finally in 1898 by forces of the South

African Republic. Before that date, they refused to be incorporated, subjugated and pay taxes.

The British, whether they actually intended it or not, made possible what the Boers could and would not have been able to achieve on their own. Although the creation of a viable modern economy in the country was still outstanding, British efforts and policies had made the now fully recognized South African Republic a reality.

But, whether a viable state could be created and maintained from this point forward was still an open question.

Part Three

Gold – the mixed blessing

CHAPTER TEN

ECONOMICS, THE GOLD STANDARD AND BRITISH POLICY IN SOUTH AFRICA

In the previous chapters, the development of the South African Republic was followed from its beginnings as the merest of white settlements to a polity with some semblance of statehood after the retrocession of 1881. Because of the major role that the white settlers played in South African history of the last seventy years of the 19th century, it would be impossible to paint a picture of events in the interior of the subcontinent without noting their increasingly dominant influence. For better or worse, the affairs of the white immigrants would be the determining influence in the lives and affairs of every inhabitant of the territory.

The mineral riches of the area would not and could not have been exploited to the advantage of all without an influx of knowledgeable and experienced prospectors and diggers and miners from all over the world, but especially from Britain, Australia and California. Despite the nascent Transvaal Boer Republic's weakness and lack of ability, the white foreigners that came to dig the gold did accept its legitimacy, chiefly because it was recognized by Great Britain. Although the gold bonanza in the eastern Transvaal delivered very little benefit to the Republic, it greatly benefited the local economy.

The gold fields of the eastern Transvaal did not have the effect of proletarianizing the local population. Rather, it stimulated the already large African peasantry that was engaged in producing a substantial surplus for the growing market. The rapidly growing digger community of the eastern Transvaal gold fields expanded the market opportunities of the local African peasants, which they enthusiastically exploited.[1]

In 1881, the most important mineral deposits were the diamonds at Kimberley, in the newly created region of Griqualand West. The very existence of the mineral exploitation and industrial activity generated by it had important consequences for the economy of the subcontinent as a whole. The exploitation of the diamond deposits in Kimberley set in motion a process of African proletarianization as black people from as far as the Pedi heartland streamed there to labour for wages. But the greatest economic reality in the Transvaal was the white immigrant's insatiable hunger for land.

The dynamics of land hunger

It would be wrong to view white encroachment on the land during this period as a process in which powerful European communities expanded remorselessly at the expense of helpless black African victims. On the contrary, there was a constant interaction between the white and black communities that can only be understood within the context of the internal imperatives of both the white and the black communities.

The Z.A.R. was a very vulnerable nascent state during the whole period, lacking internal cohesion and without a sound economic base. The Boer imperative for more land (driven by primitive agricultural practices, fixed patterns of succession by the eldest son, lack of education and alternative employment opportunities) was given vent by exploiting divisions within neighbouring African communities.

Similarly, African rulers often exploited the presence of local white communities to strengthen their own position against rivals and dissidents, who in turn resorted to the same strategy. Black Africans also exploited the divisions among the Boers, as did the Swazi during the time of Potgieter and his Ohrigstad opponents. In addition, they also availed themselves of the rivalry between the British and their South African colonies on the one hand and the Boer republics on the other.

Moshweshwe and Khama, two great chiefs of the subcontinent, employed this strategy very effectively and with great foresight. By requesting and receiving British protection from Boer pressure they founded the independent states of Lesotho and Botswana respectively. After much greater trauma, the Kingdom of the Swazi also regained its independence through and under British protection, although that only happened after the South African (Boer) War, at the beginning of the 20th century.

The gradual encroachment of whites thus proceeded by means of multiple black–white military alliances that shifted and changed throughout the period, but virtually always resulted in more land for the white farmers.

Economics in the 19th century

As against the Transvaal's local economic realities, there were the greater economic forces forging the world at large. Isolated as it was, the Transvaal could not escape the impact of these forces, since its neighbours were colonies of the powerful British Empire, but also because no people can eventually escape being part of humanity as a whole.

To fully appreciate Britain's policies in South Africa and particularly in respect of the Transvaal, we must have regard to her responses to world economic developments. Britain's policies were clearly the result of her view of her own economic interest in response to the world economic order and her relative place therein.

Circa 1880, the western world was rapidly developing from a system of mercantilist economic perceptions to capitalism. It has often been said that European imperialism was essentially a function of capitalism.[2] But, as we have seen, colonial expansion in South Africa resulted from internally generated dynamics and was not due to European or British imperial dictates, certainly up to that time. Nevertheless, especially because of the rich diamond fields,

South Africa was gaining value as an investment and trading area for Europe, but especially for Britain. This factor would start to play an ever-greater role in the further history of the region.

Although gold in large payable quantities had not yet been found, the possibility of its existence on the subcontinent had always been realized. In the early 1880s, gold was merely a South African potential, but any significant strike would impact on the world stage where gold and silver were accepted and respected as the fundamental economic values.

But although precious metals constituted the underlying value of European and North American monetary systems, Adam Smith had already denied the mercantilist view in *The Wealth of Nations* (1776) to the effect that the wealth of a nation can be measured in terms of the value of precious metals in its possession. He stated that prosperity of the community was the proper goal and measure of a nation's wealth. This might be said to have begun the 'Gross Domestic Product' (G.D.P.) measure of national prosperity in preference to measuring the value of the precious metals lying in the state Treasury.

Developments before 1870

Although Adam Smith had only made the point in 1776, economic forces were already in the process of substituting this capitalist credo for the mercantilist one from the early 19th century. It had already begun with the first industrial revolution, which had largely been a British affair.

By 1850 Britain had achieved absolute supremacy over all competitors in the production of, and international trade in, manufactured goods. She had achieved this through the manufacture of commodities in factories organized along capitalist lines and by then an enormous gap between her and her potential competitors had opened up.

It was also during these times that the doctrine of free trade was triumphant. Free trade was an economic policy that favoured British enterprise, but it also suited those countries that wished to import British-made machinery and expertise in order to increase their own rate of industrialization.

It is therefore not surprising that British colonial policies were largely aimed at achieving economic ends and protecting trade advantages, rather than military or geopolitical ones. Military and geopolitical considerations flowed from economic ones and not vice versa. In the past, numbers of historians have emphasized geopolitical perspectives of imperialist policies and actions to the exclusion of the then prevailing economic forces, not only of Britain, but also of all European powers in the latter half of the 19th century.

Thus, although some historians would have us believe that imperial expansion was a giant ego trip of military might, pomp, ceremony and self-aggrandizement, it is more likely that economic factors were the prime movers in imperialist expansion.[3] This economic determinism notwithstanding, strategic, military, philanthropic, and other non-economic drives cannot be excluded as causal factors in European, and especially British, expansion.

A wider interpretation of imperialist motives leaves room, not only for the fact that imperial policies were also directed by non-economic motives, but also for the fact that individual officers in the colonial service and politicians in positions of power were often motivated by considerations of national pride, jingoism or self-promotion in the actions they took. Even downright incompetence plays a role in any series of historical events. However, the often important result of actions based on such motivation and lack of competence notwithstanding, they remain anecdotal and do not define or describe the nature of the broad historic movement of imperialism.

Developments after 1870

The relative economic position of Britain began changing after 1870. The four decades after 1870 have been termed the 'Second Industrial Revolution'. Whereas the First Industrial Revolution had been based on small, family-run factories where the law of increasing returns to scale had scarcely begun to make its effect felt, the Second Industrial Revolution was represented by new technology, heavy industry and large capital investment.[4]

The 'comparative advantage' of economic development began to move away from Britain towards Germany and the US. Both of these countries had literally followed the British 'recipe' for industrialization and had initially protected their infant industries behind high tariff walls. These two countries also disposed of all the requirements to successfully run the Second Industrial Revolution, while Britain's very success in the First Revolution actually hampered her competitive ability in the Second.

Although Britain still retained most of her productive superiority until the end of the 19th century, it was being eroded during the whole period so that, for instance, by 1890 the US produced substantially more pig iron than Britain, although Britain still produced more than Germany by quite a large margin. However, by 1910 Britain's production of pig iron would only be the third largest in the world after the US and Germany.

Facing this increased competition for manufactures, it is surprising that Britain managed to keep a disproportionately large share of international trade. The reason for this is primarily due to her colonial policies of securing political hegemony over colonial territories with the concomitant trade primacy in those new areas. Thus, after 1870 the economic imperatives of maintaining and developing Britain's comparative trade advantages in the colonies and new states within the Empire became even more compelling.

After the discovery of the Witwatersrand gold fields, the maintenance of British political hegemony would become the dominant driving force of events in South Africa. The understanding of this motivation is the central and fundamental key to understanding events in South Africa after 1886.

British policy in South Africa – the economic imperatives

British general colonial policy can thus be summarized as follows:

- Britain's role was as a long-term investor in the new countries.
- The new countries (including those within the Empire) had to transform British investment into demand for British exports.

● European countries on the gold standard held the system's ultimate reserves and had to allow it to be drawn upon via discount rate changes.[5]

It is important to see Britain's role in the history of South Africa in this context. There was no real advantage in annexing a territory such as the Boer Republics, Griqualand West or any other colonial territory. Purely from an economic point of view, the annexation of a country or territory could hardly ever be justified because taking responsibility for governing a country meant shouldering an unwarranted, unpredictable and non-quantifiable financial burden. Whatever the view of generals and impulsive politicians, the Treasury would always act as the most intransigent obstacle.

Establishing and maintaining trade relations with politically independent states, on the other hand, was much more lucrative than running countries. In a previous chapter it was already noted that Britain had decided at the time of the Sand River Convention that informal empire was the preferred option to formal empire. But imperialism was much more than free trade with independent states.

Imperialism dictated political hegemony. The imperial power's policies would be directed to establishing a trading monopoly, amounting almost to complete trading exclusivity with the client country. By necessary implication such a relationship must limit the freedom of the client state to trade freely with whomsoever it wishes. It could thus not be allowed to raise customs or other barriers to trade against the imperial power. The levers used by imperial powers to create such a situation were military and political power, both as threat and as protection, combined with the advantages offered by investments made in the client state by investors from the imperial power.

Interference in the affairs of an independent country could thus be justified if there were valid considerations within the context of these economic imperatives. Such considerations would include the endangerment, or disturbance, of existing lucrative trade relations, or when the lives, rights and property of the imperial power's citizens within the client country were at stake.

In the case of the Cape Colony, British policy initially sought to contain the growth of white colonization and to establish peaceful borders. The Cape was a special colony, being primarily of strategic rather than economic importance. All the rest was wasted money and effort because for decades the colony had not been viewed as a particularly promising customer for British manufactures. Therefore the cost of governing the colony was required to be kept as low as possible and should preferably be made financially self-sufficient as soon as possible.

When containment of the boundaries of the colony proved impossible for a variety of reasons, including vacillation, ham-handedness and inconsistent policies by its appointed officials and by successive British Governments, which hardly paid sufficient attention to this backwater area, the confederal idea was born. The federal solution had by then already proved successful in Canada and Australia. It seemed like a sure-fire solution to the South African problem.

By the time this idea came to the fore strongly, the Cape Colony itself was already largely self-sufficient and had responsible government. The same cannot be said of Natal, which was still dependent on support from the British treasury. Additionally, Britain kept being drawn into other conflicts and conflagrations within the sub-continent. The basic idea was that a confederation of South African states, which would include the diamond fields of Kimberley, would be a self-contained, self-sufficient state capable of looking after its own defence needs. This would relieve the British taxpayer of an unproductive burden while also plugging a hole in the Treasury that was constantly leaking money into the territory. That was the aim, but it would only be partially achieved in the course of the 19th century.

Of course, for these developments to be successful and in line with the general aims of colonial imperialism, British primacy, or political hegemony in the subcontinent had to be maintained. It is for this reason that British suzerainty, a term, the meaning of which defied even the ingenuity of lawyers, had been reserved in the Pretoria Convention in 1881.

When subsequently, the London Convention was signed in 1884, this fuzziness was done away with, but its essential intent was

Plate 1. Cairn, commemorating the decision to fight the first British annexation of the Transvaal. Erected by Burghers under the leadership of the triumvirate of Kruger, Joubert and M.W. Pretorius after a meeting at Paardekraal in 1880. The beginnings of the town of Krugersdorp appear in the background.

Plate 2. A water well serving the battery at Queen's Mine, outside Krugersdorp. The site of a mine's crushing plant is known as a battery.

Plate 3. A typical wooden mine shaft headgear during the 1890s. The large wooden box on the left hand side is the ore box. The gold ore was hauled up the shaft and tipped into the box. From the box, the ore would be released by means of a trapdoor into the coco pans standing on the rails in the foreground.

Plate 4. A group of Z.A.R.P. officers.

Plate 5. Jameson's eastward march is halted at Queen's battery, forcing him to make a southerly detour after the battle. Taken from behind Boer lines, it shows the battle in progress.

Plate 6. The battlefield at Queen's battery, after the battle. Five Boer commando members were killed in the action.

PETRUS JACOBUS JOUBERT,
COMMANDANT-GENERAL AND VICE-PRESIDENT OF THE SOUTH AFRICAN REPUBLIC,
1881-1900.
Photo by C. F. Robertson.

Plate 7. Chief Commandant of the Z.A.R. and Kruger's main political opponent, Gen. Piet Joubert.

Plate 8. Cavity caused by the explosion of a train, carrying 50 tons of Lippert's dynamite, at the railway marshalling yards at Braamfontein – 19th February 1896.

Plate 9. Ready for action. Three Boer militiamen aged, from left to right, 60 yrs., 15 yrs. and 42 yrs., respectively.

Plate 10. The Krugersdorp Commando, circa 1899.

Plate 11. A typical blockhouse built in 1901.

Plate 12. Boer Prisoners of War return. Held on St. Helena Island, they returned on the S.S. Canada in 1902, after the peace of Vereeniging.

retained. In the later convention, the term 'suzerainty' was substituted by the much clearer condition that Britain would have the final say in the foreign policy of *De Zuid Afrikaansche Republiek* (Z.A.R.) as it was styled therein. Additionally, it provided that British citizens would have full freedom of access and protection within the borders of the Z.A.R. In order to justify past and future British investment in the subcontinent, it would jealously guard this political hegemony.

CHAPTER ELEVEN

WARS, CONCESSIONS AND A SHORT BOOM

After the retrocession of the South African Republic, the economic situation did not change for the better. Although the British annexation had solved the original financial problems, the base cause of those problems remained unresolved. Even the subjugation of the local population had not been completed. The problem of collecting taxes by force from an uncooperative local population, who received no advantage thereby, would remain a constant problem for the Republic. The implied threat of violence for non-payment made the system resemble 'protection money' more than it did taxation.

Two Boer leaders had come to the fore during the armed rebellion against British annexation: Paul Kruger and Piet Joubert. Although they were partners with M. W. Pretorius in an appointed executive triumvirate until the first elections could be held, these two would remain political opponents for the duration of the life of Z.A.R.

They stood against each other in the first Presidential election of 1883, which Paul Kruger won by a landslide. During the election campaign, however, Piet Joubert, who was acting as Commandant-General of the Republic, was away fighting a war to subjugate Njabela, the newly anointed chief of a neighbouring Nguni tribe. The trouble was really a continuation of the previous problems with the Sekhukhune and the Pedi, and demonstrates again the strains put on the state by its exploitative nature.

Upon taking office in 1881, Paul Kruger released Sekhukhune, the Pedi chief imprisoned by the British, from gaol in Pretoria.

Mampuru, his half-brother and rival whom Wolseley had installed in Sekhukhune's place, was not at all thrilled with this development. Consequently, he had Sekhukhune murdered together with one of his sons and thirteen of his subjects.

Mampuru then fled to the neighbouring tribe of Mapoch, a Ndebele chieftain, who gave him sanctuary and refused to hand him over to the *Veldcornet* of the district. When Mapoch died, his son Njabela succeeded him but he also refused to hand over Mampuru to the Republican authorities. Njabela's 'crime' was even greater than Mapoch's though, because he tried to reassert his tribe's independence by additionally refusing to pay 'hut tax' and to acknowledge the redefinition of his boundaries on the lines the Boers and British had agreed between themselves at the Pretoria Convention.

Thus, on 30 October 1882, a commando of 2,000 Boers set out from Middelburg under the command of Joubert. A fighting force of unknown strength, consisting of Pedi warriors who had supported Sekhukhune and who were out to get Mampuru, augmented them.

They too are human beings ...

Piet Joubert was apparently a reluctant soldier. He did not want the job of Commandant-General and protested it at every occasion, yet he kept it well into the start of the South African War in 1899. On this occasion too, he was not a happy warrior. 'I don't want to shoot any more Kaffirs,' he confided to his wife Hendrina. Emphasizing the point, he added: 'I have shot enough and it can't be good for our people to be forever shooting Kaffirs. They too are human beings after all. I will wait until hunger drives them out ...'[1] He thereupon proceeded to starve them out in a siege that lasted nine months.

Although his words and deeds do not qualify him as one of the great humanitarians of his time, they are insightful. Winston Churchill would later say that if we judge the past by the present, we shall lose the future. In this instance, then, we must judge Piet Joubert not by the moral and ethical insights of today, but against those of his time. Hence, given the time and place and the callous, rabid racism of many, if not most of his countrymen, including many English speakers, his attitude is decidedly liberal. This demonstrates the high probability that many other Boers of his time might also have shared similar insights.

Starving out his enemies was to him, probably a more humane solution, because the victims at least had some choice in the limits of their suffering. It would of course not have occurred to him, or to many Europeans of that time, that he was robbing a people of their freedom, their independence and their dignity, not only by their subjugation as such, but particularly by subjugating them to a state wherein, to his knowledge and in accordance with his own intent, they were to be forever condemned to servility without rights. 'Forever' at least, was the intention at the time, and for the individuals engaged in that conflict, also the reality.

Joubert, and especially his wife Hendrina, saw to it that there were large quantities of food available so that the people could be fed the moment they surrendered. Their surrender was hastened with the help of Nellmapius, the 'Count' mentioned earlier as the luckiest of the diggers at Pilgrim's Rest. Nellmapius used his expertise with dynamite to blow up the entrances of some of the caves that gave succour to the besieged. Some of the minor chiefs and their people started drifting out in surrender. On 8 July 1883, Njabela sent out Mampuru with his hands tied behind his back, as a prisoner for Joubert. On 10 July Njabela gave himself up with 8,000 of his people and the siege was over. Mrs Joubert immediately began directing the distribution of food to the starving.

The cost of the exercise was formidable for an indigent state. The direct expenses ran to £40,000 and over the nine-month period the Boer militia had to be relieved every two months since they were merely civilians under arms, not paid soldiers. They numbered 10,000 at one time, without counting the Sekhukhune supporters. Njabela was sentenced to death by hanging for rebellion and Mampuru received the same sentence for murder. That one can be convicted of rebellion against a state that has unilaterally assumed jurisdiction over you by overwhelming force remains a jaw-dropping legal phenomenon. The British Government complained of the harshness of Njabela's sentence and Joubert, then acting as State President in Kruger's absence in Europe, commuted it to life imprisonment.

But before Joubert stands accused of having the milk of human kindness coursing through his veins, it must be recorded that, at his suggestion, the people of Mapoch were dispersed and their erstwhile territory thrown open for white settlement. At that time colonization and settlement of territory were generally, although by no means universally, acceptable. The subjugation of colonial peoples was rationalized by most Europeans on the grounds that the 'savages' were thus receiving the benefits of Christianity and of European civilization. Apparently, so the argument goes, they were thereby 'uplifted'.

Whether such blatant expropriation of land by force was ever acceptable to civilized people must be open to grave doubt. Thus, without judging the past by the present, one can only be appalled by such an act of unmitigated piracy, but it was acceptable conduct to the Boers of that time and to a large, although constantly diminishing, number of their descendants up to the present time.

An economy built on state favour and privilege

The triumvirate of Kruger, Joubert and Pretorius faced the same basic economic problem that Burgers and Shepstone had. There was no trade and no economy, but there were pressing expenses. Imagine the financial burden of a state that had to keep the vast majority of the people over whom it had assumed jurisdiction in a state of subjugation by force and intimidation. Then further take into account the fact that, because it had neither trade nor industry, it could not pay for its imports. These were essential not only for certain foodstuffs but, because they lacked all technology and industry, also for firearms and gunpowder which formed the basis of the balance of power in their favour.

The triumvirate executive thus set out to continue an economic policy of selling concessions, which would, in the longer term, have disastrous consequences for the state. Kruger, who would later call the concessions policy 'the cornerstone of the independence of the Republic',[2] continued the policy until the demise of the Z.A.R. As previously mentioned, the selling of concessions by the Swazi kings very nearly brought that country to a permanent end as an independent state. It would not do much better for the Boer Republic, but in the short term it did save the state from immediate bankruptcy. Despite the economic deficiencies of the policy, the exploitation of the soon-to-be-discovered mineral riches would enable an otherwise feeble state to challenge the hegemony of Britain in the southern subcontinent of Africa.

The economic policy of granting concessions must be the very antithesis of a free and open economy. Its theoretical basis is that all economic activity is owned and controlled by the state. Nothing can be done unless the right to do so has been granted by the state at a price. This, in essence, means that the citizens of the state have no economic rights whatsoever, since all the rights to economic activity are owned exclusively by the state, which 'leases' them out to individuals or corporations on an *ad hoc* basis. Such an economic system of state favour is obviously incongruent with the ideas and ideals of Republicanism.

Concessionaires never became owners of the right to conduct the economic activity concerned. They were only licensed, against payment of an upfront fee and a continuing royalty, to engage in or exploit a particular economic activity for a specified period. The tendency to create this type of economy in the Boer State was evident from the very beginning. At the time of the initial settlement of whites in the Transvaal, men over the age of 16 were allowed to apply to the state for two farms of their own choice.[3] Since the farms were each, on average 3,000 morgen (about 2,400 hectares) in extent,[4] this explains the Boers' insatiable appetite for more land.

Although this practice from the beginning established the state as the repository and grantor of all economic rights, the land grantees actually did receive outright ownership of their farms.

Trading and shopkeeping were initially not subject to licensing by the state, nor was it necessary to apply for permission or concessions to participate in these activities. They escaped the net of state ownership and favour probably because it was not initially considered important to regulate small entrepreneurs.

With the advent of mineral exploration, however, the basic concept of state ownership was extended to include mineral rights. The Gold Law of 1871 provided that all minerals were the property of the state and that the right to mine minerals was also vested in the state. These principles were not changed by the substantial amendments to the law in 1885. The state was, of course, empowered to license out its rights, which it did by means of granting prospecting, digging and mining licences. The provisions causing the ownership of mineral and mining rights to be vested in the state is certainly not unique in free societies or even unwarranted, but the extension of this principle to commerce and industry was a recipe for graft, dishonesty, nepotism and disaster.

Most, but not all concessions were exclusive. Monopolistic concessions that were granted during the life of the Republic, such as the dynamite and railway concessions, would create monopolies that exacerbated an already problematic economic and political situation. The ubiquitous and enterprising Mr Nellmapius, to whom the pre-annexation Volksraad and President Burgers had already, in early 1875, granted the concession to build the road and operate a daily transport service[5] to Delagoa Bay from Pilgrim's Rest, was one of the major beneficiaries of the concessions policy.

Supported by the astute Sammy Marks, Nellmapius was granted a monopolistic concession to refine sugar and distil spirits in the Z.A.R. Since he was so skilful in the use of dynamite, as he had demonstrated in the war against Njabela, he was also awarded the monopoly to manufacture dynamite in the Z.A.R. He would later gain further and even more far-reaching concessions on transport. Nellmapius began by bottling Hatherley gin, true rotgut, that he named after his farm in the Pretoria district but which colloquially known as 'Mapius', even after the concession was sold to Sammy Marks. Exclusive rights to navigate the Vaal River and to mine in various areas were granted to one Adolph Gates, but the first truly contentious concession was granted to David H. Benjamin, in November 1881.

Benjamin, who informed the Republican authorities that he was from Cape Town, but was in truth a financier hailing from London, believed that there was a great deal more gold in Pilgrim's Rest than the diggers could extract from the alluvial diggings in the creek. He had both the capital and the guts to take action based on this opinion. Whether Benjamin was consciously aware of the political feelings of the Z.A.R. authorities at the time is not certain. What is certain, however, is that the political climate in the Transvaal favoured his plans.[6]

The Volksraad members were not the sort of people that would easily forgive or forget the actions of the Pilgrim's Rest digger community at the time just before and during Shepstone's annexation in 1877, when they embraced the cause of the failing Boer Republic with less than total enthusiasm. When Benjamin, through a local spokesman, approached the authorities in Pretoria for a sole concession to mine six specified farms in the Pilgrim's Rest district, he found a ready ear. Already in 1875 the Transvaal Gold Law had been amended to allow for mining concessions to be given to companies meeting certain requirements over areas that were no longer suitable for exploitation by individual diggers.

Mr Benjamin undertook to compensate the diggers who were still there and to pay £1,000 per year for the concession. The concession was granted without recourse to the diggers in the area and without even a cursory investigation to establish whether the area concerned met the legally required pre-conditions for the grant of the concession. The Volksraad was satisfied and only too happy that the troublesome diggers would now have to leave. But this, too, would prove to be a forlorn hope.

As can be expected, the Pilgrim's Rest diggers, who still numbered several hundred at that time, were violently opposed to the concession. Not having in any way been consulted in the matter, they were suddenly faced with a *fait accompli*. As far as they were concerned, there was no such thing as a 'worked out' field.

Nevertheless, in 1882, with the assistance of Mr E.J. Jorissen, the State Attorney of the Z.A.R., Benjamin floated the Transvaal

Gold Exploration Company (T.G.E.C.). Its first chairman was Mr G. Maynard, a farmer from Cape Town, but most of the shares were held in London.[7] It was the first gold mining company in the Transvaal and would prove to be one of very few successful ones outside the Witwatersrand area. Benjamin's faith would be rewarded and all those who had backed him would have reason to celebrate their good fortune for many years to come.

It took Benjamin two years of negotiations and is rumoured to have cost him some £70,000, but he eventually managed to reach an accommodation with all the diggers at Pilgrim's Rest. Benjamin's efforts to get the diggers to accept compensation and leave their claims were greatly assisted by other developments in the area. One of the wildest, greatest, but also shortest gold booms in history was just beginning. The gold at Pilgrim's Rest was giving out and the diggers already had their eyes on the De Kaap valley and exciting new gold discoveries being made further south, closer to the Swaziland border. They heard opportunity knocking.

Unfettered speculation

For some time during 1882, reports and rumours had been circulating of gold strikes in the De Kaap valley and of patches of gold being found on claims in the 'Duivels Kantoor' (the Devil's Office); then the Pioneer Reef was struck. The many unemployed diggers that were by now scattered all over the Transvaal, came rushing back to the eastern area of the country. With the rush of knowledgeable and experienced diggers into the gold-rich area, new strikes were made and reported as fast as the diggers' camps could be pitched.

At the announcement of every new discovery, diggers would rush over and start pegging claims. Given the multitude and richness of the gold discoveries all over the area, a further source of wealth production was quickly introduced – mining company stocks. At the new gold rush town of Barberton a stock exchange was founded. It was the second one in South Africa after the first, much older one, at Kimberley, but this was the first one in the Z.A.R. The stock exchange was a frenzy of activity and worked all day and half the night. Anybody who owned a claim or two could float a company and sometimes people who owned no claims at all also floated companies.

The Z.A.R. had no company law on the statute books, with the result that there was no control, order or legal recourse in the market place. Market volatility was as high as the area's humid summer temperature, which often pushes the thermometer over the 35°C mark. Rich patches of gold suddenly gave out, promising reefs pinched out, but new finds kept everybody's hopes up.

Apart from Pioneer Reef, some of the discoveries that fuelled the speculation in company stock were Concession Creek, Moodie's, French Bob's Reef, Barberton Reef and then in 1885 came the big one – Golden Quarry. Golden Quarry was discovered by a man by the name of Bray and through it ran the Sheba reef. Bray began developing this reef after floating the Sheba Mine. From the first 13,000 tons of ore milled by the company, 50,000 ozs. of gold were recovered. At today's gold price of approximately $320 per fine ounce, it would amount to some $16,000,000 worth of gold.

Due to its lack of ability to control the situation, the new government was as unsuccessful as its predecessors in gaining any substantial advantage for the state from the new gold discoveries. The wily and experienced foreign adventurers were not going to be done out of their finds by some far-off government that had neither the knowledge nor the resources to make any meaningful contribution to their lives or their efforts.

The growing exploitation of minerals, prospecting and influx of people did not leave the local Boer settlers untouched because it broke the isolation of their existence. The rise of gold mining in South Africa was like the rise of the same industry amongst the original Mexican settlers of California. It brought confusion to an unprogressive rural society.[8] Due to the Boers' inexperience and lack of expertise, they were quickly disheartened and became totally impoverished at the diggings. From the outset the goldmines were, for the Boers, a nursery of poverty.[9]

The unfettered speculation had to end sooner or later. It ended in 1886 when the new goldfields gave out and when most of the company stock traded on the exchange proved to be worthless. Nevertheless, after the bubble burst, there were mines left that were producing gold and they paid good dividends at that time; they would carry on doing so for many years to come.

In the meantime the enterprising Mr Benjamin had not been idle. He too had taken advantage of the boom on the Barberton stock exchange. Although the farms relating to his concession were in the Pilgrim's Rest area and included the town of Pilgrim's Rest, which was miles away from the new gold discoveries, this did not seem to matter in the high spirit of the time. But the difference was that his enterprise was a serious gold mining company. It recruited and sent over to Pilgrim's Rest to manage all the company properties, a young American mining engineer by the name of Gardner Williams, who incidentally also enjoyed the full confidence of the Rothschilds. In 1886, the company was able to announce that it had recovered gold to the value of £1,576.[10]

This was also the year in which payable gold was discovered on the Witwatersrand.

CHAPTER TWELVE

OPENING PANDORA'S BOX – MINING THE GOLD

The Witwatersrand (meaning rocky ridge of white waters) is a rocky promontory of parallel ridges, stretching some 60 miles from east to west. It stands visibly proud of the terrain lying to its north, but it rises more imperceptibly from the southern highveld to a height of approximately 2,000 metres above sea level and forms a watershed in the Southern African subcontinent between the Atlantic and the Indian Oceans. All the rivers to the south of the promontory flow westward to the Atlantic, while all the rivers to its north flow eastward into the Indian Ocean.

Many explanations are given for the peculiar name of the area. Some aver that the name is derived from the white bleached rocks along the many strongly running streams and fountains that are found on this treeless savannah. My personal preference is that the name was derived from the many small, but prominently beautiful waterfalls that spout white water down the northern cliff face of the promontory, where a number of the rivers that flow through the lowveld to the Indian Ocean have their source.

Although the area has many sites demonstrating human habitation from the earliest times, and the Tswana speakers claim it as the area of their origin, the Witwatersrand was apparently not inhabited when the first Dutch settlers arrived. It had probably been depopulated during the Difaqane. It was thus an uncontested white settlement that sprang up in the area. It is not surprising therefore that one of the earliest references to the name Witwatersrand is found in a government farm inspection report of 1841.[1] The rich grassland and fertile soils make it prime agricultural land but due to its height above sea level the area is susceptible to cold winters and severe frosts. Consequently most settlers also chose a second farm in the warm lowveld, whence they departed with their stock for the winter.

Since it lay at the heart of uncontested territory, white settlers populated it relatively densely, long before any gold was discovered. This had the result that land prices were also quite dear even before the treasure under the ground caused them to rocket. Due to the constant subdivision of farms and the large families who inhabited them, the population of the area grew apace. By 1875 it is estimated that the total population consisted of some 500 burghers (male citizens) and their dependants, which could readily amount to a white population of close to 2,500 people.

They were a self-sufficient pastoral society whose staples were mealies (corn), bread and meat. Vegetables and fruit, such as peaches, apricots, pears, prunes and grapes were also planted. They were subsistence farmers who did not produce food for the market, nor did they produce a surplus for storage. Each family annually planted one bushel of bread wheat and that kept them in bread for a year. As far as food was concerned, they were dependant on imports for cake flour, sugar, coffee, tea, tobacco, wine and spirits. These were generally supplied by travelling smouse (hawkers) who obtained their supplies in either the Cape or Natal.

There was a constant shortage of cash, so that most trade, especially between the settlers themselves, was conducted through barter and exchange. Even land rental was regularly stipulated for in agricultural products such as, for example, 20 bushels of corn, 20 rolls of tobacco and one bushel of dried fruit per year.[2]

The vast majority of people in the area had only the barest education. That education and schools were not in great demand can be implied from the fact that the first schools were erected only some 43 years after the first farms were established. The first school in the area was opened in February, 1884. A second school was erected in 1884, which was opened on 1 March of that year by D. Kern, on the farm 'Misgund', some 11 miles south of the present CBD of Johannesburg. N.H. Pannevis opened a third school in November 1884. By that time the total white population must have been substantially greater than the probable 2,500 of ten years earlier and the number of potential pupils probably numbered a few thousand. The Boers' enthusiasm for schooling was, however, severely lacking. The third school opened with only 13 pupils. As can be expected, in all of them the language of instruction was exclusively Dutch.

Prelude to the discovery

The fact that gold was discovered on the Witwatersrand in 1886 was surprising only because it was so long in coming. Among the local population it had already been known for years that there was gold. Gold in small quantities had been found all over the area and many people were out and about actively scouting and prospecting for the yellow metal. Unfortunately the necessary knowledge was possessed by only a very few people, among them being well-known prospectors such as George Honeyball, the brothers Struben, Godfrey Lys and Jan Bantjes; they were all actively engaged in feverish prospecting. Some of them were actually working certain gold strikes, but these eventually all proved to be disappointing.

The challenge was thus not to find gold, it could be found all over the area, but to find it in payable quantities. The problem appears to have been that the prospectors were all looking for gold quartz and did not recognize the auriferous conglomerate wherein lay the true treasure of the highveld. Additionally, everybody was searching an area ranging from a few miles to the north of where the main reef would eventually be discovered, to as far away as Pretoria, approximately 60 kilometres to the north. Not without reason, though, gold patches had been discovered very close to Pretoria.

The concentrated prospecting to the north of the eventual main reef was probably due to the earliest gold discovery in the area. In 1853, Pieter Jacob Marais, of whose efforts mention was made in the earlier part of the narrative, found some gold whilst panning in the Jukskei River in the area where it flows between the Witwatersrand

and Pretoria. This find probably directed the attention of later gold seekers to the area north of where they should really have been concentrating their efforts.

The discovery of payable gold on the Witwatersrand was the last act in the drama of the Transvaal's hunt for gold. However, had it not been for the previous mining developments of Kimberley, Pilgrim's Rest and Barberton, mining on the Witwatersrand might not have become such an early success after its discovery as it did.

Gold on the Witwatersrand is found in auriferous conglomerate form, which requires more intensive mining techniques to extract than alluvial gold or gold quartz, the more usual forms. Although the gold deposits were the most extensive ever found, and the gold content was very consistent throughout the deposit, the gold content per ton of ore was one of the lowest ever found. It would require great concentrations of capital in order to exploit this – simultaneously the richest and the poorest of gold strikes in history. Thus, because of the geology of the area, the Witwatersrand goldfields would never become the playground of individualistic diggers and adventurers as the eastern Transvaal goldfields had been.

The discovery

In order to make the discovery of truly payable gold, lady luck would smile on only one man out of the many who were frantically digging, crushing ore and watching the bottom of the pan. At the end of 1885 George Harrison arrived on the Witwatersrand. He was an Australian digger, but he had come to the Rand to build a house for Mr Johan Hendrik Oosthuizen on the farm Langlaagte. This farm had previously been divided into four portions and Mr J.H. Oosthuizen, together with his widowed mother, was joint owner of the easternmost portion.

It is not recorded how it happened that Harrison came to build this house. The search for gold in the whole area of the Rand was so well known that it is improbable that he, an experienced digger, did not know about it. It would thus not be too far-fetched to speculate that his real intention in coming to the Rand was probably to prospect for gold, but that he intended to tide himself over by building the house.

He certainly kept his eyes wide open; in March 1886 he came across every prospector's dream. Legend has it that he literally stumbled across the outcropping, but that is probably apocryphal. The chances are that he was prospecting around the area when he came upon the outcropping of banket reef. Being a knowledgeable prospector with many years' experience in Australia, as he later testified to the executive council of the Republic in Pretoria, he obviously recognized it for what it was and immediately sampled it for gold.

Harrison did not discover the reef on the same portion of the farm that he was building the house on. He discovered it on the neighbouring portion, which belonged to a Gerhardus Cornelis Oosthuizen. The latter's relationship with Johan Oosthuizen, for whom he was building the house, is unclear. George Harrison and his friend George Walker then entered into an agreement with G. C. Oosthuizen during April 1886, in terms of which they would each be entitled to peg a claim on the property should the strike prove to be payable and a public diggings proclaimed. Only in June, however, did Oosthuizen inform the government of the strike and requested it to declare a public diggings on his farm.

The notification put into action a chain of events that led to a flood of further discoveries of the main reef along an east–west line some 44 kilometres long. During the waiting period for public diggings to be declared, many people frantically started to position themselves favourably to obtain claims when they were proclaimed.

After the first discovery by Harrison, another key to unlocking a golden future was still missing – capital. It did not take long for this element to come to the table, however; events were developing their own momentum. Many individuals took action that alerted the Kimberley capitalists to events on the Witwatersrand. One individual who took precipitate action was Mr Jan Bantjes. While the government deputies, *Veldcornet* Meyer and *Landdros* Maré, were still making inspections to determine whether a public diggings should be proclaimed, Bantjes set off to Potchefstroom to borrow £2,000 for a small crusher. Another who took action was William Peter Taylor, the elder brother of J. B. Taylor, then a broker on the Barberton stock exchange, but more about him later.

Jan Gerritse Bantjes had been prospecting on and around the Witwatersrand for a number of years. He, like many others, had been prospecting around areas some miles north of where the main reef actually was. However, he was actually hot on the trail of the real thing when in November 1885 he, Douthwaite, Jacobson and Kauffmann concluded a contract to prospect for gold on the farm 'Roodepoort', which lay much further south.

The main reef actually runs through 'Roodepoort', but it was their bad luck that the reef made no outcropping between the farm 'Langlaagte', where Harrison discovered it, and the farm 'Witpoortjie', a neighbouring farm on the western border of 'Roodepoort'. So where Bantjes was prospecting, he searched in vain for a speck of gold on the surface. After Harrison's discovery, however, Bantjes focused his attention below the surface and to the east, toward 'Langlaagte', on the farm 'Vogelstruisfontein'. On this farm he managed to strike the main reef in June 1886, hence his trip to Potchefstroom.

The capitalist posse assembles

Arriving in Potchefstroom, Bantjes met up with W. Alexander, a trader from Kimberley. He was on his way to Barberton that still seemed, at that stage, to be in the midst of its boom. Bantjes managed to interest Alexander in his strike and on his way back from Barberton he visited Bantjes' excavations. Alexander took some samples from the Vogelstruisfontein excavations with him to Kimberley where he crushed and panned it in the presence of some of the moneyed men of that town.

Alexander's demonstration must have made a considerable impact on those present, although his was by no means the first or the only demonstration of its kind in Kimberley. Two gentlemen, who would be numbered among those later to become famous as the 'Randlords' were already on the same coach out of Kimberley to investigate the new strikes. J. B. Robinson and Hans Sauer were the first to arrive on the Rand from Kimberley and they did not waste any time when they got there. Destiny beckoned and both of them would soon be household names in South Africa.

The narrative needs to be interrupted here, because earlier developments in Kimberley were absolutely essential to the history of gold mining on the Witwatersrand.[3] Indeed, it would not be overstating the case to say that were it not for the capital formation that had earlier taken place in Kimberley, the mines in the Transvaal would not have been developed much beyond a shallow exploitation of the outcroppings, not, at least, at that stage of the 19th century. Not only was the capital accumulation that had taken place at Kimberley to prove essential for the development of the Rand, but so also would the business acumen developed by the people of the diamond fields prove to be a central factor in gaining the interest of international financiers and the international financial markets.

The diamond diggings at Kimberley were at first a jigsaw puzzle of small claims worked by individual diggers. As the diggings progressed deeper and deeper, some claims pinched out and other became unworkable, especially because the richest claims were in the middle of the diggings. The deeper and steeper the workings became, the more difficult it became to access and work the central claims. Thus, from quite early on, claim consolidation became a feature of the Kimberley diggings. By 1886, the firm of Jules Porges of Paris, Julius Wernher of London (although from Germany by birth) and Alfred Beit, also originally from Germany but of Kimberley at that time, completely dominated the market for diamonds.

Cecil John Rhodes had originally come to South Africa as a young man for health reasons. He joined his brother Herbert on a cotton farm in Natal, but Herbert was already dividing his time between the cotton farm and three diamond claims he had in Kimberley. He was not having much success with either but Cecil John eventually joined him at Kimberley. Herbert did not have the perseverance required of a digger and he returned to the farm in

Natal leaving young Cecil in charge of his claims. At the time of the gold strike on the Rand Cecil John Rhodes was already one of the major players in Kimberley. He was then in the process of amalgamating all the diamond mines of Kimberley under the umbrella of De Beers, a company in which he had a major shareholding. It would be his greatest coup and leave him rich beyond the dreams of avarice.

His backer and partner in these endeavours was Alfred Beit, who was, among other things, the local representative of Jules Porges and Co. Alfred Beit had recourse to international finance through the firm of Jules Porges & Co. in Paris. In Kimberley, if anybody needed venture capital, Alfred Beit was the man to speak to. Without Beit's assistance, Rhodes might never have achieved his dream.[4]

Alfred Beit made a name for himself in Kimberley as a diamond dealer. Before coming to South Africa, he worked in the Amsterdam branch of his uncle David Lippert's firm in Amsterdam. There he learnt the diamond trade at its international centre. From the beginning he showed an uncanny ability as a diamond sorter and valuer, talents that would be very useful in the new town of Kimberley. He was thus duly sent out to South Africa as the Lippert representative in Kimberley.

Alfred immediately recognized that in Kimberley, real knowledge of diamonds was much scarcer than diamonds:

> They bought and sold at haphazard, and a great many of them really believed that the Cape Diamonds were of a very inferior quality. Of course, I saw at once that some of the Cape stones were as good as any in the world, and I saw, too, that the buyers protected themselves against their own ignorance by offering generally one-tenth part of what each stone was worth in Europe. It was plain that if one had a little money there was a fortune to be made.[5]

Apart from his business as representative of Lippert, Alfred became the partner of Julius Wernher, who was Jules Porges' first representative on the diamond fields. With this partnership, Beit also became Jules Porges & Co.'s representative in South Africa.

Before J.B. Robinson took that Rand-bound coach out of Kimberley to the Witwatersrand, he first had a talk to Alfred Beit. Robinson had really fallen on hard times and he was up to his ears in debt. Striking a deal with the shrewd but sympathetic Beit would present him with the only way back to financial salvation. It appears that Beit was already fully apprized of the situation on the Rand when Robinson approached him. J.B. Taylor, the Randlord to be, had earlier sent his brother William to Beit with samples from the Rand that he, in turn, had obtained from Harry Struben.

Despite Robinson's reputation as a cantankerous and selfish man, he and Beit immediately formed the Robinson Syndicate with a starting capital of £30,000. The syndicate consisted of Robinson, his partner M. Marcus and Alfred Beit.[6] Beit's role, obviously, was to supply the finance for the enterprise.

So by the time that Robinson joined Sauer on that Rand-bound mail coach, he was already part of a hastily formed syndicate and entrusted with a brief to buy up farms on which the existence of the reef had been established, and where the presence of gold in payable quantities had been proved. As the journey got underway, each told the other that he was headed for Pretoria, wishing to keep secret the real purpose of their trip. But when they met on the step of the hotel at Potchefstroom the following morning, after the Pretoria-bound coach had already left, they were then obliged to admit to each other the real purpose of their visit. Others were soon to follow Robinson and Sauer, including Herman Eckstein, Barney Barnato and finally, Cecil Rhodes. Having arrived from Kimberley, Hans Sauer was being taken on a Cook's tour of the outcroppings, but Robinson was buying land. He was the first in the field and he made the most of it.

Robinson clearly had great faith in the future of gold mining on the Rand. He exceeded his mandate by buying land for the syndicate to the value of £90,000 but the drafts were duly and uncomplainingly met by Alfred Beit in Kimberley. Taylor comments that Alfred Beit was at that time probably the only man in South Africa who could advance such a large sum of money on a speculative gold mining venture.[7]

Ferreira's Camp

In the meanwhile, a shantytown was mushrooming up on the Witwatersrand goldfields. Although the auriferous reef was narrow and stretched over many miles, the main focus of all who came to the Rand was around Langlaagte and its immediate environs. Colonel Ignatius Ferreira had initially parked his wagon on the farm 'Turffontein', which also carried the reef and was the eastern neighbour of 'Langlaagte'.

Ferreira's wagon became the central point of the thousands of people streaming to the Rand. His wagon stood next to the road from Kimberley and so newcomers readily settled in its proximity. He was a natural leader, having earned his Colonel's rank in the British army during the Zulu war. By force of his personality alone, for he had no official authority, Ferreira managed to maintain law and order in this cosmopolitan community. The settlement of tents, grass houses and wood and iron buildings grew at a phenomenal rate during the month of July. It is not surprising that this settlement became known as Ferreira's Camp.

Although this is the main camp from which the City of Johannesburg grew, his was not the only one. Other camps were also being formed in the general area, such as Natal Camp and Paarl Camp, which later became known as Paarlshoop. The latter camp housed an Afrikaner community and was named after the town in the Cape Colony whence many Afrikaner fortune-seekers came to the Rand.

In the Witwatersrand area the government had much greater access and facility of control than in virtually any other part of the Transvaal. Yet, it chose to exercise very little over the day-to-day affairs of the community. Licences for wayside hotels were easily obtained, payment of the quarterly licence fee in advance being the only real requirement. It is therefore hardly surprising, given the nature of adventurers drawn to such a gold rush town, that the excessive consumption of alcohol that went on day and night soon became the biggest social problem on the goldfields.

Arthur Ballantine Edgson, one of the first to establish himself at Ferreira's, had a licence for a wayside hotel, but he was also a postal agent and a storekeeper. *The Diamond Fields Advertiser*, the Kimberley daily newspaper, described the situation in Ferreira's Camp as follows:

> For grog shops there was no place in the world more remarkable for them than Ferreira's Camp. To a population, living mostly in tents and grass houses, of about two to three hundred persons, there are fourteen so-called hotels. Anyone paying his licence money can get a license. No board or authority has to be consulted. Mr. Edgson has got the best hotel in Turffontein, but it is not yet completed.

The meeting

On 5 August 1886, an important meeting took place in the vicinity of Ferreira's wagon. It had been called by the government-appointed Commission investigating the throwing open of the area as public diggings. About 200–300 people attended the meeting and an address of welcome from the farmers and diggers was presented to the two Commissioners, C. J. Joubert, Vice President of the Republic, and Johann Rissik, first clerk in the office of the Surveyor-General.

The meeting was a precursor of things to come. Many of the people who would build the economy of South Africa were present such as J.B. Robinson, Hans Sauer, Cecil Rhodes, T. W. Beckett, J. Lever and many others. Many would still come, but the vanguard of the capitalist posse had arrived. They brought a whole new set of imperatives to the cauldron of De Zuid-Afrikaansche Republiek and this southern subcontinent of Africa.

The meeting was a great success. After Joubert addressed the meeting, setting out the basis on which the further intentions of the government would be founded, the meeting adjourned to Edgson's canteen. There the health of the President was proposed and heartily responded to by all present. The local population being hard-working, hard-living, hard-drinking men, it is recorded in the notes of the meeting that liquors of all kinds were soon sold out and nothing but peach brandy could be had. All lamented the short notice given of the meeting, not because many more people might have attended had they had sufficient notice, but because longer notice would have enabled a greater stock of liquor to be assembled.

Everything started so well and there is no inherent reason why it should not have remained so. So much more the pity then, that such an amiable and sound start to the long anticipated viable economy of a nascent state should have ended so tragically for all concerned. Although many of the imperatives were new, many others were already in place and had been developing for years. The management of these imperatives would make the difference between boom and doom.

As a direct result of the report of this Commission, the government, by proclamation in the *Staatscourant* (Government Gazette) of 8 September 1886, declared public diggings on nine farms, including Langlaagte, Roodepoort and Vogelstruisfontein.

CHAPTER THIRTEEN

THE CHALLENGE TO MINING

Colloquially, the Witwatersrand auriferous conglomerate is known as banket, since it resembles an eponymous Dutch candy containing nuts and almonds mixed into varicoloured layers of sugar candy. The conglomerate consists of a 'mass of pebbles, usually water-worn, cemented together by siliceous matter'.[1] Nevertheless, the Witwatersrand conglomerate is by no means unique. Gold had previously been discovered, and was then being mined and extracted, from similar conglomerates in Australia where it is known as 'cement rock', and particularly also on the Gold Coast of Africa.

In September 1886, Professor Henry Louis, a renowned metallurgist, visited the Rand goldfields. The *Transvaal Advertiser* published an interview with him in which he stated that the gold mining companies in West Africa were working upon reefs similar to the conglomerate reef of the Witwatersrand. He added that samples of ore from the two localities would be found to be virtually indistinguishable from each other. He also stated that the cost of working on the Gold Coast was abnormally high.[2] The difficulties and cost of extracting gold from this type of ore were thus not unknown.

Gardiner Williams, who was by then no longer general manager of the Transvaal Gold Mining and Exploration Company, but had moved to Kimberley to manage the De Beers interests there, also visited the Rand in 1886, stopping on his way to Kimberley from Barberton. Hans Sauer showed him over the outcrop and as Williams was leaving, Sauer asked him what he thought. Sauer later wrote that Williams looked at him for a moment and slowly said; 'Doctor

Sauer, if I rode over those reefs in America I would not get off my horse to look at them. In my opinion they are not worth Hell room.'[3]

Williams went further. He predicted that gold would be encountered in pyrites from a level of about 200 feet down and that the process for extracting gold could cost as much as £4 per ton of ore.[4] He accordingly advised Rhodes to be very careful of investing large sums of money on the Rand. This was probably a major factor that caused Rhodes to be one of the last of the capitalists to invest in Transvaal gold mines. Besides, he and Barnato had other fish to fry in Kimberley. Others had more faith in the future of the Witwatersrand.

Gardiner Williams was not alone in his opinion; many other expert mining engineers shared it. The outcrops were certainly gold bearing, but they were weak in quality. The general opinion was that they could not be mined to any great depth and one Australian mining engineer thought it geologically impossible for the reefs to run down further than 200 feet. If this were the case, the gold would not last very long. He was not completely wrong. The 'banket' reef would give way to pyrite reef from 180 feet down, as Williams had predicted. Pyrites would present the first real crisis for South African mining – it would not yield its gold to the old mercury covered copperplate extraction method. The bonanza could almost be gone before it had properly started.

The geology of the Rand has been compared to a very thick telephone directory. The gold reef can be viewed as one page in the middle of the book, but that page is crumpled and torn and in addition, the whole book is broken into parts. Finding that page between the thousands of other pages is only the first difficulty faced by the mines. The next problem is that the gold itself amounts to no more than the commas on that single page.

From this metaphoric description the extreme difficulty of mining gold on the Rand can be understood. It would not only demand great amounts of capital to finance the infrastructure required to mine the ore at very deep levels, but also to erect plant and equipment to extract the gold from the pyretic ore. The work would place extreme physical demands on labourers in the mine and on the skill and intelligence of the managers. Everything had to be achieved within the constraint of a fixed gold price. To achieve a conquest of all these hurdles would be like working with one hand tied behind the back, as it were, and would be a singular achievement, but it would also require a total exploitation of the labour force.

With the advantage of hindsight one can say that appearances were misleading, but the early experts were absolutely right in their opinion that the gold would be extremely difficult to find and exploit. In fact, the gold had been deposited eons ago by a vast inland sea. The gold reef it laid down was extremely thin and is now encased in the earth's surface. Unbeknown to anybody at that time, the reef dipped steeply to the south and went down for thousands of feet. It would prove impossible to mine from the surface.

The only feasible solution was to sink vertical shafts to the south of the main reef and then to dig straight down until the reef was struck. To obviate the necessity of sinking multiple vertical shafts, each giving access to the reef at a deeper level, a simpler solution was found. A single vertical shaft was sunk at a distance of approximately 1,000 metres from the reef and then, at increasingly deeper levels, horizontal tunnels, called drives, were dug in a northerly direction from the vertical shaft until the main reef was struck by each tunnel. Where a drive ran into the reef proper, the reef-bearing rock face was then systematically laid bare by widening that end of the tunnel. The gold-bearing ore could then be progressively blasted out of the auriferous rock face. The workplace at the auriferous rock face, where workers drilled and blasted the gold bearing ore, is known as a stope. This procedure enabled a company to mine the main reef horizontally as wide as their mining lease extended and vertically all the way down to its bottom.

But these were problems to be faced and solutions to be found much later. They were not the problems at the start. When mining started, the gold was on the surface and the old copperplate extraction method yielded approximately 70 per cent of the gold in the ore. Given the relatively low-tech nature of the operations, this yield was ample to deliver extremely good results and superficially at least, it seemed like happy days were here to stay.

The road to capital

In what was to be a curious repeat performance of developments at Kimberley, there was again a broad convergence of forces – legal, financial, social and technological – that would preclude the individual digger's survival on the Rand goldfields. Gold is generally less amenable to mining by individuals than diamonds, and this would be even more so on the Rand. On the reef, huge quantities of ore had to be dug and processed to obtain a meaningful quantity of gold.

An extremely important reason why large capital ruled so soon on the Rand was that an indigenous process of capital formation for investment had already taken place in Kimberley. The Witwatersrand gold rush can be distinguished from other gold rushes up to that time inasmuch as it was dominated, not by fortune-seekers, but by those who had already made their fortunes. To be sure, fortune-seekers swarmed there in droves, but they would not be dominant as they would not be needed and they did not stay long. The Rand was able to import its capitalists ready-made from Kimberley.

The Transvaal Gold Law at that time was not 'capital friendly'. It severely limited the number of claims that could be held by one person and was still designed for the typical alluvial gold digging situation, where many individual diggers exploited the deposit on small 50 ft. by 50 ft. claims. Before the power and leverage of big capital could be brought to bear on the Witwatersrand gold reef, the law had first to be changed. This challenge was soon met by two amendments.

At a meeting of the Z.A.R.'s executive council on 17 August the council received a deputation of some owners and lessees of farms on the Witwatersrand. They pointed out that it was impossible to develop and work the goldfield without costly machinery, and this would only be available to highly capitalized companies. The council accepted their arguments and it duly passed a resolution setting out the conditions under which mining leases would be granted. The minimum area of a mining lease would be 50 morgen (about 40 hectares) with no legal maximum. However, in measuring the ground for mining right leases the length and breadth of the reef would be measured, the ratio of which was not to exceed 2 to 1.

Nevertheless, on the proclaimed public diggings, thousands of small claims had already been registered. For example, In 1886 during the period 28 July–7 September, 1,207 licences were issued and the applications kept on coming; they were being issued in Johannesburg by the Mining Commissioner at the rate of 60 per day.[5]

When Cecil Rhodes visited the Rand goldfields for the first time, the idea of the amalgamation of small claims was already fixed in his mind. Due to his experience at Kimberley, he knew that those who managed the consolidation could make a fortune. He thus visited President Paul Kruger in Pretoria and urged him to allow for the amalgamation of claims without any limit.

Kruger agreed to this suggestion. He argued that it would also be easier for government to deal with a few large companies than to deal with probably thousands of individual claim holders.[6] The Transvaal Gold Law was accordingly amended to allow a person or entity to hold an unlimited number of claims. This took the principle accepted with the granting of Mining Right leases a step further.

Mining could thus be carried on either on a claim with a digger's licence, or on a designated piece of land on the reef by virtue of a mining lease. Rhodes was not the only one who realized the advantages of claim amalgamation early on. Syndicates were quickly formed to acquire claims in proximity to one another, thus forming amalgamated blocks of claims. This development allowed the flotation of companies with large enough gold reserves to justify the solicitation of sufficient share capital to meet the onerous investment requirements of plant and machinery. The way had been paved for the founding of those famous institutions of the Rand – the mining houses.

The Corner House

The first and foremost gold mining house was known as the Corner House. It came into being as a direct result of that first trip of J.B.

Robinson to the Witwatersrand on behalf of the hastily formed syndicate with Beit.

Hermann Eckstein, the German-born manager of the Phoenix Diamond Mining Company near Kimberley, had made a very favourable impression on Beit. In 1887, Beit asked him to move to the Rand to take charge of Messrs. Porges' interests there. Those interests were, of course, the properties bought by the Robinson syndicate.

At the same time, J.B. Taylor was sending negative reports to Beit about the future of Barberton. On the strength of these reports, Beit sent Gardiner Williams and Curtis, 'an eminent mining expert of considerable experience in the United States of America'.[7] Their report confirmed Taylor's pessimistic view and Jules Porges, Alfred Beit and Hermann Eckstein paid a personal visit to the properties of the Robinson Syndicate on the Rand and then visited Taylor at Barberton, where they inspected the local mines there.

Jules Porges thereafter thanked Taylor for his good advice and offered him a partnership. He proposed that Taylor and Eckstein open a new firm on the Rand under the name and style of H. Eckstein. This firm would take over, at cost, the Porges firm's share in the Robinson Syndicate. This was duly done and the Corner House was founded in Johannesburg.

Mining houses all operated on the principle that each mining lease, or group of amalgamated claims held, would operate as a separate company. The 'House' then became the holding company of each of the separate operating companies and it also assumed the financial management of all the companies in the group. In this way the Corner House group floated off, *inter alia*, the Robinson Gold Mining Company, the Randfontein Gold Mining Company, the Langlaagte Gold Mining Company, and the Bantjes Gold Mining Company.

It is important to note how this first mining house was financed. It was unique among the mining houses of Johannesburg because its capital was not raised by means of public subscription. The firm of Jules Porges & Co, in cooperation with their friends on the Continent, found the working capital. The firm had great influence among the banking houses of the Continent, having previously introduced diamond shares in Vienna, Berlin, Paris, Hamburg and

Amsterdam. The reputation of Jules Porges & Co. was so good that a large number of Continental investors stood ready to invest in any flotation it sponsored.

When the Rand gold mines started, there was very little interest in them in London. Fortunately, because of the good offices of Jules Porges & Co., the Corner House did not have to raise capital there. However, the situation was different with the other mining houses that would presently be founded.

Boom and bust

In 1887 very little gold was being milled. In that year only some 23,125 ounces were actually produced on the Rand, because for several years only a minority of the gold-mining companies produced any gold at all. The young directors of the Corner House had to spend most of their time in the struggle for power and position by buying claims and dealing on the vigorous new Johannesburg Stock Exchange.[8] The greater part of the correspondence among members of the Corner House group consisted of news of share dealings. Indeed, there was a charging bull on the loose in the Johannesburg Stock Exchange.

For the first several years, the majority of the incomes of most mining companies were derived from share dealings, and not from the production of gold. Mining houses and individual capitalists were accumulating yet more capital whilst at the same time gaining equity interest in the numerous mining companies being floated. In this way the affairs of most of the mining houses became inextricably linked, since, to a greater or lesser extent, they all held stock of each other's gold mining companies.

By 1888 a lot more gold was being produced. That year saw production of 10 times more than the previous year. The Robinson mine was working a wonderfully easy, rich ore that was being taken from the surface out of a wide reef. It was a simple operation to mill and extract the gold from the crushed ore. The charging bull on the stock exchange became a stampeding bull. Share prices rocketed from August onwards. It was a market driven by often less-than-honest news and sometimes by downright fraudulent claims.

It was also the year in which Barney Barnato arrived on the Rand. The consolidation of Kimberley diamond mines into De Beers was nearly complete. He and Rhodes had started that process as protagonists and ended up as colleagues. Like Rhodes, diamonds were Barnato's passion, not gold. Nevertheless, always the opportunist, he agreed to send an agent to Johannesburg for Barnato Brothers, albeit reluctantly. He then returned to Kimberley to see to his financial and political affairs, but he was back in Johannesburg by November.

Upon Barnato's arrival in Johannesburg, scenes of mad excitement on the floor of the stock exchange greeted him. 'Men (were) taking their coats off and shrieking like maniacs – fortunes were made and lost in hours.'[9] Robinson G.M.C. shares went up to £80 and a former clerk, later to be the first mayor of Johannesburg after the South African War, made £20,000 in one day on the exchange. Barney realized that this was too good an opportunity to pass up.

He immediately wired his brother Harry and his nephew Jack Joel, who were both in London at the time, that he would be investing heavily on the Rand. He went ahead and did so without delay, but nothing he did on the Rand improved his reputation for honesty, nor was it intended to. Nevertheless, it was the start of another mining house that was called 'Johnnies' and it would also spawn the later success story of Johannesburg Consolidated Investments (J.C.I.).

The bull market had, by the end of February 1889, become a bubble that was ready to burst. The total capitalization of Rand gold mining stock was approaching £25 million and between January and April, bank advances increased from £300,000 to in excess of £1 million. Most of the stock trading was done on margin and borrowed money, and although bank managers, like the manager of Standard Bank in London, condemned the gambling madness, there was nothing he or they could do to stop it.

The bubble burst when Gardiner William's prediction came true. Before the founding of the Corner House, Beit had been advised of Williams' opinion that great difficulties would be encountered at a level of some 200 ft. down. Beit's only reply was: 'We will deal with that difficulty when we get to it.' And deal with it they did.

According to Taylor, pyrites were first reached in the City and Suburban Mine at 180 feet. Upon receiving the news, he and Eckstein wired their firm in London to find out whether or not they should proceed with the work. Beit immediately cabled back that they should carry on without delay, for as long as the gold was there, means would be found to extract it. While Taylor and Eckstein ordered mining operations to continue, Beit sent to America for Charles Butters of California.

The discovery of pyretic ore did not remain the private knowledge of the Corner House for very long. One mine after another struck the same problem as they dug deeper. The character of the reef changed as it went down and the change took place at the same depth over the whole length of the reef. The news shocked Johannesburg out of its euphoria. The problem now was that the gold could not be extracted from the ore by the normal methods.

Up to then gold extraction had been a simple, low-tech process. The pulverized ore would be mixed with water to form a thickish slime. In the slime, gold particles would be in suspension, mixed together with fine particles of rock. The slime would then be passed over a series of copper plates coated with mercury. While the rock particles would wash over the mercury, the gold particles would form an amalgam with the mercury, which would be scraped off the plates. The mercury could then be separated from the gold and reused. The process only recovered a maximum of 70 percent of the gold in the ore, but it was deemed adequate at the time.

The pyretic ore, also called refractory ore, could not be treated with mercury. It contained iron, copper lead and zinc that combined with the mercury without extracting any gold. Although there was an even distribution of gold in the reef, it only contained half as much gold as the banket reef. This was not payable gold – it was impossible to mine at a profit. Share prices immediately collapsed. One stock that stood at £50 at the height of the boom could not be sold for one tenth of that by the end of 1889 and by March 1890, the total market capitalization of gold shares was down to 40 per cent of its value a year earlier. People fled from Johannesburg – the gold rush reversed.

According to Percy Fitzpatrick, grass grew in the streets of Johannesburg. It did not grow long, however, because the answer had already been found. Similar refractory ores were being successfully treated on the North American and Australian goldfields. It was for this reason that Beit had sent for Charles Butters – he was an expert in dealing with refractory ores. He immediately erected a chlorination plant on the Robinson mine and put up 'frue vanners'* to collect the concentrates.[10]

Although the discovery of pyrite ore on the Rand had burst the bubble on the stock exchange, it was more an emotional shock than a financial one. In that boom, as in all booms on financial markets, expectations tend to rise way out of proportion to reality. The discovery of pyretic ore did not have much of an effect on the actual gold production of any mine. Most of the ores mined at the time were still the free-milling concentrates of the banket and there was enough of that to keep the mines in production for years. Even by as late as 1894, 70 per cent of the ore was still being treated by the old mercury process, simply because it was cheaper and yielded sufficient gold. There was thus more than enough time to develop alternative methods of refining the pyretic ore, but it certainly threw a scare into over-optimistic investors.

The chlorination process consisted of dissolving the pulverized ore in chlorine, which then precipitated the gold. Although the process was only partially successful on the Rand, it was sufficient to keep the deeper mines in production. The Robinson Company even bought the pyrites of other mines at their assay value and then extracted the gold. They would keep on doing so until

---

* The 'frue vanner' is a travelling, inclined belt used for collection of heavy metal particles in pulverized ore. It is a continuous moving belt which is inclined in two directions. Its motion is upwards in the major inclined direction, with a slight tilt to the side. Pulp (pulverized ore mixed with water) is discharged onto the top of the inclined belt. Waste material runs down over the belt into a launder. Heavy particles become trapped, and get taken up with the belt. Over the return roller the belt runs through a washing tank and the heavy metal particles are washed off and collected in the tank sump. Introducd about 1890 for tin ores and later adapted for gold ores.

technology came up with a better solution. Even the better solution had already been found – in Scotland.

Technology saves the day

A Scotsman by the name of John Jack was one of the pioneers on the Witwatersrand. He took a trip to Glasgow, carrying a sample of Rand ore, and there he visited two brothers, Robert and William Forrest who were both doctors. They had been collaborating as speculative scientists with a chemist, J.S. MacArthur. Together these three Scotsmen had found the best answer to the treatment of gold ore.

The essential discovery that the three collaborators had made was that gold had an affinity for cyanide. Thus, if crushed ore, pyretic or not, was dissolved in a solution of cyanide of potassium, the gold in the ore will precipitate onto zinc shavings. The gold then readily lends itself to recovery and further refining from the zinc shavings. The process proved successful on the Rand ore samples that Jack had brought with him and the rest, as they say, is history.[11]

Although the process was patented in 1887, the first installation on the Rand was set up on a mine called the Salisbury. The problem was that although the process had been invented, it still required industrialization before it could be used on an industrial scale. J. B. Taylor avers that experiments for treating slimes by cyanide were carried out largely on the Robinson mine. He probably means the experiments with the machinery required to make an industrial process out of the basic invention, because he goes on to record that 'the machinery for doing this was designed by the experts employed by our (the Corner House) firm, and the success was largely due to Charles Butters and his staff'.[12]

Taylor nowhere acknowledges the contribution of MacArthur and the Forresters, although their pioneering work is well recorded. In fact, the process is officially termed the MacArthur-Forrest process. His 'oversight' may well be due to the later history concerning royalties. The mining houses at first paid royalties to MacArthur and the Forrests, but they soon decided that the payments were too high and took them to court. Expensive and protracted litigation then followed, which eventually led to the overturning of their patent rights. The mining houses saved every penny they could in their bid to contain overheads.

Recovery

As in any market collapse, the weak fall first and are absorbed by the strong. So it was in the case of the Corner House. It was the strongest mining house before the bubble burst and it was even stronger when the recovery began. It had not only increased its holdings along the main reef, but it had, with great circumspection and secrecy, been acquiring blocks of land well to the south of the outcrop. This area was known as the deep-level zone.

During the darkest days of the market collapse, Lionel Philips had arrived in Johannesburg to join the Corner House. Already in January 1890 he wrote to London that 'the more I see of the Rand the more the more I become convinced that deep levels are of the utmost importance to the parent companies. Mr. Jennings will, I think, concur with me.' The 'Mr Jennings' referred to in the letter, is Henner Jennings, one of the brilliant American mining engineers brought to Johannesburg by the Rothschilds.

It was very fortunate that Messrs. Jules Porges & Co. were so well connected. They had originally persuaded the Rothschilds to invest in De Beers and they again persuaded them to invest on the Rand. The Rothschilds wanted to make absolutely sure that they would be served by the best possible advice in their continuing and further investments. It was thanks to them therefore, that a succession of brilliant American mining engineers was sent out to South Africa.

It started with Gardiner Williams who, having first been sent to Barberton and then lured by Rhodes to manage the De Beers interests in Kimberley, played an important role during the early discovery of the goldfields. Charles Butters, Hamilton Smith, H.C. Perkins, Henner Jennings and Captain Thomas Mein, among many others, followed him to South Africa. Many of these men had cut their teeth on gold mining problems at El Callao, one of the mines owned by the Rothschilds in Venezuela.

Hennen Jennings was the chief consulting engineer to the Corner House, being responsible for the layout of the mines of the Robinson Syndicate. Taylor credits him with being the ablest mining engineer that ever came to the Rand and Jennings collected all the ablest men from America and elsewhere to assist him.

It would thus be fair to say that the eventual and long-term success of the mining operations on the Rand was principally due to Continental finance and American engineering expertise. Without the catalytic input from these two sources, gold mining on the Witwatersrand might never have taken off and would certainly never have been the viable industry that it is today and has been for more than a century.

The production cost challenge

When the recovery began, deep level mining was still some years in the future, but a number of things had already become clear. Although not all believed that there were virtually limitless supplies of gold under the ground, it was apparent that there was no foreseeable end in sight. All indications were that there was enough gold on the Witwatersrand to keep up production for decades. Equally clear, however, was that mining would be horribly expensive.

Gold had one advantage over other commodities – it had a fixed price. Diamond mining in Kimberley for instance, had short cycles of boom and bust as the price of diamonds shot up and tumbled down. It was one of the reasons it had been so important to establish the De Beers' monopoly. By means of the monopoly, greater control could be exercised over the total supply of diamonds on the international market. Thus greater price stability could be assured. The idea was so successful that even non-De Beers-controlled diamond producers and countries such as Russia fell in line with the company's diamond marketing strategy. It was not only price stability that could be ensured, but by controlling the total supply, price levels could be adjusted to maintain a reasonable profit margin over production costs.

Price manipulating strategies were not available to the gold mining industry. The commodity's price stability presented its producers with their most serious challenge as the price was fixed, not by the ebb and flow of supply and demand, but by the international monetary system and ultimately, politicians. Production costs were virtually the only variables. In order to show a profit, the mines were thus forced to manage production costs very carefully.

Even then, the industry had more control over some elements of production costs than over others. Mining a very low-grade ore, at ever-deeper levels under the geological conditions of the Rand would be the most challenging mining enterprise undertaken to date. The best shaft-sinkers would be sought from all over the world and brought to Johannesburg. It was thus always clear that keeping a profit margin alive on the mines of the Witwatersrand would be a penny-pinching, cutthroat affair.

Materials, transport and labour

The mines saw their overhead costs as consisting of only two broad elements – labour and materials. Materials included all the machinery and equipment required to operate the mine-embracing an astounding array of manufactured items, from the gargantuan machinery required for the shaft headgear and stamp batteries for pulverizing ore, to miniscule weights for the chemical scales in the assay offices. Each and every item, from the largest to the smallest and most insignificant, even including materials such as structural steel, had to be imported, either from Europe (mainly Great Britain), or the US.

Materials also included coal, for energy, and water for a multitude of purposes. Fortunately, there was initially enough water, but the area is subject to cyclical droughts. There were occasions when drinking water needed to be physically transported to the Rand, but the supply was generally adequate.

The area was fortunately also well endowed with coal. Coal deposits were discovered at Springs, which is at the easternmost end of the reef, and at Witbank, less than a hundred miles further east. There was also coal in Natal, at the town of Newcastle, so named because of the coal deposits. All the coal discovered was of a very low grade, but there was a limitless supply that could be mined easily and quite inexpensively. Given the necessary transport infrastructure, there was thus an adequate energy supply available.

Materials and transport

The mines' supply of materials was strategically dependent on an efficient transport system. It follows therefore that they were extremely vulnerable to transport costs, but also to import and customs duties, and excise tax. The transport infrastructure was negligible. There was no transport system except for a few wagon roads to the Witwatersrand. This lack, and the fact that the first rail link to the outside world would, for political reasons, take many years to realize, was a major inhibiting factor in the initial development of the Rand. For a transport system, the mines would be utterly dependent on the government.

Again, due to the geology of the Rand, probably the most strategic material required by the mines was dynamite. One very experienced shaft-sinker at the time complained that it required a third as much more explosive to cut through the rock of the Witwatersrand than it would take to do the same job in Australia.[13] Whereas the surface banket reef was easily mined with picks and muscle power, the underground pyrite reef would yield only to dynamite.

As with transport, the mines were delivered to the monopolistic economic policies of the government. The government had granted the dynamite concession to Alois Nellmapius, but he sold it to Edward Lippert, a nephew of Beit. The mines dealt with this monopoly reluctantly, but they were without any alternative. Dynamite could of course not be imported into the country because of the concession.

All of these matters would be contentious issues and play a prominent role in future political developments.

Labour

The final element in the cost structure of the mines was labour. From the outset the overwhelming majority of the workforce was black, transient and migratory, rather than permanently settled and proletarianized. This was a result of several complicated, and interwoven factors, but it was ultimately, the best solution for the mining houses, though not for the black workers.

The migratory labour system was made possible first, by the availability of a large black labour force that could be recruited from a well-functioning rural society. Second, the mines made use of labour-intensive techniques that did not require a long or expensive period of training.

> Although the gold mines on the Rand were not unique in their employment of labour-intensive techniques, they were unique in responding to cost inflation by perfecting the recruitment and organization of the system of migrant labour, which was the singularly central feature of the labour structure on the Rand.[14]

The mines did not regard unskilled labour by whites as a viable option. They were not of the opinion that the indigenous white population was suitable for this type of work, as were the white populations in America and Australia, because 'in these countries the white man has, by experience and necessity, been trained to do all the hard manual labour – the pick and shovel work – himself.'[15] In the same passage, the brochure continues by pointing out that 'the gold output of both America and Australia has been seriously declining of recent years (referring to years recent to 1924), and the principal cause of this decline has been the high rate of wages paid to labour.'

In order to squeeze the maximum amount of manual labour out of the labour force at a minimum wage, a highly coercive and exploitative system of industrial relations was developed. It must be pointed out that the term 'cheap labour' is a misnomer.

The labour of rural blacks was 'cheap' only for the mine owners. As Norman Levy has shown, the system was based on exploiting the social security inherent in the extended family of the male mine-worker who came to work on the mines unaccompanied and for whom extensive single-male hostels were provided on mine property. He would always be able to return home and be cared for if he was sick, or became unemployed or unemployable through injury or sickness.

The migratory system relieved the mines not only of providing and paying for social security services, but it also allowed them to pay wages based only on maintaining the single unit of labour who came to the mines. The worker's family continued to take care of themselves back home. The mine wage therefore did not need to be structured to pay for the housing and maintenance of a whole family, but of only one man.

In effect, then, the mine owners were reaping the rewards of a successful agricultural and social system developed by the indigenous black population of the region. In economic terms, they were using the surplus produced in the rural areas to depress the wages of black miners to below their normal economic value. The surplus production of the rural areas was thus converted to profits for the shareholders of the mining companies.

The perfection of this system required the active cooperation of the state. In this regard at least, the mine owners had no difficulty with the Transvaal government, or for that matter, with the British administration that took over after the South African War. The Transvaal government would never be found wanting for enthusiasm when called upon to exploit black people as 'labour units'.

Notwithstanding the government's willingness to cooperate however, the availability and control of black labour would remain an issue between it and the mine owners. This was due simply to the government's ineptitude and incompetence in carrying out the policies to which they so readily agreed.

However the problems were being handled, the mines were clearly set to continue. There was no final bust on the horizon such as happened in the eastern Transvaal. Gold mining was there to stay. The only question was whether the Transvaal polity would now be able to make a success of its statehood; now that a very promising and vibrant industry had been founded, albeit with foreign capital and foreign expertise.

The sad thing is that the local Dutch population could not contribute to the industry either in capital or labour. They were unable to receive much benefit from the boom. They had no commercial experience, no technical expertise, no knowledge of finance or economics and they were unfit for, and unused to, manual labour.

In this last category, the large black population of South Africa could at least come into their own. The mines could not survive without their labour; just as as it could not survive without the capital and expertise of the *Uitlanders*. This then was the great irony – those who had arrived first to set themselves up as masters of all they surveyed, were, with one exception, totally irrelevant and wholly sidelined when a viable industry was found and had to be established.

The only exception was that they had been placed in control of the political machinery, by courtesy of Great Britain. Civil administration was all they could contribute, albeit through Kruger's Hollander mercenaries. Political power was their only power and they would use it to the full – but to what end and with what result?

Part Four

Intrigue and confrontation

CHAPTER FOURTEEN

AFRIKANER NATIONALISM AND RAILWAY POLITICS

While the Transvaal Boers, with little evident success, had been busy trying and failing to set up a viable state north of the Vaal River, their cousins, the well-settled, reasonably prosperous Afrikaner community in the Western Cape colony, had been busy developing an identifiably separate cultural identity. This development was not directly mirrored in the Transvaal, but it would soon spread throughout the region.

However, it took Netherlands-born and Netherlands-educated people to see the potential of the patois language that had developed at the Cape. They started promoting it as a separate language. Over the next few decades, it would become accepted as the Afrikaans language, but in the process of fighting for its acceptance, its promoters would hitch its fortunes to a more powerful vehicle – a virulent and aggressive nationalism. This would supply much of the foundation of the road to war.

To start with, educated Dutch speakers at the Cape did not accept this watered-down version of Dutch as a language worthy of the name. They condescendingly referred to it as 'kitchen Dutch'. The appellation had a basis in fact. The language had developed naturally from a Dutch linguistic basis through interaction between the Dutch settlers, Malay, Khoi, other coloured people of the Cape, who had never mastered high Dutch in the first place. There was also a substantial number of the Cape Dutch who had only had a rudimentary education and who were in the process of losing their ability to speak proper Dutch.

Since the Malay and coloured people were generally servants of both the educated and the uneducated 'white' part of the community, the interaction that spawned the Afrikaans language took place largely, although not exclusively, in the kitchen – the primary preserve of servants. The educated Dutch-speaking settlers would only speak this 'corrupted' form of Dutch to the servants in the kitchen, hence the derogatory term.

That the language found much greater acceptance among this lower, 'servant class' of the population is borne out by the fact that the first book to be published in Afrikaans, in 1856, was a Muslim catechism for children. People of the Muslim religion first came to the Cape as slaves and although many of them became wealthy shopkeepers and traders after emancipation, the 'Christian White' community summarily regarded all of them as belonging to a class below their own.

However, the language was not merely watered-down Dutch – it was liberally peppered with words and grammar imported from Malay, various Bantu languages, Khoikhoi, French and German. By 1880 it had already been under development for two hundred years. In the 1680s the Dutch Commissioner, Van Rheede complained about the colonists' perversion of the Dutch language and the wholesale importation of foreign phraseology.

The movement to develop this patois into the modern Afrikaans language was initially undertaken by three eminent, well-educated Dutch immigrants – Dr Arnold Pannevis, a philologist and preacher, C. P. Hoogenhout, a schoolmaster and Dr Johannes Brill, rector of Grey College in Bloemfontein, the capital of the Boer Republic of the Free State. In 1875 they started a movement called *Die Genootskap van Regte Afrikaners* (G.R.A.) (The Society of True Afrikaners). The movement was founded in the town of Paarl, in a predominantly Dutch-speaking rural area that was also a prominent wine and grain-producing area.

They set themselves the aim of developing a national consciousness among Afrikaans speakers and adopted a policy of defending Dutch rights against the Anglicization policies of the British administration at the Cape. They published their own newspaper, *De Patriot*, which they used to demonstrate the expressive ability of the new language, to proselytize their socio-political views and to encourage their readers to come out and use Afrikaans.

Their purpose was to unite all the Afrikaans-speaking people in South Africa as a self-conscious national group, but their classification was based only on language, not on race. Dr Pannevis for one, was chiefly motivated by a desire to translate the Bible into Afrikaans, mainly for the benefit of the coloured people who could neither read, write nor understand the high Dutch of the Bible. This applied also to the less educated majority of the Dutch-speaking white community at the Cape.

For their purposes they identified three types of Afrikaners – Afrikaners with Dutch hearts, Afrikaners with English hearts and 'true' Afrikaners, those who identified with their own point of view and who had adopted their agenda. Their battle to have the language accepted was a difficult one and would only be completed in the second decade of the twentieth century.

Although their agenda trespassed on political terrain, they did not see themselves as a political party. They did, however, lend impetus to another development, the Boeren Beschermings Vereniging (BBV) – initially at least, a political pressure group more than a party. Recruiting its members from the wine and grain farmers in the Western Cape, it was founded in 1878 as a lobby to combat excise duties on wine and spirits. Since these farmers were generally Afrikaans speakers, it follows that there would be an overlap with the agenda of the G.R.A. Jan Hofmeyr, nicknamed 'Onze Jan', led the movement from the start. He had been, up to that time, a precocious and successful journalist in the colony.

Two of the colonial-born founding members of the G.R.A. were the brothers S. J. and D. F. du Toit. Stephanus J. du Toit was a minister in the Dutch Reformed Church and he had a rather radical political agenda. His vision was that of a united South Africa dominated by Afrikaners under its own flag, i.e. not in any way linked to Britain. This credo would eventually find almost general approval among the Boers in the republics. Given the political and economic realities and the prevailing circumstances in the Cape Colony at that time, this was far-fetched and radical indeed. The Free State and Transvaal were, of course, the role models for this ideal.

Despite du Toit's adoption of these two Boer states as his role models, the Boers did not initially share all views. Although there probably existed a reasonably pervasive desire among the Boers to have a united South Africa under its own flag, it was not yet a strong motivating force in the early 1880s. Most importantly, however, the Boers did not regard themselves as anything but Dutch speakers. The language called 'Afrikaans' and the identity of 'Afrikaners', were ideas restricted to the Cape colony and not adopted by the Boers of the Republics at that time. They both regarded and referred to themselves as 'Boere' and Dutch was their language.

S.J. Du Toit was a demagogue and given to violent outbursts of rhetoric. Instead of being merely pro-Afrikaans, his position became more and more anti-English. Nevertheless, in 1880 the two du Toit brothers founded the Afrikaner Bond with a programme of radical principles, espousing the cause of a united South Africa under its own flag, free from Britain. This was a dangerous course to set. In the Cape Colony, it could be construed as treason.

In the meantime, however, the B.B.V. had already established itself as a credible political party with a solid block of supporters in the Cape Parliament. Quite correctly, Hofmeyr saw the new movement as a challenger for his own position. He was able to outmanoeuvre S. J. du Toit and arranged a union of the Afrikaner Bond and the B.B.V. in 1883. This united movement retained the name Afrikaner Bond, but Hofmeyr had in fact hi-jacked the party out of du Toit's control. Du Toit removed himself and his political activities to the Z.A.R., where he would in due course become an embarrassment to Paul Kruger.

The Bond became a party of Afrikaans, Dutch and English speakers with a much-moderated set of principles. It would strive for a united South Africa and accepted the hegemony of Britain and the fact, of course, that a very substantial portion of the white population of the colony had direct ties with that country. The policies of the Bond relating to non-whites reflected Afrikaner attitudes more than it did the more liberal English ones, but it always supported a non-racial, qualified franchise. Although it never enjoyed an outright majority in the colonial Parliament, it would be the single most influential force in that body. Whoever governed, would only be able do so with the support of the Bond.

This applied also to Cecil John Rhodes when he became involved in Cape Parliamentary politics. His involvement came about as the result of the incorporation of the Kimberley diamond fields into the Cape Colony. The Keate award originally created the separate territory of Griqualand West when the issue of jurisdiction over the newly discovered diamond fields was in issue between contending South African states. The newly created territory was then reluctantly annexed to Britain, but with a sweetener of some £200,000 it was successfully passed on to the Cape Colony in 1880.

Incorporation into the Cape meant representation for the area in the Cape Parliament. Rhodes was not slow to respond to the opportunity of marrying his growing financial power to a solid base of political power. He thus made a successful bid to have himself elected to Parliament for the constituency of Barkly West at the very first opportunity.

He was an enigmatic man whose unbridled personal ambition was driven by an almost mystical belief in the destiny of the 'English race' and a cynical reliance on his own ability to 'fix' his opponents.[1] He was an unrepentant imperialist, devoted to the ideal of bringing all of Africa, from the Cape to Cairo under British rule. Apart from the resistance to be expected from local inhabitants to such subjugation, Rhodes' greatest opponent would in fact be the imperial power of Britain itself. As discussed elsewhere, colonization policies had particular economic advantages in view and it definitely did not include the mere acquisition of more slices of undeveloped real estate with a concomitant increase in responsibility for governing more colonial people. Governing people costs money.

But Rhodes had great personal charisma and he could bully, cajole and coerce people around him to a great extent. His very success in everything he had tackled made it extremely difficult to gainsay, never mind oppose, him. When in 1880, Rhodes became a member of the Cape Parliament, representing the constituency of Barkly West, he and Hofmeyr very soon entered into a political alliance. This alliance, uniting English-speaking imperialists with the politically more pragmatic men of commerce and conservative Afrikaner farmers, would last until 1895 when Rhodes' boundless ambition caught up with his lack of prudence, scuttling his political future.

Afrikaners and Boers - family politics

Not only was there a divergence of views on language and culture between the Afrikaners of the Cape and the views of the Boers in the Republics, they did not always think their economic interests coincided either. It would obviously have been to everybody's advantage, Cape Afrikaners and Republican Boers alike, to create one economy for the whole subcontinent. But Boer Anglophobia and the apparently easy acceptance by Cape Afrikaners of life in a British colony set the two groups at odds, especially in the early years of the Z.A.R. Boer opinion, as represented by Paul Kruger, seemed to be that whatever was to the economic advantage of the Cape Colony must, in principle, be disadvantageous to the Transvaal.

This basic divergence must not be allowed to obscure the fact that many Cape Afrikaners, especially young men who would not inherit the family farm, held the republicanism of the Transvaal and Free State as an ideal. Many emigrated there and wrote with fierce pride of how good it was to live in a 'free' country. Nevertheless, Paul Kruger distrusted Cape Afrikaners and followed a so-called 'Hollander policy', of appointing Hollanders to all the senior posts in the civil service.

There were virtually no Transvalers with sufficient education to occupy such posts and while there were suitably qualified Cape Afrikaners available, Kruger's distrust of their cosy relationship with the British prevented him from appointing them. He was much criticized by Piet Joubert and the 'progressives' in the Transvaal Volksraad for this policy.

Procrastination, railways, and economics

The one technological advance that had the potential of uniting the subcontinent economically was a railway, but railway construction was slow to take off in South Africa. At the beginning of 1884, less railway track had been laid than in New Zealand, a much smaller country. Most of the track had been laid in the Cape, but some miles of track had also been laid in Natal. There was, however, not an inch of track in the Free State or the Transvaal.[2]

By the end of 1884, the track was approaching Kimberley, but it could progress no further without Transvaal cooperation. Neither the Transvaal nor the Free State could raise the capital to finance an extension of the line. The railway was an important factor in the growing economy of the Cape, especially as a result of the economic impetus created by the diamond mines in Kimberley. Natal was showing economic promise with its active harbour at Port Natal and a growing sugar industry, but the lagging pastoral agricultural economies of the Boers could neither afford nor sustain a rail link. Nevertheless, they did realize, and had done so for many years, that a railway would be an essential facility to allow them to create and sustain their political independence.

Hendrik Potgieter already saw the establishment of a railway line between the Transvaal and Delagoa Bay as an essential lifeline for an independent Boer Republic in the Transvaal. President Burgers accepted this view and he tried, with great folly, to execute it. The Delagoa railway line would also be a driving ambition of President Paul Kruger, even to the detriment of the Transvaal's prosperity.

After preliminary contacts in 1883, Kruger met with Dutch capitalists in 1884 with a view to the building of a Pretoria to Delagoa Bay railway line. The meeting took place when he and his deputation visited the Continent after negotiating the London Convention with the British Government.

However, in 1885, before the discovery of gold on the Witwatersrand, Kruger, probably acting against his own instincts and without abandoning the Delagoa Railway line idea, approached the Cape government to propose a South African customs union. The customs union with the Cape was not an ideal solution to his mind, but his state was in dire straits. In 1886, after the discovery of gold, he again mooted the idea, adding the undertaking that in return he undertook to allow the Cape railway to run a line through to Johannesburg.

This was an eminently sensible suggestion and would probably have avoided a lot of heartbreak in the later history of South Africa. However, with the singular lack of vision that so often afflicts dedicated mediocrities, the Upington administration at the Cape declined the proposal on both occasions. Kruger would never forget or forgive what he saw as a personal insult. He, unfortunately, also lacked the wisdom to distinguish the men who refused his overtures, and accused Merriman, a later Cape colonial Prime Minister who had nothing to do with the refusal, of slapping him in the face.[3]

Since, immediately after the discovery of gold, the state was still indigent, no progress could be made despite the fact that the mines in Johannesburg urgently required an efficient and viable transport system. Kruger, still smarting under the Cape's refusal of his entreaties, doggedly proceeded with the slow-moving Delagoa Bay project.

He had, under the circumstances, a strangely ambivalent attitude to the development of the mines. Although he must have realized that they were essential for the economy of his otherwise problematic state, it is not clear that he fully appreciated that their success was the Z.A.R.'s only hope of continued existence. His approach to their problems and requirements was always unforthcoming, parsimonious and condescending, as if doing the people of Johannesburg a favour. An example of this attitude occurred during his second visit to Johannesburg on 24 September 1887. In a speech he declared that he did not discriminate between the old and new populations of the Republic but this undertaking did not include his attitude to the question of voting rights for *Uitlanders* (outlanders, or foreigners). During the same speech, he declared that although he was disposed to accommodate them regarding a rail link to the outside world, this would have to wait until the completion of the Delagoa Bay railway line.[4] A rail link to Johannesburg was obviously not an accommodation of the *Uitlanders* – its early completion was a national necessity.

The Delagoa Railway line was not about to be completed, however. When Kruger visited Europe after the deliberations with the British government that resulted in the London Convention, he also concluded a concession agreement with Dutch capitalists. In August 1884, the Volksraad ratified the concession agreement. Under the agreement these Dutch capitalists were granted a monopoly of railway construction in the Transvaal. Unfortunately, among the concession agreement's many serious deficiencies was the absence of a price for the building of the line to Delagoa Bay and the date for its completion.[5]

The granting of the concession did not immediately result in a viable railway company, however. Despite the fact that the Government of the Z.A.R. guaranteed the investors a 5 per cent per annum dividend, Dutch investors were extremely difficult to persuade. In addition to the deleterious effect on their enthusiasm caused by the recent collapse of some US railroads, their reluctance stemmed from other considerations as well. The major consideration was probably that it was unclear exactly what commercial activity in the Republic would create the traffic for the line to carry. The parlous state of the Republic's finances was well known and therefore the state's guarantee of a 5 per cent per annum dividend did not carry much weight.

As the would-be railway operators gave up hope of raising the necessary capital to exploit the concession, the first concessionaires transferred the concession to another group of entrepreneurs, who in turn transferred it on in 1886. Eventually, the concession landed in the hands of R. W. van den Wall Bake, who was increasingly focussing his capital-raising efforts on the German, rather than the Dutch, capital markets.

Bake's efforts were eventually rewarded when the Witwatersrand goldfields proved to be exceedingly rich. This development enticed two German banks, the Berliner Handelsgesellschaft (B.H.G.) and Robert Warschauer, Cie., to subscribe the capital for the floating of the Nederlandsche Zuid-Afrikaansche Spoorweg Maatschappij (N.Z.A.S.M.) in June 1887. The company then proceeded to raise the vast majority of its capital via the issue of bonds (debentures) on the Continent, which, in terms of the concession agreement, it could write off at a half per cent of their nominal value for amortization purposes. Thus when, as an 'accommodation' to Johannesburg, Kruger conceded a railway connection to the outside world subject to the completion of the Delagoa Bay Railway line, the company that held the concession was still in its infancy and far from being sufficiently capitalized to undertake that particular project.

The concession to the N.Z.A.S.M. was not merely to build the Delagoa Bay line from Pretoria to Lourenço Marques; it was a total monopoly on the construction and running of railway service between the Z.A.R. and a seaport. This was an extremely valuable monopoly, but because of its inherent manipulative economic power, it was also an extremely dangerous one – as it would later prove. It was a political time-bomb that would explode later with some considerable force.

Along with the realization that the Witwatersrand gold mines were both rich and permanent came the recognition that the whole economic balance of power in South Africa had shifted to the Transvaal. The Witwatersrand would henceforth be the economic spindle of the whole region and access to it therefore became a central issue for the two coastal colonies. The most economical route of a line linking the port of Cape Town with the Witwatersrand would run from Kimberley across the territory of the Orange Free State and so that particular republic was not neutral in this issue. Kruger's preference for the Delagoa Bay line was certainly not in the economic interests of his Free State brethren.

The building of the Delagoa railway line was not solely in the hands of the N.Z.A.S.M. The Portuguese had given a separate concession to another company for the building of the line from Lourenço Marques to the Transvaal border. This part of the line progressed very slowly, having started in 1883 and, after six years of getting nowhere, the Portuguese government eventually took over the project itself. Nevertheless, the N.Z.A.S.M.'s part of the line was not progressing at all, as the company was still trying to sort out its finances.

By 1890 there was still no railway link to any seaport in sight of Johannesburg, or Pretoria, for that matter. During the early months of 1890 the then newly formed Chamber of Mines petitioned President Kruger, asking for a railway link to a port. They stated:

> ... the burden from which relief is most urgently required is the
> heavy cost, uncertainty and delay of transport caused by the

absence of railways ... The sum paid during the year of 1889 by the Witwatersrand district alone for the carriage of goods, exclusive of produce from the coast, is estimated at £2,750,000. The cost of importing the same goods by railway from the coast to Johannesburg would be £1,150,000. Thus an actual cost of £1,600,000 was borne by the fields in a single year.[6]

In order to placate its creditors at that time, the N.Z.A.S.M. was trying to raise capital on the Continent through the good offices of Labouchère, Oyens, Cie. and the Berliner Handelsgesellschaft. The company was forced to explore other avenues as well. Verwey, then the N.Z.A.S.M.'s director in Pretoria, negotiated an agreement with the Cape Railway in 1891, which became known as the Sivewright agreement.

The agreement provided that in return for a loan from the Cape Government of £650,000 secured by company debentures paying 4 per cent interest, the Cape Railways would be allowed to complete their line from Kimberley, which was already poised on the Transvaal border. The N.Z.A.S.M. undertook to build the line from the Transvaal border to Johannesburg, but until 1884 the Cape would be allowed to operate the service from her ports to Johannesburg and to fix the carriage rates through to the destination.[7]

The Cape wasted no time and their railway line reached Johannesburg one year later. The gold fields were finally connected to the sea by rail, six years after their proclamation. There can be no doubt that the long delay in linking the gold fields by rail to the sea seriously delayed the coming into being of a modern industrial state in South Africa.

The Sivewright agreement did not result from the doings of politicians, but it was a great disappointment to Kruger, who had desperately backed the Lourenço Marques line. His political opponents seized the opportunity to accuse him of having sold the Republic in 'bondage to England'.[8]

The economic realities had changed the political scene dramatically. Instead of having two political power blocs of the British colonies set against the two independent Boer Republics, as might be expected, the subcontinent divided into competing economic blocs, with the Transvaal and Natal on the one side and the Cape and Free State on the opposing side.[9] The business generated by the Witwatersrand gold fields was the prize and the Cape made the first breakthrough, – but Natal was not to be left behind.

Other than the Delagoa Bay route, the shortest route from Johannesburg to a viable port was to Durban, the port of the Natal colony. By 1891, when the railway deal with the Cape colony was concluded, the Natal railway was also hovering on the Transvaal border. On a visit to that colony in April of 1891, Kruger was feted and 'sucked up to' by the Natalians in an effort to promote their own railway and port as an outlet to the sea.[10]

Their efforts were rewarded and they signed the Charlestown Convention in 1894, giving them permission to extend their railway line from Durban to Johannesburg. This action could be considered a move contrary to broad imperial considerations as it made Natal economically dependent on the Transvaal – by then the chief threat to British interests in South Africa. Nevertheless, Natal borrowed £9,000,000, invested £1,000,000 on harbour works to enable them to handle the expected traffic from the Rand, and then expended a further £7,000,000 on extending the rail link.[11]

The interest payments on the debt were substantial and amounted to £180 per annum per head of the Natal population, and the only source of revenue that could be counted on to service the interest was goods traffic to and from the Rand. Natal was thus totally at the mercy of the Transvaal, a situation that most of the population did not savour, but which could not be avoided in their quest for economic development.

The Lourenço Marques line to Pretoria was eventually completed in 1894 – two years after the line from the Cape, but it only reached Johannesburg, and became operational from there, in 1895. By this time the Cape and Natal were already earning substantial amounts from trade with the Rand. Given the terms of the Sivewright agreement, it is not surprising that the Cape enjoyed almost a monopoly of trade with the Transvaal. In 1895 the *South African Mining Journal* wrote that 'the greater proportion of these receipts (from all the railway lines in Natal and the Cape together) came from Rand trade'.[12]

But before the story of railway building and economic rivalry could continue and deliver its peculiar political crisis, other events would impose their own priorities. In the years after 1886 trouble had been brewing and simmering between the Randlords, the *Uitlanders* and the Kruger regime. In 1894 Rhodes was Prime Minister of the Cape, and at the height of his considerable powers. He was more impatient with Kruger and his obstructionist policies than most others. He also believed, quite correctly as it turned out, that he did not have long to live and he was a man in a hurry. It was time for a daring plot to overthrow the Z.A.R.

CHAPTER FIFTEEN

A TALE OF TWO CITIES

From its very beginnings Johannesburg was destined to live uncomfortably with its older neighbour, Pretoria. Pretoria was in the Z.A.R. and is still in South Africa, the seat of administrative and executive power. In the Z.A.R. it was also the seat of the legislature, which was still called the Volksraad.

In the time of Paul Kruger it was only a small town, but it largely measured up to Boer expectations of what a town should be like. In contrast to the much maligned, but necessary evil of the impious, tennis-playing, fun-loving Hollanders that Kruger found necessary to employ in order to staff the higher echelons of the civil service, the town had the sedate, almost solemn atmosphere that the Boers regarded as appropriate to the serious business that is life. Pretoria was thus both the seat and the symbol of the Transvaal Boer's political power.

On the other hand, only some 40 miles to the south, lay the mushrooming city of Johannesburg, populated by a fast-growing number of people from all over the planet. As all political power resided in Pretoria, so all economic power centred in Johannesburg. The city and its people were a festering sore in the side of Boer society. Boer society, in common with other pioneer societies at that time, was generally suspicious of cities and city slickers, but Johannesburg was especially beyond the pale.

Economically the Boers could not survive without Johannesburg, but they had great difficulty in living with it. To most of them, Johannesburg was like a foreign growth in their little paradise. It was not merely that it was predominantly English, since most towns, including Pretoria, had always had predominantly English-speaking inhabitants. It was that the Boers found the vibrant, shoulder-rubbing, wheeler-dealing residents of Johannesburg unacceptable because they represented the antithesis of the backward, easy-going, secluded lifestyle that the Boers revered. These people were *Uitlanders*.

Moreover, over a period of time the majority of Transvaal Boers came to regard Johannesburg as a threat to the independence of their Republic. This fear would be so compelling as to become self-fulfilling. In fact, the foreigners who streamed to the gold fields were not a united body of people in any way. They were a polyglot lot, coming from all over the world. Whilst it cannot be denied that the majority of them were British, nevertheless there were a substantial number of Germans, Americans, Australians, Baltic Jews, Poles and other Europeans.[1] English was commonly understood and was therefore the spoken language of the city, which probably explains why the unsophisticated and undiscriminating majority of Boers regarded all *Uitlanders* as English. Culturally and linguistically they were, however, cosmopolitan.

First stirrings of strife

It was evident from the outset that problems were going to arise from the presence of *Uitlanders* in the Boer heartland of the Transvaal. The newly proclaimed village of Johannesburg (probably named after Johannes Meyer, the *Veldcornet* of the district in which it was situated and who had exerted himself mightily in organizing and securing its establishment) lay immediately to the north of Ferreira's Camp. It was formally laid out on a triangular piece of government-owned land, previously known as Randjeslaagte. Randjeslaagte joined directly onto the northern border of the farm Turffontein and Ferreira's Camp.

Much to the chagrin of the town's population, the new town was denied the normal forms of local government that operated in the other villages and towns of the Republic. Also, land tenure in the city was initially by five-year leasehold, later extended to 99 years, but it was a substantial deviation from the freehold title available elsewhere in the Z.A.R.

At least there was, from the start, a Diggers Committee to run the affairs of this boomtown. The Diggers Committee was soon replaced by a Sanitary Committee, which remained the local authority for the better part of the following 10 years. Johannesburg became one of the fastest growing urban areas in the world at that time and from its very beginning it was the heart and soul of the economy of the sub-continent, a position it holds to this day.

Nevertheless, the arrangements for local government in Johannesburg fell far short of what was required of such a fast-growing community. Numerous requests to Pretoria for a proper municipal authority fell on deaf ears and the lack of a proper, representative municipal authority was an issue causing much dissatisfaction among the population, virtually from the moment of the founding of the city. One of the main complaints was that the city's water supply was totally inadequate and resulted in recurring water shortages. Water had then to be brought to the city by ox-wagons from the Vaal River. People were of the opinion that only a fully-fledged municipal authority, in which they had proper representation, would be able to handle the growing city's problems. But Paul Kruger's reluctance to give the *Uitlanders* in Johannesburg any political power at all, extended even to local government. Nothing came of their entreaties to Pretoria and this was one of the sources of increasingly strained relations with Pretoria.[2]

The matter would only be addressed in 1897 by the grant of substantial municipal powers, but by then it was a case of too little too late.[3] The Republican regime's unwillingness to give full municipal privileges to Johannesburg increased the tension and mistrust between it and Pretoria considerably, to the extent that it constituted an important factor in the outbreak of general hostilities in South Africa in 1899.

The Johannesburg *Uitlander* community, whose very background, culture, education and system of beliefs were not only foreign to, and different from, that of the Boers, was totally unacceptable to the great majority of them. They regarded themselves as God's own people[4] and it follows that all the rest were sinners and their deeds an abomination in the eyes of the Lord. Indeed, there was a lot of sinning going on in the city of gold.

In addition to the rampant gambling (which, although prohibited, was irregularly enforced) and other vices of the demimonde that took place in saloons and bars all over town, the 'ladies of the night' were very much in evidence and conducted a vigorous business. By the second half of 1896 a significant portion of central Johannesburg was exclusively devoted to organized vice. One of the local papers, the pro-Kruger *Standard and Diggers News* lamented that 'our best residential streets and our most important thoroughfares are dedicated to [vice]'.[5]

It was not only Boer sensibilities and those of the *Standard and Diggers News* that were offended by such goings on. Some of the residents approached the local magistrate with a petition to exercise strict control over prostitution. This worthy thereupon drew up a set of regulations that he sent to State Attorney Esselen in Pretoria for approval. Esselen did not take any action, but returned them with the suggestion that the Sanitary Board of the city first approve them. In the upshot, the Sanitary Board drafted regulations and in late 1895 sent them to the then new State Attorney, Dr Herman Coster, in Pretoria. He, being a Hollander of liberal views, was not particularly taken with these proposed regulations. He strongly doubted the value of attempting to legislate on matters of morality. He was therefore not inclined to take any action on the matter.

There is no doubt that such activities and the proliferation of vice would not have been allowed to develop or exist in any other Boer town. The uncontrolled situation in Johannesburg became a source of concern and grievance to the locals regarding the Republican government. Its inaction was seen as a direct sign of its lack of concern with the well-being of Johannesburg's citizens and its disdain for their wishes and best interests.

The city was also not particularly well served by its police force. Johannesburg and the gold fields were in fact the only area in the Transvaal that had a police force. Thus, although it was really a gold fields' municipal police force, it was controlled from central government in Pretoria. It was officially named the Z.A.R. Police

Service, but generally referred to as the 'ZARPS'. The low esteem in which the force was held had a lot to do with how it was constituted, trained and managed after its founding.

Many of the poorest of the Transvaal Boers had come to Johannesburg to seek their fortune. Unfortunately they had no skills that were of value in the mines or in any of the peripheral trades, industries or professions. Many of them became self-sufficient as small entrepreneurs in the transport business and later as brick-makers when the government licensed brick-making on the farm Braamfontein immediately to the west of the city. But many more of them became totally impoverished, almost to the point of destitution. Kruger's government insisted that only burghers were eligible for service in the police force and this, by definition, excluded the *Uitlander* population of the city. Many of the young Boers, who might otherwise have been destitute, were thus taken into the 'ZARPS' despite the illiteracy of a fair percentage of them.[6]

It is therefore hardly surprising that the police force, that was supposed to serve the citizens of the city, and the citizens themselves were distrustful of each other. The people of Johannesburg did not see this badly-trained and ill-disciplined band of young men, who were in many ways unsympathetic to the residents, as protecting their persons or property in any way. Indeed, they often saw them as a threat. This perception was exacerbated by Paul Kruger's tactless and indefensible appointment in late 1887 of Adriaan de la Rey as commandant of the police on the gold fields. De la Rey had a criminal record and the residents demanded an immediate reversal of his appointment. Kruger was disinclined to give way in this matter and did not.[7]

The appointment of de la Rey was piled onto Kruger's own ill-considered words and actions earlier that same year when he was in Johannesburg on his first, two-day visit. On this first visit, in February 1887, President Kruger was driven to Johannesburg from Pretoria in his *'Staatskoets'* (State Coach). The residents of the city, who had erected a triumphal arch for his coach to drive through, greeted him with great enthusiasm. The arch had been erected by Joseph Buxton and adorned with six large flags – two *'Vierkleurs'* (the ZAR's official flag), and one each of the British, German, US and Orange Free State flags. A mounted guard of honour was sent out to meet him and escort him to the office of the special *Landdrost*, where his arrival was saluted with loud cheers. He received addresses from various communities on the Witwatersrand, each setting out their concerns and hopes for the future.

The address from the elected representatives of the merchants, storekeepers, standholders (residential property holders) and other residents of Johannesburg stressed five major concerns for which they requested his intervention. Their first request was in respect of the five-year leasehold of land in force at that time. They wanted to be given 'fixity of tenure in all purchases of town lots from the government'. Second, they requested that, as regards the monthly licence fee on town lots, Johannesburg be placed on the same footing as other Transvaal towns. Third, they asked for the granting of a municipality and licensing board for the proper government of Johannesburg. Fourth, they called for the *ad valorum* duty on merchandise to be reduced to 5 per cent and that mining machinery be exempt from all duties. In conclusion they asked for an improved, daily postal service to the city. Having received the addresses, Kruger made a short speech in Dutch and announced a later meeting to be held on the veranda of the Mining Commissioner's office, scheduled for 4 o'clock that afternoon.

At the afternoon meeting Kruger gave an address in Dutch again which was translated into English for the crowd. He first assured them that he would treat the 'new' population on equal terms with the 'old' population, although that did not extend to franchise rights. At that time citizenship and the franchise were available to anyone upon application after a five-year residence. It was not an issue, except with respect to the municipality they desired. Kruger was, in effect, giving notice that he was not going to leave it as it was.

He stressed, however, that he expected them to support the 'old residents' and the independence of the Republic. He added that he loved them all and would treat them as his children. Then, in a crude attempt at humour,[8] he made some unfortunate remarks. He told the large crowd that he had secret agents in Johannesburg who kept him informed of all developments there. He added that if there were any disturbances he would have the miscreants arrested by the diggers themselves or otherwise call up his burghers and deal with them as rebels.

A typical highveld thunderstorm then burst overhead and came down in torrents on the crowd, ending the meeting and the embarrassing harangue.[9] When later in the year, the convicted de la Rey was appointed to command the exclusively Boer ZARPS on the Rand, it hardly served to reassure the local residents of Pretoria's good intentions.

Regarding the residents' other requests, Kruger's parsimony to the 'foreign' city of Johannesburg was as evident on the following morning as ever it was and would always remain. Apart from promising a slight reduction in the monthly stand licence payment, he informed those gathered to hear his reaction to the previous day's addresses that he expected the language of the country (Dutch) to be used as far as possible at all meetings, that he regarded two postal deliveries per week to be adequate for their needs and that he could not reduce other licence fees as the money might be required to pay his burghers in case he had to call on them to quell a disturbance.[10] It is not recorded whether this remark was another spontaneous outburst of jocularity from the President. Needless to say, the residents of Johannesburg did not remember his visit with any warmth.

Despite these disappointing aspects, on his second visit to Johannesburg, the residents received Kruger very heartily and in a festive spirit. The second visit would, however, be even more disappointing than the first. It was on the occasion of this visit that he informed them, *inter alia*, that although he was disposed to granting them a rail link to the outside world, it would have to wait until the completion of the line from Lourenço Marques.

He added further insult to injury that evening when he arrived late for a dinner that was given in the city in his honour. The apparent disdain with which he had treated both the people of Johannesburg and his hosts on this occasion, caused an uncomfortable atmosphere which prevailed throughout the dinner.[11] The soured atmosphere was not improved by a rowdy protest that was in progress in the street outside the hotel. The protest concerned the previously discussed appointment of Adriaan de la Rey as police commander and the crowd was demanding the reversal of the appointment.

The noise got so bad that the hosts, the British Consul and the President were compelled to repeatedly leave the dinner and address the crowd outside in an attempt to calm them. In a further show of bad manners, the President left long before the conclusion of the function. This was the first public demonstration of dissatisfaction with Kruger and his way of doing things. Although a third visit in December of 1888 went off without any untoward incident, public discontent in Johannesburg was endemic and was destined to grow worse.

The heart of the discontent

Not a full year had passed since the proclamation of the Witwatersrand gold fields and the 'foreigners' in Johannesburg were already becoming a political issue. It would become the dominant political issue in the Z.A.R.

The anti-*Uitlander* feeling was more than Boer misanthropy, of which Kipling spoke so eloquently:

His neighbours' smoke shall vex his eyes, their voices break his rest.
He shall go forth till south is north, sullen and dispossessed.

It was fuelled by the fear that the influx of great numbers of foreigners would undermine the political power of the Transvaal Boers in general, but of Kruger in particular.

Kruger and the *Uitlanders* simply could not talk to each other.[12] The distance between them was too great for that to be possible and Kruger obviously sensed that. Upon his return to Pretoria, after his first visit to Johannesburg, his report to the Volksraad soberly commented on the fast developing gold fields and their portent for a prosperous future for the state.

Nevertheless, being an experienced politician, and sensing the chasm between himself and the *Uitlanders*, he knew that, when they were enfranchised, his candidacy would not receive much support from those quarters. He then privately began harbouring fears that the *Uitlanders* would soon outstrip the numbers of his own people and that he would find it very difficult to govern with the support of only a minority of the enfranchised population.

As things stood, the first *Uitlanders* on the Rand had arrived the previous year and within another four years they would have citizenship and the franchise. He therefore began to fear *Uitlander* demands for political rights, which he thought would place the independence of the Republic in jeopardy.[13] However, Kruger did not take any action immediately. First, the second of the five-yearly presidential elections had to take place and he had nothing to fear from any *Uitlander* vote in 1887. Piet Joubert, who conducted a negative campaign, again opposed him; Kruger won the election by a handsome margin.

Contrary to Kruger's fears, the *Uitlanders* were not a homogenous political interest group as later events would fully demonstrate. Those hailing from Britain, America and Australia were generally of a democratic persuasion but they had no clear, uniform political agenda. The substantial numbers of non-British immigrants were not particularly keen to live under the British flag; to some of them, especially those arriving from Germany and the US, the idea of living under the British flag was completely anathema.

The *Uitlanders* did not represent a single economic interest bloc either. By 1890, most of the hardy adventurers and fortune-seekers had either settled down or left for greener pastures. Most of the immigrants were by then skilled labourers, artisans, traders, shopkeepers, professionals and entrepreneurs. Since their numbers were thus divided between members of the skilled proletariat, small businessmen and professionals, it follows that their economic and commercial interests were often as much at odds with each other as were to be found anywhere in Europe or America.

Consequently, Kruger's fear that the *Uitlanders* would form a monolithic political voting bloc who would lead the Republic to wheresover they wished had no foundation in fact. Unless united by a very strong threat to them as a group, such as Kruger himself was about to supply, the *Uitlanders* were extremely unlikely to have one common or overriding political will. Kruger sensed that he would never manage to develop a proper rapport with them and in this, his assessment was quite correct.

Although there were among the *Uitlanders* a number of vociferous British jingoes who were given to raising the Union Jack and singing 'God Save the Queen' at the slightest provocation, everybody, including Paul Kruger, agreed that these elements were always a non-representative minority.[14] Nevertheless, because of their high profile and their vociferousness, many Boers gained the impression that their views represented the views of *Uitlanders* generally. The perception among the *Uitlanders*, on the other hand, was that they were being discriminated against, and they were right.

The franchise fiasco

Up to 1882, the Transvaal required only a one-year residency before full citizenship could be attained. This requirement was changed in 1882 to the more universally accepted requirement of five years residence. Thus, at the time when Kruger started worrying about the number of foreigners streaming to the Witwatersrand, the law in the Z.A.R. required a five-year residency before foreigners could attain citizenship and, if they were adult males, the suffrage. After his successful re-election campaign in 1887, and driven by his fears, Kruger set about gerrymandering the residency requirements in order to protect his own power base.

In February 1889, at the instance of Kruger, a draft Bill was published in the Government Gazette[15], amending the Constitution and the Electoral Act in order to prevent the imminent enfranchisement of those *Uitlanders* who had arrived in 1886. These earliest arrivals would have qualified for citizenship in 1891 and would consequently have been able to vote in the next Presidential election, which was due in 1893.

The scheme Kruger cooked up to suit his political ambitions was probably intended to be a political masterstroke, but it was so unsubtle as to fool no-one, at least, no-one of the *Uitlander* community. Under the guise of giving them 'some say' in the political affairs of the country at an earlier date than the existing five year period, he proposed a 'Second' Volksraad with very limited powers; so limited in fact that it would be no more than a consultative body. Real political power would remain in the 'First' Volksraad. New immigrants would be eligible to vote for the 'Second' Volksraad after only two years residence, but they would first have to accept naturalization status. Then a further period of ten years residence would have to pass before full citizenship was granted, including the franchise to vote for the 'First' Volksraad.

Kruger then caused a Bill to be published, which, in essence, contained these proposals. Surprisingly enough, there was substantial opposition from the Transvaal burghers who sent in memorials in response to the publication. It appears that most of them were of the opinion that the laws were quite adequate as they were, while a decided minority of memorialists was opposed to the *Uitlanders* ever obtaining the franchise.[16]

During the three-day debate on the proposals in the Volksraad sitting of May 1889, substantial opposition from members of that body also became evident. Jan Cilliers, a Volksraad member and editor of the influential *De Volkstem*, a Pretoria newspaper, damned the proposal as 'class legislation'. The so-called 'liberal' wing, consisting of Piet Joubert, the young Schalk Burger and a few others, preferred representation for the *Uitlanders* in the existing Volksraad. Kruger, having a personal stake in the outcome of the matter, defended the proposed amendments in one of the best speeches of his career. He started by assuming full, personal responsibility for the proposed amendments in the Bill. He declared that the proposal did not emanate from the Executive Council and members of the government were therefore free to vote against it.

Being Kruger, his whole speech was laced with quasi-religious arguments involving 'God's people' and the independence of the Republic, the responsibility for which had been placed in his hands by God and so forth. Indeed, a listener might be excused for concluding that the proposed amendments had been handed down to him directly from Mount Zion. However, the gravamen of his argument was that times had changed and that the old laws were no longer good enough.

He claimed that there was no country in the world where such a turnaround (in population) had taken place. The discovery of enormous treasure drew a stream of new residents who had been brought up with different customs and mores, and who were not familiar with the Republican form of government. In five years, their numbers would be five times greater than the numbers of the 'old' inhabitants who had striven and suffered for independence. However loyal they were, their upbringing was different. With their sympathies for their own countries of origin, they would be able to lead the Republic wherever they wished, once they were enfranchised.

Then Kruger made an important point that, although it might not have had much persuasive power at that time, places one facet of events at the end of the century into greater focus. He warned that there already existed a strong movement in favour of a South Africa united under the British flag. As against that, he stated, there is another movement, to which he had joined himself, that proposed to unite South Africa as an independent country. That independent country must have the Transvaal – its heart – as its point of departure. He asked the Volksraad members whether they would look on while the 'new population' gained the upper hand and made the Republic part of a united South Africa under a royal flag.[17]

With this argument and speech he had firmly and unequivocally nailed his flag to the mast of getting Britain out of South Africa altogether. Given Britain's involvement in South Africa at that time for close on a century, whether for better or worse, which had begun even before the Great Trek, it was a presumptuous and arrogant statement to make. It could not do otherwise than sour relations with Britain. Thereafter, this sentiment of Kruger's must have been constantly in the back of the minds of British Colonial Office officials, and must have contributed greatly to their growing spirit of distrust of him and his regime.

Only a few members of the 'old guard' supported Kruger's Bill, however, and after a somewhat acrimonious debate the Volksraad decided by simple majority to refer the Bill to a commission. The commission was to report to the Volksraad after consultation with the executive Council. With the next sitting of the Volksraad, in June 1897, the Bill, in slightly amended form, was passed by a large majority. The passing of the Bill into law can be ascribed to the great personal influence of Kruger, especially his lobbying behind the scenes.[18]

Law 4 of 1890 introduced the second Volksraad and Law 5 contained the new electoral law. The law now required a total of 14 years residence before an immigrant could attain citizenship and be fully enfranchised. It provided that new residents could be naturalized after a two-year residence and after a further two years would become eligible to vote for and sit in the second Volksraad. A further waiting period of ten years was required thereafter before full citizenship and the franchise for the First Volksraad could be attained.

The legislation was a patently dishonest ploy to take away the existing rights of the new arrivals, thus keeping them from exercising political power. It incidentally also had the beneficial effect of protecting Paul Kruger's own power base. Kruger was already in his mid-60s and with the 14 years respite he thus obtained, he might well have argued that any *Uitlanders* enfranchised after that period, would only be able to exercise their votes in the Presidential election of 1903 at the earliest. That would keep him safe for at least another two terms and, with the increase in Boer voters coming of age during that time, he might well be safe even for a third term. Thereafter the *Uitlander* vote would not be his problem anyway.

The franchise and citizenship of the Z.A.R. had not been an issue among the new immigrants until Kruger made it an issue. His patently self-serving actions, and his arguments in justification thereof, could never have been calculated to leave the new arrivals cold, nor to make them feel welcome or wanted. They knew as well as anyone that they were the economic heart and soul of the Z.A.R. They also knew that their taxes and licence fees were the lion's share of the state's revenue; that indeed, the state could not exist without them. Cheating them out of the Transvaal's existing, internationally accepted norm for enfranchisement, especially by arguing that they were not assimilable or acceptable to the people who before could not generate any economic activity worthy of the name, was a certain invitation to disaster. It would not be the last time that dishonest manipulation of franchise qualifications would take place in South Africa.

Suddenly the franchise was an issue among *Uitlanders*. Whatever their previous complaints and grievances, everything was now worse. Where previously they demanded only a representative municipality for their city, they now demanded a say in the political organs of the country that had treated them so shabbily. Even while the debate on the Bill was still in progress, people's feelings had been aroused. Kruger again visited Johannesburg while the Volksraad was in recess, after his initial speech in support of the franchise proposals and while they were awaiting the report of the committee to which the Bill had been referred.

In shrill contrast to his first three visits, when Kruger was, with one exception, the only one guilty of less than courteous behaviour, his visit to Johannesburg on 4 March 1890 turned into a fiasco. His visit coincided with the first economic downturn in Johannesburg, which lasted only for some twelve months between 1889 and 1990, but at the time seemed to spell catastrophe. The most important cause for the slump was the discovery of the pyrite reefs at deeper levels that held no free gold and the inability of existing technology to refine gold from that ore. This loss of confidence in the industry was aggravated by the absence of a rail link to the outside world and the gross over-speculation that had taken place on the local stock exchange. Indeed, a severe drought caused serious food shortages which made it difficult for the mines to feed their workers. The Chamber of Mines appealed to Pretoria and food was imported by the wagonload to relieve the shortage. Understandably, a spirit of doom and gloom pervaded the streets of Johannesburg.[19] Kruger seemed to be of the opinion that the community had brought the problem down on their own heads and he showed neither understanding nor sympathy for their situation.

Before his arrival at the Wanderers grounds, the British contingency in a 10,000 strong crowd was singing 'God Save the Queen' and 'Rule Britannia'. Nevertheless, when Kruger arrived in the midst of a cavalcade sent out to meet him, loud cheers greeted him as he took the podium. After Kruger agreed to meet with deputations from the Sanitary Committee and other bodies that evening, the meeting dispersed.

However, a part of the crowd was not yet mollified. Rowdy public meetings were held, where the *Vierkleur* was ripped down from its staff in front of the Magistrate's offices; thereafter the angry mob descended on the home of the German-born Captain Carl von Brandis, the competent and well-liked special magistrate of Johannesburg, where Kruger was huddled in talks with the various deputations. It is understandable that many of them felt angry, insulted and cheated. Many others of course, just did not give a damn.

Inside the house Mr. Liebman, a deputy, called the Volksraad's licence fees ridiculous and accused the President of treating the people with disdain. Kruger became angry, stating that he had no disdain for the people, but that he had only scorn for him, Liebman. Adding that he would not allow the Volksraad to be disparaged, he refused to discuss the matter further. Liebman thereupon left the house and was received by the crowd outside as a hero. The crowd then became even more unruly, trampled the garden and only dispersed when the ZARPS arrived.[20]

Although the rowdy demonstrations were due to the actions of only a fraction of Johannesburg residents, the dissatisfaction of the *Uitlanders* must be seen in the context of their economic contribution to the country. In this connection it is necessary to keep in mind the difference that Johannesburg and the inhabitants of the Witwatersrand were making to the finances of the Republic.

The returns for the month of September 1887 show that Johannesburg contributed an amount of £10,964 11s. 3d. to the Republic's revenue, while Roodepoort contributed £3,484 13s. 1d. and Elsburg £2,754 4s. 5d. This brings the total contribution of the Witwatersrand gold fields for the month of September to £17,203 8s. 9d., close to the annual income of the Republic before the discovery of gold.[21] The state's revenue from the gold fields was increasing from month to month and transforming the once precariously perched Boer polity into a viable, although not yet modern, state.

The Presidential election of 1893 was not another cakewalk for Kruger. Piet Joubert once again opposed him, but this time Johannes

Kotzé, the young Chief Justice of the Republic, joined the fray. The number of voters in the Republic was pathetically small, but this election would prove to be the only one where Kruger's paramountcy was in some doubt. The contretemps with the *Uitlanders* probably had some influence and some burghers might have though that a more 'progressive' policy was in order. As it turned out, Kruger won the election, polling 7,854 votes against Joubert's 7,009, and Kotzé bringing up the rear with a humiliating 81 votes.

Had some *Uitlanders* obtained citizenship and the franchise before the '93 election, as they would have done were it not for Kruger's gerrymandering, the election would most probably have had a totally different outcome. The franchise fiasco was thus a watershed event in the history of South Africa. Progress on the road to war was then set to continue unabated.

A heat build-up in the kitchen

With the series of events that took place between Kruger and the *Uitlanders* in the period 1887–90, the battle lines had been drawn. In 1892 the Transvaal National Union was born from Johannesburg residents' frustrated municipal ambitions. With some wise statesmanship, much could still have been saved, but none was forthcoming. The grievances of the *Uitlanders*, real and imagined, mounted month by month. Many, including Rhodes, who sought to achieve their own political and financial ends, were ready to exploit such grievances to the full. The five years after 1890 would see the first stirrings develop into full conflict.

It was not only the *Uitlander* man in the street who was experiencing difficulties with the Kruger regime, more importantly perhaps, the Randlords were having more than their fair share. In late 1887 it had already became clear that as long as the mines had no collective body to deal with the authorities, they would pay insufficient attention to their needs. The idea seems to have originated with Edward Lippert,[22] the man who bought the concession to manufacture dynamite in the Z.A.R. from Alois Nellmapius.

Lippert was not in good standing with most of the Randlords because of what they believed to be his underhand dealings concerning the dynamite monopoly. Nevertheless, J.B. Taylor (representing the Corner House of Herman Eckstein & Co.), John X. Merriman (representing J.B. Robinson), W. Y. Campbell (representing the interests of Sir Donald Currie, a London shipping magnate who initiated the mail ship service to South Africa) and Lippert had a meeting from which resulted the first Chamber of Mines. Membership was by individuals rather than mining companies and it was fissiparous from the start. The mining share boom of 1888–89 caused the final collapse of the body. The *Diggers News*, a Johannesburg paper generally supporting Kruger, commented that 'prosperity killed it even as depression had given it birth'.[23]

Sure enough, when depression came round again in 1889–90, the Chamber was reformed as the Witwatersrand Chamber of Mines. Membership was now by the mining houses themselves and the leading houses, the Corner House, Rhodes' Goldfields and Barnato's Johnnies', formed its backbone. Through a process of continuous succession and name changes, it thrives to this day as the South African Chamber of Mines.

There would not be a body of men on the Witwatersrand to rival the Executive Committee of the Chamber. It consisted of eleven members meeting monthly. The first President was Hermann Eckstein, who would be succeeded by Lionel Phillips, also from the Corner House. Kruger was made honorary President of the Chamber, but it was not an honour that he regarded highly or at all.

The new body's first success was its intercession with Pretoria to relieve the food shortage on the Rand. Thereafter, for the duration of the life of the Z.A.R., its main preoccupations would be the dynamite monopoly, railways, the food supply and the recruitment and control of black labour.

Mines in labour

Skilled white labourers were not a problem. 'Hard rock' men from Cornwall, known on the Rand as 'Cousin Jacks', joined with men from England's north-west and Australia to sell their skills in explosives, as samplers, underground surveyors and managers to the mines; they could demand high wages and they got them.

Black labour, however, was the key to the success of the mines. They were required as unskilled, manual labour working at first with picks and shovels. As the activity went deeper and deeper underground they used hand-drills, but by their sweat and muscle power the gold was wrested from the rockbound bowels of the earth.

When gold was discovered on the Rand, the nearest black community large enough to supply some of the new industry's labour needs, was situated some 70 miles distant, just north of a town by the name of Rustenburg. It was also close to this town that Paul Kruger had had a farm since his young days. Blacks soon came in numbers to work in the mines, as it was one of the few places they could actually earn cash. But they came only to earn enough money for a particular purpose, such as to buy a few head of cattle, or a piece of land and then they returned whence they came. This casual situation did not suit the mines at all.

They soon began recruiting on the periphery of the Transvaal, especially in Mozambique. In this matter they required the cooperation of the Transvaal Government, which they got. The more intractable problem was the wages paid for black labour. Because of the fixed price of gold and the other economic circumstances created by the politics of the Z.A.R., black wages were the only large overhead that the mines believed they had any chance of successfully manipulating to be lower. The first part of the problem was that members of the Chamber were in competition with each other to obtain this scarce resource. Many agreements fixing maximum wages for blacks were tried, but none could hold good when labour shortages put pressure on managers. The problem, in short, was how to lure labour to the mines while holding wages steady or even lowering them.[24]

They prevailed upon the government to implement a system of 'passes' among black labourers in order to control their movement and to prevent the 'theft' of labourers from one mine by another. Such a pass system had already been implemented with great success in the diamond mines of Kimberley for a similar purpose.

This callous manipulation of people, regarded more as 'labour' than as humans, was to be the blueprint for the pass system that South Africa's later apartheid government would use to control the lives of virtually every black person in South Africa.

The Chamber formed a Native Labour Department that cooperated with Pretoria regarding the implementation of the pass system. However, the pass system was not a great success in the Transvaal, not because the government was unwilling, but because it was difficult to implement due to a lack of sufficient government funding and the general inefficiency of the Republic's civil service, including the ZARPS. By 1892 the number of black labourers on the Rand stood at approximately 19,000, almost as many as all of Kruger's burgers in the Transvaal. Nevertheless, the supply and wages of black labour remained a thorn in the side of the mining houses and a perennial complaint to Pretoria.

Dynamite, explosions and deals

The other very real perennial problem was the dynamite monopoly held by Edward Lippert. In this matter, however, the even shrewder Nobel would outdo the hard-nosed Randlords. The dynamite concession was very enticing for the international dynamite manufacturers and they would play their cards well to get a piece of the action.

Apart from its general preference for having access to a competitive market for dynamite, the Chamber had two complaints against the dynamite monopoly: the quality of the dynamite and its price. They also suspected that Lippert was underhand and that he imported low-grade, finished dynamite and resold it to them at a huge profit. This suspicion would be tested in 1892.

An increasing number of mine accidents had raised serious concerns about the quality of the dynamite being supplied. In its first annual report, the Chamber vented its anger at the quality of Lippert's dynamite, complaining of 'its want of uniformity and the frequency of partial explosions; ... its want of power; ... the loss of time and injury to health by its fumes'. Although the government summarily dismissed all complaints, by April 1892 it was obliged to appoint an investigatory commission. The evidence of increasing mine accidents was irrefutable.

Lippert of course held a concession to manufacture dynamite in the Transvaal, not to import it. Already in late 1889 Nobel's agent in Cape Town alleged that Lippert was not only importing raw materials for the manufacture of dynamite, but also the finished product itself. In a consignment of 'raw materials' destined for Lippert's company on board the *Baron Ellibank* in Cape Town harbour, finished dynamite was found after a search. The Z.A.R. took no action.

Then, on a tip-off from the Chamber, the Z.A.R. government in May 1892 inspected the cargo that came off the *Highfield*. In July it was announced that the cargo imported by Lippert had indeed been found to be finished dynamite. He was importing dynamite and selling it to the mines as Transvaal manufactured goods at a 200 per cent profit. Lippert's lame excuse that he knew nothing of the matter inspired a Johannesburg wag, adopting Madame Roland's words, to exclaim: 'O Lippert, E! What crimes are committed in thy name!'

Lippert's concession was revoked in August, but Kruger was not about to relinquish such a valuable source of income. By agreement with the British, French and German consuls, the government allowed the importation of 45,000 cases of dynamite – 15,000 cases from each of the three countries. This was only allowed as a temporary measure until the Volksraad could grant a new monopoly to the government. The government would then find a new concessionary.

The Volksraad took its time and only granted the concession in September, by which time a serious shortage of dynamite had developed, further straining relations between Pretoria and the Mining Houses of Johannesburg. Lippert had in the meantime, formed the South African Explosives Company to tender for the new concession but the Chamber of Mines put in its own tender after negotiating favourable terms with Nobel. This resulted in Lippert's belated resignation from the Chamber's executive where his position had long ago become untenable.

The Chamber's tender was more generous to the government that Lippert's, paying the same 5 shillings per case royalty, but offering half the profits compared to South African Explosive's 20 per cent. Nevertheless, Lippert's tender was accepted and the question of the dynamite concession was unresolved.

Unbeknown to the Chamber, the Z.A.R. and the Randlords, a new company was floated in Europe in May 1893. In the new company, Nobel owned 220,000 shares and Lippert 25,000. Nobel and Lippert had outmanoeuvred the Randlords and they now firmly clasped the dynamite monopoly.[25]

Fifty-one miles of trouble

In the Z.A.R.'s brother Republic of the Free State, life was much quieter and far better run. Their President since 1864 was the sagacious and moderate Jan H. Brand, who was honoured in 1872 by Queen Victoria with a knighthood. In British circles he was known as Sir John Brand, GCMG. For some 20 years he presided over what was on its own terms, a model republic. He managed to establish and maintain a tranquil political situation in which the Boer majority lived in peace with their English-speaking compatriots and, although black people had no rights in the Republic, good relations between the races prevailed.

Brand was not as gung-ho about a united South Africa under its own flag as were Kruger and his cronies. Although he maintained friendly relations with Paul Kruger and the Z.A.R., as he did with his other neighbours, he had severe reservations when it came to closer cooperation with the Transvaal. This was evident in 1885 when some Free Staters expressed a wish for such closer political cooperation.[26]

The Free State was economically dependent on the Cape and Brand wished to maintain his republic's position as the gateway to the Transvaal gold fields. It was possible to reach Johannesburg from Cape Town via Kimberley without passing over Free State territory, and it was likewise possible from Natal via Newcastle and Standerton. He therefore tried to negotiate with Kruger in 1887 to allow the rail links to be built over Free State territory, but Kruger was little concerned with his Free State brethren when it came down to what he perceived to be his own interests. He would try to delay the Cape and Natal lines to everybody's disadvantage in order to give preference to his Delagoa Bay line.

When the Sivewright agreement was eventually entered into by the N.Z.A.S.M., Kruger had to capitulate. Brand succeeded in getting his way when the Cape line was extended from Colesberg in the Cape, via Bloemfontein in the Free State to Johannesburg. The later Natal line, however, did not pass over Free State territory. The agreement gave the Cape railways the right, not only to operate the railways from her ports of Cape Town and Port Elizabeth to Johannesburg, but also to fix the carriage rates through to their destination.

The Sivewright agreement led to the Cape Railways enjoying a *de facto* monopoly of rail traffic to the Rand, but it was due to expire at the end of 1894. The railway line from the Vaal River to Johannesburg in fact belonged to the N.Z.A.S.M. and after the expiry of the Sivewright agreement, the NZASM would be able to fix the rates on these portions of the routes from the Cape. On the Cape line, the portion of the total route under the control of the N.Z.A.S.M. stretched from the Vaal River to Johannesburg and amounted to only 51 miles out of a total distance of close to 1,000 miles. These 51 miles would soon precipitate another crisis for Johannesburg and for Kruger.

Van Bake, who had done so much to realize and finance the N.Z.A.S.M., was still the kingpin of the company in Europe, but the director at the company's helm in Pretoria was G. A. Middelberg. Middelberg negotiated with the Cape government for an agreement on the Cape line's share of the rail traffic to Johannesburg. The negotiations came to nothing and in January 1895 the Cape lowered its tariffs in order to compete against the soon to be commissioned Delagoa Bay line.

Middelberg retaliated by raising the N.Z.A.S.M.'s tariff on its 51-mile section of the Cape line. The Cape government then arranged that goods from the Cape would be transported by rail to the Vaal River, where they would be transferred to ox wagons for the remainder of the trip. There were no road bridges over the river and the wagons therefore had to cross the river via 'drifts', the name for shallow parts of a river where, under normal circumstances, men, animals and vehicles could cross safely. The result was of course, that instead of diverting traffic to the Delagoa Bay line, as was its intention, the N.Z.A.S.M. now did not make a penny on the lucrative Cape route.

In a note to Middelberg on 8 March 1895, van Bake reminded his colleague that 'our origins are anti-English (and) our goal is to make the Z.A.R. economically independent.' He stated that it was in the company's best interest to divert as much traffic as possible via the Delagoa Bay line and added that 'Delagoa Bay should have 5/12 of all Rand traffic, while Natal and the Cape should only have 4/12 and 3/12 respectively – should the maritime colonies find this unacceptable, we will have to get tough and transport all traffic via the bay for some six months.'[27]

Thus in April 1895, a conference of all the South African Republics and Colonies was held in Cape Town. Nothing positive came of the conference since the N.Z.A.S.M. would not agree to the share of the traffic demanded by the Cape. Meanwhile, Middelberg was encouraging Kruger to close the drifts through which the goods imported through the Cape were moving. To this stratagem Kruger eventually agreed and by proclamation he closed the two drifts concerned for all goods imported from overseas, effective from 1 October 1895.[28]

This action by Kruger really set the cat among the pigeons. The Cape cabinet immediately appealed to Westminster, arguing that closing the drifts was essentially a breach of the London Convention. In Cape Town and Johannesburg uproar in the press followed immediately and the Chamber of Mines as well as the Johannesburg Chamber of Commerce swiftly issued stern protests. The Free State also raised its voice in complaint as it stood to lose heavily through this action. Kruger again proved that he did not regard the interests of his Free State brethren at all when the chips were down, but within four years he would call on them to shed their blood in a war that actually did not concern them at all.

Kruger stubbornly refused to listen to anybody. Presently, however, he was forced to listen when the British government, having received certain guarantees it had sought from the Cape government, threatened war. Kruger climbed down and reopened the drifts. He really had no choice, since he could hardly face a war with Britain when everybody in the subcontinent, including the Free State, was against him.[29]

The drifts crisis and Kruger's loss of face were a low point in his career. He had been trapped by his own creation and it was to play a vital role in his and his Republic's eventual downfall. The drifts crisis, added to all the other highly emotional political events of the decade up to then, had directly contributed greatly to the polarization of the white communities in South Africa. It was not only a matter of the Transvaal Boers vs. the *Uitlanders*; Kruger had also managed to alienate the Afrikaners of the Cape and the Boers of the Free State. Most of this damage would soon be repaired, however. Kruger was about to be saved, temporarily at least, by his enemy – Cecil John Rhodes.

CHAPTER SIXTEEN

THE CONSPIRACY AND THE RAID

As Prime Minister of the Cape government during the drifts crisis, Cecil John Rhodes was intimately involved in the development and eventual resolution of the whole matter. The drifts crisis, perhaps more than any other single event, soured relations between Kruger and Rhodes. The two had frequently met before and Rhodes had usually been conciliatory, but his imperialist dreams were no secret. The drifts crises and Rhodes' role in securing the support of Britain in resolving it in favour of the Cape caused Paul Kruger to fear him as the greatest danger to his Republic.

Rhodes was an idealistic imperialist and had already played an important role in expanding the Empire in South Africa. His personal income exceeded £1,000,000 per year. De Beers, the company he had so successfully put together at Kimberley was by 1895 one of the largest and richest corporations in the world and Rhodes was its chairman. His company, Goldfields, was one of the largest and most successful mining houses on the Witwatersrand. It was also one of the most sought after shares on the London Stock Exchange. He was the undisputed head of the British South Africa Company (B.S.A.C.) which held a Royal Charter to acquire land in Africa wherever it might be had. This wealth and financial muscle, added to his political power as Prime Minister of the Cape, allowed him to translate at least some of his dreams of empire into reality.

In very dubious dealings, he had managed to obtain for the B.S.A.C., through his agents, the right to all mineral exploitation in Mashonaland, which was the land of the Matabele north of the Limpopo River. He had blocked expansion of the Transvaal across the Limpopo with this acquisition, which had been achieved in the course of a thoroughly disreputable enterprise.[1] The territory so acquired by the B.S.A.C. would later form the eastern part of the later country of Rhodesia.

To the west and northwest, Transvaal expansionism was blocked by the wisdom of the Tswana chief Kgama, who had requested and received British protection for his lands. The territory then became officially known as the Bechuanaland Protectorate and later, the independent country of Botswana. With this move, Kgama had also stymied the ambitions that Rhodes had held for this tract of land, but Rhodes did manage to reserve a narrow corridor of land for the British South Africa Company all along the western border of the Transvaal. It linked the Cape with Rhodesia territorially, but especially by means of a rail link. It appears that Rhodes had in mind that a campaign against the Transvaal might very conveniently be launched from there.

Talking intervention

When the most influential man on the continent starts talking of intervention, other people tend to listen. Rhodes first advanced the case for intervention against the Transvaal on a visit to London in 1893. His extraordinary persuasiveness, fortified as necessary by the judicious distribution of shares at substantially less than market value, combined with the sweep of his vision of a British Africa from the Cape to Cairo, won widespread support.[2] His appeal was made more credible since it came hard on the heels of despatches of the British High Commissioner in South Africa, Sir Henry Loch.

In 1893, Loch visited the Transvaal for discussions with Kruger to finalize the Republic's borders. At the time of his visit, he came to realize the depth of feeling between the *Uitlanders* and the Kruger regime. Certain *Uitlander* activists, such as Percy Fitzpatrick and

Lionel Phillips, the new captain in charge of the Corner House, convinced Sir Henry that discontent was reaching fever pitch and could turn to open rebellion at any time. Without underestimating the frustrations and humiliation felt by many of the residents of the Witwatersrand, the imminence of open rebellion was a gross overstatement.

Nevertheless, in June of the following year, Sir Henry experienced the high feelings of the *Uitlanders* up close and personal. He arrived in Pretoria for discussions with Paul Kruger on a different issue. In terms of an existing Transvaal statute, the Republic had called up British subjects for military service in one of their interminable campaigns against black tribes. This time it was to bring a Northern Transvaal tribe and chieftain to heel. The disenfranchised *Uitlanders*, who had only recently been told that they were not deemed fit to govern the country on an equal footing with the 'old' inhabitants, were not charmed at being railroaded into military service to fight the Republic's wars.

On that day, Sir Henry and Kruger travelled in the same horse-drawn coach to Loch's hotel in the city. On the way a boisterous crowd of people, who were waving British flags and singing patriotic British songs, stopped the coach. They unhitched the horses from the coach and, singing and cheering all the way, they dragged the coach to the hotel. There, at the crowd's insistence, Loch got out to hear a loyal address read to him by the leaders of the crowd, while Kruger was left, deeply humiliated, to brood sombrely in the now horseless coach. He was saved by some of his burghers who dragged the coach further to the government buildings where Kruger was able to disembark with what was left of his dignity.[3]

Following this incident, Kruger relented on the call-up of foreign nationals for military service. Piet Joubert was said to have commented that 'you can't hunt foxes with unwilling hounds anyway'. However, the events of this visit did nothing to improve relations between the Boers and the *Uitlanders*, but it did reinforce the words of Phillips and Fitzpatrick in the mind of Sir Henry. Under the circumstances he can be forgiven for claiming in his report to London that the 'political atmosphere was charged with such an amount of electricity that any moment an explosion was imminent'.[4] He also included a few suggestions of ways in which a rebellion might be assisted.

In 1893, the B.S.A.C., with troops under the command of Dr Leander Starr Jameson, crushed a rebellion by the Matabele against the company in a particularly bloody fashion. This 'victory' was particularly due to the devastation sown by the new Maxim machine gun when arraigned against a massed enemy. '*The Maxim is something ...*' the troopers sang at the time '... *we have got ... and they have not.*' In the process, however, Dr Jameson developed an unwarranted opinion of his own military leadership abilities, while his success also had the salutary effect of raising the value of B.S.A.C. stock in London. Dr Jameson's inflated opinion of his own prowess no doubt played a great role in the reckless ego trip he would soon embark upon.

Although some mineral deposits were found in Rhodesia, Rhodes' venture north of the Limpopo proved to be a financial damp squib. He had hoped to discover a second Rand, but there was none. This he reluctantly admitted after visiting the area with his American mining adviser, John Hayes Hammond. Things were not going his way and Rhodes was becoming frustrated. A lot of animosity had developed between him and Kruger over the years. At the end of 1894 Phillips told Beit that Kruger had developed a deep fear that the *Uitlanders*, of whom he regarded Rhodes as the head, would gradually buy up the whole country and oust the Boers. In response, Beit informed Phillips in December 1894 that he had had a very confidential talk with Rhodes and that he, Rhodes, would not stand for Kruger's government for long.

Conspiring against Kruger

Rhodes knew very well all of the *Uitlanders'* complaints, but he knew even better the complaints of the mine-owners. Apart from the monopolies and the fact that Johannesburg had by all accounts become the most expensive place in the world to live, which was directly attributable to the monopolistic concessions and the policies of the N.Z.A.S.M., the mine-owners complained that both government and justice were corrupt and partial. Of course, the mine-owners joined enthusiastically, but certainly not joyously, in the wholesale bribery and corruption that was going on. On the other hand, their choices were limited. It was the only way to get at least some things done. During the Volksraad elections of 1893, Phillips told Beit that he thought they could influence the elections with a fund of £10,000. But, he added, it would have to be secretly subscribed, for, if Kruger found out there was £10,000 behind the so-called 'progressives', he would put up £20,000 out of the secret service funds. The latter amount ultimately also came out of their pockets.[5]

The Corner House had several senior government officials in their pockets, including judges. Even the young Chief Justice, Johannes Kotzé, was not beyond reproach. He had been one of the 'friends' who received shares at par when Rand Mines was floated and early in 1895, Phillips recorded that Kotzé owed Corner House £4,289, adding with a straight face that they had helped him 'out of pure good nature, without any ulterior motive'. But bribery costs money. It increases costs and, for the Randlords who counted costs in pennies, it was not a situation they wished to see prolonged unnecessarily. Every hindrance, every obstruction and every frustration was piled on top of another and Rhodes had fertile ground for his conspiracy.

The long, dry, highveld winter of 1895 dragged on with the powdery dust from the mine dumps swirling in the August winds, sifting through the cracks of windowpanes and doors; nothing was proof against it. It settled on furniture, floors and permeated upholstery. But Johannesburg was quivering with excitement through all of this. After the depression of 1889–90, investors had been slowly regaining their confidence in the Rand gold mines. For five years, there had been a slow but steady recovery in share prices. Shares in South African gold mines became known as 'Kaffirs' on the London Stock Exchange.

By mid-1895, winter in the Southern hemisphere, there was a full-scale boom in South African gold mining shares, which was soon dubbed the Kaffir boom. For the already exceedingly rich Randlords, the boom was an opportunity for consolidation. The Corner House used it to winnow the wheat from the chaff. The chaff they sold off at ridiculously high prices and used the cash to consolidate their deep-level mining operations. Rhodes benefited greatly by selling heavily and hoarding the cash for the schemes he was brewing. He was already conspiring with the other Randlords to take action against the Kruger regime.

At the same time, Rhodes was liasing closely with the new Colonial Minister in London, Joseph Chamberlain. For this purpose, he made use of the services of Rutherford Harris, a medical doctor who had come out from England to Kimberley and then moved from medicine to business. The idea was that the mine-owners would make common cause with the Reform Committee in Johannesburg. The Reform Committee was a *Uitlander* organization with political aims, working to gain full political rights for the *Uitlanders* on an equitable basis. It also served as the political mouthpiece on all matters for the *Uitlanders*. It did not represent the Randlords and the mine-owners. Although he was a Randlord himself, Percy Fitzpatrick was one of the movers and shakers of the Reform Committee. All discussions between the conspirators took place in great secrecy and the uprising was called a 'flotation' so as not to arouse suspicion.

The real problem was that the Randlords did not agree among themselves what the aim of the insurrection really was. Indeed, not all the Randlords were involved. Conspicuous by their absence especially were J.B. Robinson, Barney Barnato and Woolf Joel, Barnato's cousin and business partner. Not only was there dissension among the Randlords, the body of *Uitlanders* in the Reform Committee was even more strongly divided, especially on the 'flag' issue. Phillips suggested a new state under quasi-imperial control like Egypt at that time, but this was not universally acceptable. Others preferred to reform the present Republic into an open democracy under its own flag. The Americans, and especially the Germans, in the reform movement were in a difficult situation. None of them had a particular desire to live under 'British bunting' and with the then current manoeuvrings of German diplomacy, it seemed that the long amity between it and Britain was being strained to the utmost. Instead of resolving these internal issues, Rhodes preferred to ride roughshod over everybody. After all, he wanted a united South Africa under the British flag and he was financing the rebellion.

He arranged for Dr Jameson to gather some 1,500 troopers at Pitsani, a railway station in Mafeking in British Bechuanaland, there to await instructions. Phillips and the Reform Committee apparently thought that Jameson was under their command, but he was not. The idea was that there would be a popular *Uitlander* uprising in Johannesburg. When the insurrection was well under way and Kruger's burghers rode in to put it down, Jameson and his merry men would arrive on their steeds, fall upon the Boer host and save the day for Queen and country. That, at least, was the theory, but the details were vague, the command structure virtually unknown and Rhodes too shifty to make his intentions clear.

The position of the Americans became even more difficult because of developments in the Americas. A long-standing border dispute between British Guiana and Venezuela would now complicate Rhodes' plans even further. Venezuela had all along skilfully sought US support for its position and in December 1885, just as the Rhodes conspiracy was nearing its climax, the Venezuelans succeeded in getting US involvement in the dispute. On 17 December, President Grover Cleveland sent a message to Congress, which amounted to an ultimatum to Britain: a commission would be appointed by the US to settle the border dispute and its decision would, in the name of the Monroe doctrine, be imposed on Britain – by force if necessary.

The Americans in the *Uitlander* community were now potentially at war with Britain. Rising against Kruger to overthrow the Republic in order to become a British Imperial colony was out of the question for them, as it was for many others in the community. The unease among the conspirators became so palpable that it was felt even in London. The next day, 18 December, Sir Robert Meade, the Permanent-Secretary at the Colonial Office wrote to Chamberlain on the matter. He urged the Colonial minister that 'the *Uitlander*

Movement' be postponed at least for a year or two. Others in the Colonial Office, like Edward Fairfield wanted the rising postponed indefinitely. Chamberlain's response was that the rising should take place immediately or be postponed for a year or two at the very least. Of course, it was not the Colonial Office's uprising, and they were not in control, but their being privy to the matter was certainly very compromising and politically very dangerous.

In Johannesburg, however, the feeling was unequivocal. One of the leading conspirators, George Farrar, visited Leonard, a co-conspirator, early on Christmas morning. He stated his position strongly and directly: 'I have induced every man who has joined me and who is helping me in this business to go in on the basis that we want a reformed Republic.'[6] Leonard and Frederic Hamilton left immediately to give Rhodes that message, but Rhodes took no immediate action. He was really the only one that could have controlled Jameson, but he failed to act. His failure might have been due to another misunderstanding between him and Jameson. On the evening of 28 December Rhodes told another confidant that the rising he had been financing had 'fizzled out like a damp squib' partly due to the flag issue; Jameson would do nothing, he asserted. Much relieved, the confidant returned home for the prospect of a quiet Sunday. Rhodes might have been under the impression that Jameson would do nothing unless specifically instructed, but his previous telegraphic instruction to the good doctor had already lit the fuse: 'Company will be floated next Saturday'.

Everything about this disorganized, ill-conceived adventure that hardly had any hope of success at its conception, then proceeded to go even more wrong. Jameson had only managed to assemble less than 400 men with less than one day's rations. The rising in Johannesburg, which was the precondition for Jameson's invasion, did not take place and never did. Not mindful of such small details, and not waiting for the signal that was supposed to come from Johannesburg, the swashbuckling hero crossed the Transvaal border on 30 December 1895 and undaunted, proceeded to lead his men to dismal disaster.

On and on they blundered

Jameson did not have the element of surprise as he naively thought he had. They were followed and sniped at by Boer patrols from the moment they crossed the border. The British High Commissioner in the Cape, Sir Hercules Robinson, knew what had happened and so did the British agent in Pretoria. They both, independently sent messengers to intercept Jameson, begging him to turn back. Yet, he proudly blundered on. He was in for more surprises. The Maxim guns that gave him such ribald confidence, and a victory over the massed Impi of the Matabele, were no good against the Boers.

The Boers were not soldiers, but they were hunters. They knew all about stalking, keeping out of sight, blending with the countryside and shooting from cover. How do you fight an enemy when all you can see are odd little puffs of smoke rising from the empty savannah all around you? And every puff of smoke signalled a man down on your side.

Just west of the town of Krugersdorp, the Boers had assembled a large enough force to halt Jameson's eastward march. He then tried to bypass this force by heading south towards Randfontein and around towards the east again. He thought he had managed to evade them but, only a few miles east of Krugersdorp, he found he could continue no further. At Doornkop, on 2 January 1896, still some 20 miles from Johannesburg, the farce ended.

Having suffered many casualties, Jameson's troops raised a white flag. The 'flag' was a white apron that they had somehow managed to obtain from a black matron somewhere in the vicinity – desperate times require desperate measures. The survivors, including Jameson, were taken off to jail via Johannesburg. There the Reformers were sitting in the sumptuous luxury of the Rand Club, talking and having a few drinks, watching Jameson and the other rag-tag survivors being brought in and marched around Market Square before being taken to jail in Pretoria.

When the Reformers first heard of the invasion before its ignominious end at Doornkop, they belatedly decided to put up some sort of a show. They raised the Transvaal flag upside down to signal the new Republic and distributed some guns. It was all to no avail. Phillips led a deputation to see Chief Justice Kotzé in Pretoria. The latter spoke gently, but requested proof that the Reformers were the true voice of the *Uitlanders*. Unsuspectingly, but disastrously, Phillips agreed to give him a full list of members' names. On the night of 9 January, 64 Reformers were arrested at the Rand Club on warrants for their arrest that had been issued in Pretoria.[7]

Sir Hercules Robinson arrived in Pretoria and immediately found himself without any political or moral leverage. Instead of making demands on behalf of the Reformers, he was taking orders from Kruger. Robinson had to tell the Reformers to cooperate with the authorities or forfeit the sympathy of the British government. Rhodes, whose complicity was crystal clear, resigned as Prime Minister of the Cape the following day. Kruger, the old man of the Transvaal had been politically redeemed from his loss of face during the drifts crisis – redeemed by an overzealous and imprudent adversary.

Kruger's redemption unfortunately put South Africa more firmly on the road to war. Emboldened by Britain's embarrassment, the idea of chasing Britain out of South Africa now gained greater currency among the Free Staters and many of the Cape Afrikaners. Expectations were rising that with a little bit of effort, they would be able to achieve a united South Africa, free from British hegemony. It would prove to be a dangerous delusion.

CHAPTER SEVENTEEN

POWER POLITICS

Afterthe fiasco of the Jameson raid, the era of power politics finally arrived. While Chamberlain was trying to hide his prior knowledge and complicity in the raid, the Boers were gloating over their victory and many were baying for revenge.

Immediately after the arrest of Jameson and his troopers, Kruger pleaded with his officers and burghers that they should not be summarily executed. After some four hours he, with the help of two deputies sent from the Free State and eventually with the support of Schalk Burger, managed to convince them of the prudence of Kruger's suggested plan. The meeting then decided by majority vote that the miscreants would be deported and, since they were all British citizens, handed over to the British authorities for punishment.[1] In Britain, the perpetrators, including Jameson, received and served various gaol terms. By neatly putting the ball in Britain's court, Kruger sidestepped any possible criticism for meting out too harsh a punishment and, under the circumstances, gained much stature as a wise statesman.

Matters were different when it came to the 64 Reformers from Johannesburg. They seemed to present the Republic with an ideal opportunity to play politics. After all, it had under lock and key a man like Lionel Phillips, who was chairman of the Corner House and President of the arch-enemy, the Chamber of Mines, as well as George Farrar, Frank Rhodes (the brother of Cecil John) and John Hayes Hammond, Rhodes' American mining adviser. However, when one of the awaiting trial prisoners committed suicide by cutting his own throat, Kruger realized that he could not play cat-and-mouse indefinitely. Two weeks later, the lesser offenders were released on payment of a £2,000 fine.

The four 'ringleaders' of the Reform Committee were put on trial for high treason before Judge Gregorowski, not a native Transvaler either. He was a barrister of Gray's Inn, the son of a German pastor and married to a Scotswoman.[2] The four pleaded guilty, were found guilty and sentenced to death. Kruger wasted little time in commuting the death sentences to short terms of imprisonment, a fine of £25,000 and a ban on entering the Z.A.R.

Cecil Rhodes turned out to be no cad. He picked up the tab for all the fines and it is estimated that he paid something in excess of £300,000 as a consequence of the raid. He was straining every muscle to regain his influence, but he was a spent force. Although he was still immensely rich and would become even more so, he had his own private colony in Rhodesia and he played no role in the further fortunes of the Z.A.R. Nevertheless, he still served as a handy bogeyman for Kruger in the next presidential election – 'Beware of Rhodes and keep your powder dry', was to be his slogan.[3]

A disastrous year

But 1896, which had begun so dramatically in January, had not yet done with the Z.A.R. That year would become known as a year of disasters, for after the Jameson escapade there occurred three more disasters, but they tended more to temper the feelings between Boer and *Uitlander* than to drive them apart, as Jameson had done. The first tragedy happened on 19 February, when a train loaded with dynamite exploded in the railway marshalling yards of the N.Z.A.S.M. in Braamfontein, causing major loss of life and extreme damage to property. The second was the outbreak of the *Runderpest*, a terminal African horse sickness, which drove many of the farming community into poverty. The third catastrophe happened in June of the year, when, on a trip between South Africa to England, the *Drummond Castle*, one of Sir Donald Currie's mail liners, sank near the coast of France with the loss of 242 lives, many of them from Johannesburg.[4]

The train explosion in Braamfontein was probably the most traumatic and, although the disaster struck almost exclusively Boer and black families in Johannesburg, the event was relevant to some of the main grievances of the Johannesburg residents in general. The marshalling yards in Braamfontein were right in the middle of the area that the Z.A.R. government had previously proclaimed open for brick-making. Many impoverished Boers had come to Johannesburg and started making bricks on a very small, cottage-industry scale. When the explosion rocked Braamfontein, not only their lives and homes were first in line of the devastation – it was their very livelihood. The people of Johannesburg immediately rallied and a committee to assist the devastated families was established. Over the next few months the citizens of Johannesburg, including the mining houses, gave unstinting of their support in material and money.

The presence of great stocks of dynamite in the middle of the steadily growing Johannesburg had been a source of great unease for many years. It was discussed in meetings of the Sanitary Committee as early as October 1893, but nothing was done by Pretoria, while the committee in Johannesburg had no power to remedy the situation.

It seems again that the arrogance created by monopolistic concessions lay at the heart of the disaster. The problem of the presence of great quantities of dynamite in the city was worsened because the N.Z.A.S.M. and Edward Lippert could not reach an accommodation regarding appropriate times for delivery and receipt of consignments. Lippert was not prepared to accommodate anybody; he would receive dynamite only at his own convenience. Thus, whole trainloads of dynamite often had to stand for hours in the hot summer sun, waiting to be rerouted to the magazines.

It was clear that, directly or indirectly, the explosion was due to the joint and several negligence of the N.Z.A.S.M., the Delivery Company and the South African Explosives Company. Exactly how the explosion occurred could not be determined, since those most intimately involved with it had all disappeared. Nevertheless, on 24 April the surviving victims of the explosion were very distressed to learn that the government's commission of enquiry had decided that nobody was responsible for the explosion. Since

they were all burghers, they called on the First Volksraad for assistance. All aid was channelled through the Johannesburg Committee for Assistance, which at the end of December 1896 closed its activities with a surplus of £32,522 0s. 10d., after having paid all claims lodged. It was agreed that the victims, apart from the tragic loss of life, were, at least as far as housing was concerned, better off after reparations than before the explosion.

Although the tragedy had, as one newspaper put it, 'submerged' questions of race and politics, it expressed the hope that 'when political questions re-emerge, both sides will mitigate their rancour with an enduring remembrance of the common bonds of human pity which unite them in face of the ghastly tragedy through which we have passed'. Unfortunately, it was a forlorn hope. The event underlined and heightened the mine-owners' complaints about the quality of Lippert's dynamite and the competence of all the concession companies concerned, while it apparently had little effect on the perceptions of those most intimately affected. Indeed, in many ways developments in South Africa were now taking a more ominous tone.

A new order arises

As the discovery of gold had dramatically reordered the economic balance in South Africa, so the events of the Jameson raid had brought about a new political alignment in South Africa. It was ominous because it made war with Britain very difficult to avoid and virtually certain in the medium term. The problem was not the *rapprochement* between the Boers of the Transvaal and the Free State with each other and with the Afrikaners of the Cape, but the fact that its driving spirit was the expulsion of Britain from a united South Africa. Much emboldened by the military successes of the Boers against the British since Majuba Hill, and lacking any proper perspective on matters military, the confidence of Afrikaners grew to the point that they believed they were powerful enough to drive the British out by force if necessary.

In the Transvaal, which they saw as the heart of the envisaged new South African Dutch Republic, the Boers were now more determined than ever to keep the country exclusively Dutch and be damned with the rest. The income from taxes, derived mostly from the industry of the *Uitlanders*, was now used to rearm the Z.A.R. Using the Jameson raid as an excuse, the Transvaal was preparing for war. Its budget for 1897 included an amount of £614,000 'for war purposes', excluding salaries and wages.[5] The Republic proceeded openly to arm itself at an ever-increasing rate over the next few years, building one fort in Johannesburg and three others on hills overlooking Pretoria, at an enormous cost. None of the forts offered any military advantage since they were poorly sited and none of them was ever used in the war. The fort in Johannesburg only served to further raise the suspicions of the *Uitlanders*, who saw it more as a threat against them than as being a defence of the city.

Kruger also started taking a hard line with the compromised Joseph Chamberlain, who would now find it more difficult to put pressure on the Z.A.R. to act fairly and justly toward its immigrants, other than Cape Afrikaners and Boers from the Free State. In January and February of 1896, Chamberlain invited Kruger to come to England to discuss the questions that gave rise to the present discontent of the *Uitlanders* and for which they were unable to gain constitutional redress.

In his reply, Kruger stated flatly that he would not suffer any interference in the internal affairs of the country; thus articulating the precursor of the National Party's oft-repeated refrain in the 20th century, when it sought to protect its repressive apartheid policy from condemnation by the outside world. Kruger added that if he were to come to England, he would wish to discuss many other points, including the withdrawal of the London Convention of 1884. It was clear that Kruger had no serious intention of dealing with any of the *Uitlander* grievances.

Nevertheless, the raid had made him and his government aware that matters could not just be ignored. He therefore attempted to administer palliatives as he had with the introduction of the second Volksraad, when he took away the rights of immigrants

under the subterfuge that he was granting them some say in government. He proposed, and passed, a law that gave Johannesburg a municipality, but its net effect was to place real power in the hands of a small Dutch minority and the Transvaal Government. He then argued that he had addressed some of the grievances of the disenfranchised immigrants, although in substance nothing had changed.

In that same year of 1896, the Volksraad, at the behest of Kruger, proceeded to pass further laws, such as the Press Law, the Education Law and the Aliens Immigration Law. The laws made the position of those who were not Dutch-speaking, and who were purposely kept outside the pale of citizenship, even more untenable. Chamberlain protested that the Aliens Immigration Law was in direct contravention of the London Convention, but in the end he did not press the matter and reserved the right to protest individual proceedings that might be taken in terms of its provisions.

Foreign fears for Britain

Compounding Britain's situation in South Africa were the actions of some of its European competitors who obviously revelled in her embarrassment. This was especially true of Germany; Britain had already been excluded from Bismarck's system of European Alliances and the development of German colonial policies in Africa was nervously watched. As far as the British were concerned, the agreement on the division of Africa into spheres of influence, between the European colonial powers as negotiated by Lord Salisbury in 1890, had been in final settlement of all these matters.

But the German Kaiser, to aid Germany's own diplomatic and political purposes, could not resist gaining some mileage from British embarrassment at the Jameson raid. He sent a telegram of congratulations to Kruger for having dealt with the crises without outside aid and seemed to imply German military aid if the Z.A.R. required it in future. On 6 February, in an audience with Dr Leyds, the Kaiser went even further. He assured the State Secretary that British suzerainty did not exist, and that if the Transvaal had been unable to repel the raid, 'he would have made it a *casus belli*'.[6] Fortunately, nothing was ever revealed about the audience, for this telegram was like a slap in the face for Britain; it had come not from an enemy, but from an old friend.[7] Being naively uninitiated in international diplomacy, it also gave Kruger unwarranted confidence in German support in his future dealings with Britain. Britain's European contenders, such as Germany, France and Russia, did not leave Kruger unmoved by their exaggerated displays of admiration and support for him and his Republic.[8] He was unable to see these attentions in their proper perspective and to evaluate them objectively. After the uproar over the Kaiser's telegram, however, France, Russia and the US quickly acknowledged British hegemony in Southern Africa. It was easy for them of course; they had no ambitions in the region.

These delusions of unrelenting support and admiration might also have precluded Kruger from giving due weight to the warnings of Leyds, the Republic's minister plenipotentiary travelling in Europe, but stationed in Brussels. Already in 1897 he warned Kruger not to expect any help from France in the event of a confrontation with Britain; he would repeat it again in 1899 with respect to Germany, but Kruger gave these warnings no heed.

The British Colonial Office had long felt that German commercial penetration of the Transvaal was closely allied to Germany's feared political ambitions in the area. Kruger's 'Kaiser Kommers' speech in January 1895, coupled with the Kaiser's telegram was seen as both substantiating Germany's political ambitions and the Kruger regime's willingness to support them. The Germans in fact encouraged these perceptions by stressing, in their dealings with British diplomats and politicians, the considerable German financial investment in the Transvaal, not only in mining, but also in the N.Z.A.S.M., and by claiming that some 15,000 Germans lived and worked there. But these claims by Germany were probably calculated more with later diplomatic concessions from Britain in mind, than with any real political ambitions in a geographical area where British hegemony had been vested for almost a century.

The British Colonial Office, however, was wary. The value of German trade with the Transvaal increased from £94,086 in 1893 to a whopping £339,452 in 1897. They regarded this growing German trade with apprehension and the N.Z.A.S.M. with suspicion. Their misgivings were strengthened by the events following the drifts crisis. The N.Z.A.S.M.'s tariff war with the Cape and, to a lesser extent, Natal, did not end when Kruger reopened the drifts. The Cape's share of the traffic fell rapidly from approximately 85 per cent in 1895 to only 28.4 per cent in early 1898. The Delagoa Bay line, which was then known as the *Oosterlijn*, saw its share of traffic increase from 28 per cent when it opened in 1895, to 37.06 per cent in 1898. The main reason for the shift in traffic was because the N.Z.A.S.M. decided to charge 7.7 pennies per ton per mile on its section of the Cape route compared to the 7.2 pennies charged by the Cape in 1892.[9]

The tariff war inflated the prices of goods and materials on the Rand, and the Colonial Office noted how the N.Z.A.S.M., and its German backers, not only discriminated against British trade, but also made life difficult for the colonies of the Cape and Natal. At the same time, however, and probably unbeknown to the Colonial office, some of the German interests on the Rand had, since 1893, been making strong representations to their government against the Kruger regime.[10]

While some mining companies were wholly British-owned, others were wholly German-owned. There were many shareholders and investors in Paris, and in the rest of the Continent, where the Corner House group of companies recruited most of their investment funds. If there was one thing that all investors agreed upon, be they British, German or French, it was that the state had to play a supportive role in achieving their own financial objectives. They required a pliable polity with an efficient administration and one would have expected them to get it as mining was the only economic activity which was driving the prosperity – and it was responsible for the very existence of the Z.A.R. itself. Without it, all other commercial and industrial activity ceased.

It is certain, therefore, that Kruger's policies towards the *Uitlanders*, and the gold mining industry as a whole, did not only upset the often-blamed British jingoes who, it was argued, would never have been satisfied with anything less than a British takeover anyway. The Z.A.R.'s short-sighted, short-term, and in the end, self-defeating policies would increasingly alienate the international investing community and, in the longer term, their governments.

Cometh the hour, cometh the man

Meanwhile, a British Parliamentary Committee of Inquiry had whitewashed Joseph Chamberlain in its investigation of the raid fiasco. In its report, the Committee acquitted the imperial authorities of complicity, but it roundly condemned Rhodes. Although intimately informed of the whole intrigue from its inception, Chamberlain was only on the periphery of what had in essence been Rhodes' plot, but to all concerned he pleaded ignorance. The proceedings of the Committee apparently did not fill observers at the time with any great confidence and British parliamentarians generally referred to it as the 'lying in state at Westminster'.

Despite the whitewash, Chamberlain was not satisfied. Most people suspected, and a number in the Colonial Office knew, of his involvement in the raid. The lack of evidence as to the extent of his involvement led only to it being exaggerated. Bringing the Boers to heel now gained a much higher priority on Joe Chamberlain's agenda of things to do. When Sir Hercules Robinson was due to retire, the Colonial Secretary personally selected the new man for the job – he was Sir Alfred Milner, the star of British officialdom.

Milner was a bachelor, having lost the love of his life to Lord Asquith, intellectually brilliant and with an immense capacity for work. Although he was of mixed British and German stock, he had been brought up by his mother in Germany where he had received most of his childhood education. Later, he completed his schooling in England, after his mother returned. Although he thus lacked the advantages of birth and wealth in Britain, he was also unencumbered by the experience of the full rigours of an English education. His academic and civil service record was impressive. He was a Balliol scholar, a Fellow of New College, Oxford and he had already been made a Knight Commander of the order of the Bath for his exemplary service in the British Colonial Service.

At the age of 33 he had effectively been charged with sorting out the muddle of Egyptian finances, a task he accomplished within three years. Thereafter he was made Chairman of the Board of Inland Revenue, with the responsibility of assisting the Chancellor of the Exchequer in preparing the budget. He was still in his thirties when he was acclaimed as the most distinguished public servant of his day: 'There never was a man who gave himself with a more complete self-devotion to a great task, or who set a higher example of public service and duty, than Lord Milner.'[11]

Milner maintained a cool and disciplined exterior, being seen as a reserved and silent man, and he operated well within the highly structured imperial civil service, where everybody knew their place. Being a figures man, he was probably too rigid in his approach to matters to be a successful diplomat, which was what was largely required of a High Commissioner in South Africa at that time. But when the job at hand is to balance the books, there is no room for compromise – it balances to the penny or it does not.

Chamberlain first offered Milner the post of Under-Secretary of State for the Colonies, but this he declined. Then, on 18 January, 1897, he offered Milner the succession to Lord Rosmead, the peerage that Sir Hercules Robinson had been raised to on his visit to Britain the previous year. The offer of the latter appointment Milner accepted.

After the disaster of the Jameson raid, Milner's brief was clear and unambiguous – to protect and secure British hegemony in South Africa. British hegemony, often also referred to as paramountcy, primarily meant the primacy of Britain as an investor and exporter of goods to the region. This necessarily implied free access as well as fair and just treatment for all its subjects anywhere on the subcontinent. It also required economic policies by all concerned that would enhance cooperation and mutual support between the states in the region and, finally, it implied a measure of control over foreign relations, at least to see that in dealings with other countries, Britain's interests would be given due consideration and its established trade ties not discriminated against. These conditions were, in essence the main rights that Britain reserved to herself and her subjects in the London Convention of 1884. It was with this mission uppermost in his mind that Milner arrived in Cape Town in May 1897.

Upon his arrival, General Goodenough handed him a memorandum setting out the general political situation in the country. Goodenough referred to the propaganda against Britain that was being spread throughout the country at that time. Milner was also apprised of the effect that it was having, not only on the Afrikaners of the Cape Colony, but also on some of the English speakers in Cape Town itself. Many of the South African-born English speakers, it appeared, had had their loyalty to the British Crown shaken by the weakness and vacillations exhibited by successive British governments. The General went on to say that 'the growing spread of this propaganda must, it is believed, have latterly influenced H. M. Government and made it feel that whilst they were looking at the Transvaal, the old Colony itself was slipping away from its allegiance'.[12]

Afrikaner nationalism rampant

It is quite enlightening to look at the nature of the propaganda to which Milner was referred. Although, in general terms, the political idea being advanced by the propaganda was a united South Africa under its own flag without any particular allegiance to Britain, the arguments presented in support of the idea were not based on anything approaching the universal principles of human rights, liberty or the principles of republicanism. Rather, the arguments were based on quasi-religious considerations such as claiming that the Anglican Church was hardly distinguishable from Romanism, and that perfidious Britain aimed to elevate the natives to equal rank with the whites for the sake of industrial profit, in direct conflict with spiritual authority.

Included in their armoury of claims was the assertion that South Africa belonged, by right, to the Afrikaner nation and that the British government was the usurping enemy of the Boer nation. In justification of this claim the contention was proffered that the Cape Colony was 'transferred to the British Government by *force majeure*, and without the consent of the Dutch nation, who had renounced all claim in favour of the Afrikaner or Boer nation'.[13] That this was generally believed and widely preached by Boer and Afrikaner leaders is supported by the reiteration of this contention in the book written during the first half of the 20th century by an eminent Afrikaner leader and member of Parliament, General Kemp.[14] While vehemently repeating these allegations and contemptuously dismissing any possible contradiction, he nevertheless neglects to present a single argument in its favour, much less one iota of evidence to support it.

These contentions might have been popular heresies among those who sought to fish in troubled waters and who sought too gain political power from engendering hatred between Boer and Brit, but it was a dangerous argument for the Afrikaners. Apart from the fact that it was factually devoid of all merit, the premises of the contention were potentially disastrous for the Boers. If they truly and honestly contended that *force majeure* could not bestow the right to govern a territory forcibly occupied, and if they were thoroughly convinced that people could not lose the right to their land and be governed and taxed without their consent, then, by the same token, they themselves could hardly claim to be entitled to govern one square inch of South Africa outside the Cape peninsula.

In the aftermath of the raid, the distinction between Afrikaner and Boer was disappearing. Dutch and Afrikaners were consolidating into one conscious ethnic group. The Afrikaner Bond, the party of Hofmeyr in the Cape, broke its long-standing link with Rhodes and sought the future of what they saw as an Afrikaner nation, with Kruger and his Republic. Afrikaner national feeling gained strength and even Paul Kruger's mistrust of Cape Afrikaners disappeared. He would no longer hesitate to appoint young Cape Afrikaners to key government posts and the charge that he followed a Hollander employment policy was heard no more. In May 1898

Kruger appointed the academically brilliant young Cape Afrikaner, Jan Christiaan Smuts, as State Attorney of the Z.A.R. He was destined to play a major, often contentious, role in the affairs of the Transvaal and especially in the later Union of South Africa.

Closer cooperation with the Free State was also on the agenda. The wise old man of Free State politics, President Jan Brand was no longer there and had been succeeded first by F. W. Reitz, and then, in February 1898, by Marthinus Theunis Steyn. Reitz moved across to the Transvaal after his term as President of the Free State and was appointed State Secretary of the Republic. Steyn was, like his predecessors, an English-educated lawyer, but unlike them, he was both dour and doleful. He also did not share the reservations of the late Sir John Brand about closer cooperation with the Transvaal; indeed, he was a protagonist of closer cooperation. Thus, in September 1899, Kruger easily inveigled him into a close military alliance.

The general national awakening by Afrikaners and Boers, inspired by Paul Kruger, meant that in any future contest, Britain would, much more so than in the past, have to contend with resistance by the Afrikaner nation as a whole. Henceforth Paul Kruger would be much more than the head of state of the Republic north of the Vaal River. He would be the symbol of the autonomous national striving of a whole nation.[15]

Gathering of the clouds

Much fire has been poured onto Milner's head from historians and other commentators, proving and arguing in one way or another that he was a bellicose warmonger. Some have even claimed that the South African War at the end of the century was Milner's war. They claim that he had a hidden agenda and that, as an imperialist, his only wish was to make the Boer Republics part of the British Empire.[16]

As a highly intelligent and very conscientious civil servant and an expert on financial matters, it would be surprising if he totally ignored the decisions of the British Colonial Conference of 1884

and the position of the Colonial League, a body advocating colonial interests. These bodies foreshadowed a confederation of self-governing British colonies united in preserving their common interests. Neither the Transvaal, nor the Orange Free State was numbered among the envisaged colonies.[17]

There was absolutely no reason why Milner, Chamberlain, or any other British imperialist would specifically have coveted the Transvaal as a territorial possession. Britain in fact tried its best to divest itself of such overseas possessions. It preferred self-governing colonies and countries within the Empire that could turn British investment into demand for British exports.[18]

There was also no need for Britain to exert itself to corner the gold production of the Transvaal, which landed in the pool of the European gold standard anyway, by whatever route it might be exported. In any event, the doctrine of *laissez-faire* and minimal government interference in business and financial affairs was the ruling philosophy for most of the time. London was the main centre of the international gold market, as it is today; the international gold standard played like a well-practised orchestra, with the Bank of England as the conductor. The gold standard operated in a congenial economic and political environment, while the hegemony of the Bank of England kept the system functioning under all circumstances, managing international cooperation and acting as lender of last resort. Economic growth continually bailed out policy errors and international cooperation could be taken for granted rather than depending on painful and conditional support.[19]

Imperial interests therefore did not dictate possession of the Transvaal, its mines or its gold production, but they did demand the primacy of Britain as investor in and exporter of finished goods to it. As the economic engine room of Southern Africa, British interests also demanded, as a necessary corollary to the foregoing, that the Transvaal did not discriminate against the British colonies in the region, but rather that it cooperated in their economic growth and advancement. These considerations then weighed heavily in favour of intervention in the Transvaal.

There was also a further factor favouring intervention, which is unrelated to any notion of imperialism and colonialism; it is the interest that any country has in the fair and equitable treatment of its citizens in another country. In the Transvaal, the preoccupation was with all of the resident international community. In a way, Britain felt responsible for all those who had wound their way into the subcontinent, fully under the impression that the British writ would run to protect their persons and their interests.

The probabilities are that it was Milner's intention only to carry out the brief that had been given him; that was protecting and strengthening British hegemony in South Africa, by whatever means possible, including, as far as he was concerned, war. Milner was convinced that the vacillating and weak-kneed policies of the past had brought about the present impasse. He was not going to repeat them. He would be inflexible in this approach to the solution of the problems as he saw it.

Whatever the merits of the criticisms and accusations against him might be, it cannot be denied that he faced an enormously difficult task in South Africa. The forces that were destined soon to rip the country apart were already arraigned against each other before he arrived: the protection and maintenance of British hegemony in South Africa vs. Afrikaner nationalism. War is never inevitable, but circumstances do make it more or less probable from time to time in a particular place. At that time, in South Africa, the probabilities of war were mounting with or without Milner's contribution because the arraigned forces were, on the face of it, irreconcilable. The maintenance of British hegemony was not merely a point of policy or an attitude emanating from government circles in Britain, there were many people in South Africa as a whole and in the Transvaal in particular, absolutely demanding it.

From the British point of view the abandonment of the two self-governing colonies to the Boers was inconceivable. The British view was succinctly, and probably correctly put by General Goodenough in his letter to Milner, when he wrote that

> to establish South Africa as it is, England has spent blood and money untold and all men have to realize that it is a wild dream to suppose that Britain, with all its latent spirit and in the plenitude of its wealth and power, would fail to be roused

to a campaign, aye and not one but many campaigns, as Lord Beaconsfield said, if it were a question of maintaining her interest and that of those who have gone into the country under her rule.[20]

To maintain Britain's interest in South Africa and of those who had come to the country over the period of a century, expecting their interests to be so protected was Milner's brief and his personal mission. From Milner's private correspondence it is apparent that he was deeply aware of past British blunders in South Africa and feared that they may be repeated, especially by him.[21] He regarded, quite justifiably from his point of view, the threat to British paramountcy in South Africa to be the direct result of past blunders of British administration and governments.

These blunders, inconsistencies in administration and vacillating policies were well-known frustrations of the Colonial Office and had been so for many years. Already in 1885, Edward Fairfield of the Colonial Office began a long and sarcastic memorandum as follows:

> Colonel Stanley has asked for some notes of instances in which there has been vacillation in the policy of this country towards South Africa. To tell the story in full would be to rewrite the history of the country.[22]

But for a year Milner would remain studiously passive. He learnt to read Dutch newspapers while he travelled around the country and simply observed, keeping his opinions for his correspondents. At times he was frustrated by the attention bestowed on him as the representative of the British Empire by the 'Progressives' in the Cape Parliament, to whose ranks Cecil Rhodes had recently added himself. Also, he was by no means inclined to take seriously all the complaints that reached him from the Rand.[23]

A well-directed shot in the foot

In 1897 Kruger would not have everything his way, however. There was a vocal and influential minority, also known as the 'Progressives' in the Transvaal (but unrelated to the eponymous movement in the Cape) which opposed him and his politics in the Volksraad. Chief among these was his old political foe, but still Commandant General of the Republic, Piet Joubert. Kruger was about to receive an unexpected jolt from these 'Progressives'.

In his intended window-dressing efforts to address the grievances of the mining companies, Kruger, on 5 April 1897, appointed an Industrial Commission consisting of six members of the Volksraad, with Schalk Burger, a member of the Executive Committee and one of the Progressives, as its chairman. The Commission's report was published in July and its findings were painful but true.

The Commission tackled its job in a thoroughly professional manner, as any commission should. It gathered all the available evidence, called and examined witnesses and sought experts on specific issues to advise it. Its findings were well argued and fully substantiated by the evidence presented to it. The problem for Kruger was that it validated every complaint that the gold-mining industry had laid before the government over many years.

Among the Commission's findings was that during the previous year there were 185 gold mines in the Republic, of which 79 produced gold to the value of £8,603,821, while the other 106, for various reasons, produced no gold at all. Out of the gold-producing mines, only 25 declared dividends to a total amount of £1,718,781. The commission found that the main reason why so many of the gold-producing mines did not pay dividends was the high cost of production.[24]

In the past Kruger had often shrugged off the problems of the mines with the contention that through their over-speculation on the stock exchange, they were the cause of their own problems, a wholly facile contention. The government, he always argued, was not in any way to blame for that. The Commission neatly deflated that argument by saying that '... neither does the question of over-speculation or over-capitalisation affect the case ... there are only 25 companies who declared a dividend out of their profits while the rest work with a very small profit, and in many cases do not cover the cost of production'. It then went on to say that 'A company might be over-capitalised, but the costs of mining their

property is in no way affected thereby.' The same might be said of over-speculation.

The Commission then set itself the task of solving the question of 'what must be done to reduce the cost of production so as to leave a margin of profit upon the article produced, and this is a problem apart from any complications as between Government and nationalities'. It stated unequivocally that it was the duty of the government to cooperate with the mining industry, especially when it is considered that up to that time, the mining industry must be held as the financial basis, support, and mainstay of the state.

In its report, the Commission also expressed itself very strongly against the policy of concessions, adding that at that stage, the economy of the country was being hampered thereby. It took this heresy even further by stating that the country had arrived at a stage of development that will only admit of free competition 'according to Republican principles'. It then went into detailed findings and recommendations concerning labour, transit duties (finding them unfair and recommending their abolishment), import duties (recommending that they be abolished on foodstuffs, since 'at the present moment it is impossible to supply the population of the Republic from the products of local agriculture'), explosives (condemning the unsatisfactory evidence adduced on behalf of the South African Explosives Company and then validating every charge ever brought against that monopoly by the mines), railways (finding the N.Z.A.S.M.'s tariffs and fees exploitive) and a number of other matters of lesser importance.

Obviously, Schalk Burger and his five colleagues had totally misunderstood Kruger's intentions with the appointment of the Commission. He did not want to hear the truth; he wanted to hear the gospel according to Paul Kruger. The Commission was supposed to support his position, not that of the mining industry. It was supposed to be a ruse, not reality. Kruger lost his temper with Schalk Burger and they had a raging row.[25]

Kruger, in a ploy to hide these unpleasant truths, then appointed a second commission to consider the report of the first commission. The second commission understood its task much better. It did not even attempt a professional approach. It produced a toned-down version of the first report, but even its attempts at obfuscation and evasion could not hide the truth of the original. Significantly, two prominent members of the second commission, Louis Botha, later to be the first Prime Minister of the Union of South Africa and Barend Vorster, dissented from its findings and did not sign the report. Unfortunately, they did not issue a dissenting report, but indicated that they would discuss their reservations with the Executive Council in committee.

The report of the Industrial Commission presented the Z.A.R. with a last, and very credible, opportunity to redeem itself internationally. Milner applauded the report and called it surprisingly liberal but Kruger's reaction, and his unwillingness to give meaningful effect to its recommendations, were a self-inflicted shot in the foot. It effectively ended the possibility, insofar as it ever existed, of receiving international assistance and support in a confrontation with Britain.

It had by then become clear to all concerned, and particularly to the German government, that the Kruger regime was incapable of establishing a well-ordered polity able to satisfy the economic needs of the partly German-owned mining industry. It was not merely the stubbornness, inefficiency and inability of the Transvaal government to establish such a polity; the rank corruption was more than most European institutions were prepared to live with. Thus the Deutsche Bank was discouraged to proceed with a proposed loan, because they could not reconcile rank bribery with their position.[26]

While Kruger and Leyds had always relied on their contacts with the German government, through the good offices of the N.Z.A.S.M. and its supporting German banks, to act as a counterbalance to British pressure, the N.Z.A.S.M. was not even close to being Germany's largest investment in the Transvaal. As was pointed out to the German government on several occasions by its own citizens, their investment in the N.Z.A.S.M. only accounted for some £2 to 3 million of German capital, while their investments in the Transvaal totalled some £25 million. Apart from direct investments in mining, German industrial and commercial capital was rapidly dominating the electrical and mining machinery industries in the Transvaal.

All these investments were ultimately dependent upon the continued success of the mines.

When the Z.A.R. failed to act on the Industrial Commission's recommendations, by late 1898 German capital interests had come to view both the Republic and the N.Z.A.S.M. as the main obstacles to the continued efficient and profitable exploitation of the Transvaal's mineral resources.[27] They were joined by French interests, which also rushed to inform their government that their interests were being neglected.[28] Thus, in the following year, the threat of international intervention in Southern Africa was removed from Britain.

Germany and Britain entered into negotiations concerning the future of the Portuguese empire. Portugal was in severe financial difficulties and the two powers agreed to grant it loans to alleviate those problems. It was also agreed between them that if Portugal defaulted on the loans, Britain would be allowed to control Delagoa Bay and the rest of Portuguese Africa south of the Zambezi River, while Germany would gain control of the rest, being the lion's share, of Portugal's African empire. In the agreement Germany specifically and explicitly acknowledged British hegemony over the whole of Southern Africa. With this acknowledgement, all the European colonial powers and the US had fallen into line and British hegemony internationally was not in issue.

In German financial circles, with connections to mines on the Rand, the agreement was well received. In a number of articles on the agreement, the *Kölnische Zeitung*, representing the views of Ruhr mining interests with connections on the Rand, applauded the agreement and the anticipated increase in Britain's influence on the Rand.[29] As far as the international community was concerned, Kruger and his Republic stood isolated and Britain had a free hand to deal with the situation as it deemed fit. Although it is difficult to believe in the light of the widespread publication and acclamation of the agreement's terms in Germany, it is alleged that Kruger did not know that the strong arm of the German government, on which he had been relying so heavily, had been removed at, for him, a critical moment.[30]

Last gasp on the road to war

February 1898 was Presidential election time again in the Z.A.R. Paul Kruger approached it with some trepidation. He had not taken any action on the recommendations of the Industrial Commission and his own people did not let him off unscathed on that issue: meetings of burghers were held and petitions for the nationalization of the railroad and cancellation of the dynamite monopoly were drawn up. The dynamite monopoly survived by only a single vote in the Volksraad. Even the loyal Hollanders in the civil service complained and the Volksraad threw out three government measures in quick succession.[31]

Kruger was opposed in this fourth and last presidential election of the Z.A.R., by his old adversary, Piet Joubert, but now also by Schalk Burger. That was a strategic error for the Progressives, because the two candidates split the vote, thereby making Kruger's re-election a cakewalk for him.

Piet Joubert's campaign was uninspiring. His approach was negative and amounted to no more than a disagreement with Kruger. Schalk Burger, probably in an attempt to woo the majority of voters, diluted his liberalism to an alarming extent: he indicated that he was against any extension of the franchise. He said that he favoured an alliance with the Free State, but added ominously that he would not advocate a union even with that republic, for he was working for a united South Africa wherein an independent, dominant and untrammelled Transvaal was the centre.

Kruger merely relied on his record and the slogan: 'Beware of Rhodes and keep your powder dry'. That was enough to have him re-elected by an overwhelming majority. Immediately after his re-election, Kruger took ominous and decisive action in the long-standing judges' crisis. It centred on a judicial debate concerning the existence of a testing right over Volksraad legislation and the independence of the Supreme Court. Kruger of course denied that any such testing right existed; modern jurists have tended to support him on this issue. Justice Kotzé, however, was the main contender that the Supreme Court did have such a right and reclaimed it immediately after the presidential election. After 20 years service, Kruger abruptly dismissed him under Law No. 1.

This abrupt treatment of the Chief Justice and the appointment in his place of Justice Gregorowski, the hanging judge in the trial of the Reformers, did not inspire confidence in the *Uitlanders*, who had at least always felt that the courts in the Transvaal would treat them fairly. The campaign platform of Schalk Burger had also come as a shock to most people. It appears that they could hold out no hope of a fair deal even from the more liberal Boers.

There can be little doubt that these events in the Transvaal must have greatly influenced Milner's perception of the problem and its solution. After Kruger's landslide victory and the abandonment by his opponents of all conciliatory policies and liberal principles, he in turn abandoned the prospect of reaching a peaceful, negotiated settlement with the Transvaal. It was most likely at that stage that he decided that intervention and rigid, unswerving demands to set matters straight would be the only way to avoid the vacillating failures of the past. Either Kruger would reform his rickety republic, or there would be a contretemps. It would be a case of 'my way or no way' – a clear choice between reform and war. Milner personally thought war the most likely outcome.[32]

In deference to Chamberlain's wishes he had kept quiet for a year after his arrival in South Africa, but in March of 1898 he uttered his now famous words: 'Loyal! Of course you are loyal. It would be monstrous if you were not.' This was said at Graaff Reinet in response to declarations of loyalty in a welcoming address at a Bond meeting. He then called upon those present to urge the Transvaal, which he described as the cause of all the unrest in South Africa with its talk of threats outside its borders and its toleration of internal abuses, to bring its institutions and policies into line with just and fair principles of government.

In March 1898, Chamberlain stated to Milner in a letter that 'for the present our greatest interest in South Africa is peace ... our whole policy should be directed to that end'.[33] That policy Milner had followed diligently, but it seems that by the end of his first year in office he could no longer abide the wisdom of such passivity. Thus, in November of that year, he undertook a working holiday to Britain during which he would make a significant effort to press the views he had developed on the South African situation.

He realized that this self-imposed mission would require him to be doubly diplomatic. His first task would be to disabuse Chamberlain and the Colonial Office of their rose-coloured illusions about South Africa. He would have to prove to them that time was not on their side; things were not about to fall into place by themselves. Second, he would have to prepare the Press and other politicians for a more interventionist policy as far as the Transvaal was concerned. The support of British public opinion was a precondition for successful intervention in the Transvaal.

When, on 22 November, Milner had an interview with Chamberlain in his office, he put his case directly. A crisis must be engineered he argued, time was not on their side. After his re-election, Kruger had become even more autocratic. It was even possible that the Cape Colony could come under attack if, later, Britain became engaged in a European war. These considerations occupied Milner's mind, but Chamberlain was against war. The time was not ripe. In effect, Kruger must first be given enough rope; war could only be contemplated if Kruger was flagrantly in the wrong.

Milner did not agree, but at least, Chamberlain had not given an unequivocal no. London's anti-war stance did not appear to bind him hand and foot. To take matters forward from here on would be in his own hands. He was reasonably satisfied.

War manoeuvres

At the end of December 1898, just before Milner's return to South African shores, Pretoria was the scene of a military victory celebration. Piet Joubert had just returned victorious from another one of the interminable 'Kaffir' wars. This time his victim had been a chieftain by the name of Mpefu. This was only the latest of about half a dozen such wars in as many years.

Victories over local black tribes were even easier to come by since the Republic's aggressive rearmament policy. The most modern

French Creusot-artillery, with smokeless ammunition, could now be tested against the backwardly armed black tribes. Even so, the Transvaal's writ did not run throughout all the territory they claimed. Their military forces were unbeatable, but they weren't everywhere. And they ruled the black peoples only where their *force majeure* was present and persistent.

Upon his return Milner put his own plans into action. Meeting after meeting and conference after conference were held to reach some compromise on his demands for reforms. Milner, continually kept informed on Transvaal matters by Percy Fitzpatrick, was clearly not in favour of reaching any compromise agreement.

A number of suggested reforms emanated from the Transvaal Government, but they were all hedged around with conditions that Milner found unacceptable. Milner rejected them all, seeing either a trap or a ruse, or an impossibility of performance on Kruger's side, given the composition of the Volksraad. The Afrikaner Bond of the Cape and the Free State governments all tried to act as honest brokers. They urged Kruger and his government to agree to meaningful reforms. Proposals and counter-proposals were exchanged, but no agreement could be reached.

The last conference that Milner reluctantly agreed to was held in Bloemfontein. The conference started On 31 May 1899 in a congenial atmosphere. But four days later Milner declared it closed, announcing to all the delegates that none of the parties had incurred any rights or obligations arising from the discussions. Chamberlain was not amused at Milner's precipitous action in ending the conference so abruptly. He was for accepting the seven-year residency offered by Kruger at the conference, but it was too late. By the time Chamberlain heard of the offer, Milner had already rejected it.

It appears that whereas Milner had previously seen war as the alternative to reform, he now no longer believed that reform was a viable option. War was the only way. He had apparently made up his mind that the problem of the Transvaal could only be solved by means of annexation. In this matter neither the British government, nor Chamberlain, nor the Colonial Office was in agreement with him, but Milner was playing his cards well.

Chamberlain at last realized that Milner's policy had only one object in view – to force war on the Transvaal and to incorporate it into the Empire by annexation. This was contrary to his own policy, which was to reach a genuine agreement on the franchise issue and to conclude a new convention whereby the Z.A.R.'s independence, as far as its internal affairs were concerned, would be guaranteed.[34] Under Milner's deft orchestration of events from the Transvaal and the pressure and influence of his friends in Britain, Chamberlain and the British Cabinet would have little choice but to acquiesce as events unfolded. The frustration that this process caused is evident from Lord Salisbury's now famous words in a letter to Lord Lansdowne, the Secretary for War: 'Milner and his jingo supporters would force the government to make a considerable military effort – all for a people whom we despise [the Randlords], and for something which will bring no profit and no power to England.'[35] But he was gloomily determined to push on for the sake of British hegemony in the subcontinent.

Almost at the last moment, Kruger made a final proposal. He accepted the retrospective five-year residence qualification that Milner had demanded in Bloemfontein, but made it conditional upon the removal of British suzerainty and agreement not to intervene on behalf of British subjects in the Z.A.R. Milner saw it as no more than a continuation of the horse-trading that had been taking place all along.

Milner's view had always been that years of horse-trading had landed the British Empire in the mess that it was in. In this case, despite his increasingly emotional and unappreciated despatches to the Colonial Office,[36] he managed to persuade Chamberlain, who in turn persuaded the Cabinet, that such conditions were unacceptable. That does not mean that Milner had swayed them to his point of view that the Transvaal should be annexed. As late as 6 October 1899 Lord Salisbury insisted that he was prepared to face war 'sooner than not get out of Kruger terms that will secure good government at Johannesburg and make the Boers feel that we are, and must be, the paramount power in South Africa'.[37]

Milner had been pleading for some time for more British troops to be sent to South Africa to give him more leverage in negotiations.

There was very little sympathy for this call in Whitehall and it was only in September, in preparation for an expected outbreak of armed conflict, that additional troops were sent. The number of troops at the disposal of Britain in South Africa had not grown by much in the two years of Milner's tenure. Some 10,000 troops sailed from Bombay to the port of Durban after the British Cabinet had finally, on 8 September, decided to augment British forces. After the addition of the troops from India, the total British force in South Africa would number some 22,000, with some 15,000 of them deployed in Natal. These forces were totally inadequate to face the combined 40,000 burghers of the Transvaal and Free State's militia, armed with the latest German five-shot Mausers, smokeless ammunition and supported by state-of-the-art artillery, including 20 of the revolutionary British-made one-pounder 'Pom-pom' guns.

Things were also moving briskly in the Transvaal and Free State. The inclusion of the Free State into this equation was largely due to the long-standing efforts at closer cooperation by Kruger and President Steyn's willingness to be included. In this he was supported by many of his own burghers. But while the origins of the Free State's feeling of solidarity with the Transvaal is understandable, their military alliance is difficult to comprehend in the face of their divergent interests. Their political interests did not coincide either. Even if the independence of the Transvaal was threatened, as many perceived it to be, that of the Free State was totally secure. The issues that gave rise to such a threat in the Transvaal, if such it was before the war, were wholly absent from the Free State.

Also, the British government and the Free State had not been at odds for many years and there were no issues outstanding between them. The Free State too, was a major beneficiary of trade between the Transvaal and the Cape and of the Transvaal's imports and exports through the Cape. The issues between the Transvaal and the British government did not really concern the Free State directly, but insofar as they did, the Free State stood to benefit more from British success than vice versa. Indeed, the Transvaal had often acted contrary to, and with complete disregard of, the Free State's economic interests such as the recent matter of the drifts crisis. The true reason for their military alliance should be sought not in the economic interests of the Free State, but elsewhere.

In the Transvaal, the imminence of war was as clear as in Cape Town and London. Already on 4 September 1899, Jan Smuts, the young, precocious State Attorney of the Z.A.R., had written a secret memorandum for the Transvaal Executive Council:

> South Africa stands on the brink of a terrible blood-bath from which our people will emerge either as the carriers of water and the hewers of wood for a hated race, or as victors, the founders of a united South Africa, one of the great empires of the world ... an Afrikaner Republic in South Africa, stretching from Table Bay to the Zambezi River.[38]

Frenzied war preparations were in progress from 2 September onward, although President Steyn was hanging back. He was not totally convinced that war was the only way out. He would only be convinced at the last moment, when threatened by a revolt from his burghers led by Christiaan de Wet. Thus, the mobilization of the Free State only commenced on 2 October while Kruger and his Transvalers, unwilling to wait on their allies any longer, started mobilizing on 28 September. War fever was pervasive throughout the Transvaal; many burghers really believed that they could drive the English into the sea and proclaim an Afrikaner republic from Table Bay to the Zambezi. But the war psychosis was not such that it can be said that Transvaal public opinion forced Kruger into the war. He could readily have brought the hotheads to heel, had he so wished.

Smuts prepared the initial military strategy, which would eventually be only partly accepted by Kruger and Steyn. He was very sanguine and he foresaw that the key to the campaign was to throw all the burghers at Natal, where they would enjoy a numerical superiority of almost three to one. The point would be to take Durban with its harbour before the British troop ships could land. This coup would inspire the Cape Afrikaners to proclaim a third great Republic. The international repercussions, Smuts concluded, would be dramatic. A very important part of the British Empire would have been shaken to its foundations and Britain's enemies – France, Russia and Germany – would rush to exploit Britain's collapse.[39] It is clear that at that stage of his life, Smuts' youthful exuberance, combined with his lack of experience of international diplomacy, was far outstripping his undoubtedly great intellectual abilities.

By this time it was clear to all concerned that war was inevitable. It was not only clear to those in government; the war psychosis was palpable on the streets of Johannesburg. Ever since August, a stream of refugees had been arriving in Cape Town from Johannesburg. As the political situation worsened, the stream became a river, until, by October, it became a flood. People got on to the first train they could, not only to Cape Town, but also to Durban. There were insufficient passenger coaches so the refugees piled into cattle trucks, coal trucks and whatever rail cars they could find, whether open or closed. It is estimated that some 60,000 people fled from Johannesburg in those short weeks. Then the giant wheels of the headgears on the gold mines stopped turning and the crushers fell silent. With the *Uitlanders* gone, there could be no mining.

Milner arranged with Herman Eckstein and his colleagues to start a refugee fund in Britain, on a scale last seen for the relief of the famine in India. Between Alfred Beit, Julius Wernher and J.B. Robinson they would contribute £10,000, but Rhodes only contributed £700. But the *Uitlanders* would not remain refugees. Two *Uitlander* regiments were raised at Milner's suggestion. The Imperial Light Horse (I.L.H.) was raised in Durban on September 21, 1899 from refugees there, while the South African Light Horse originated in Cape Town. In terms of the numbers involved in South Africa, these two regiments virtually amounted to a *Uitlander* army. They eventually numbered 20,000 officers and men, commanded by the very men who were *Uitlander* leaders before the war. *

---

* These regiments served with distinction throughout the war, with three Victoria Crosses awarded to men of the I.L.H. Stationed in Johannesburg after the war, the I.L.H. served again in Flanders in WWI. In WWII, having become an armoured car unit, the I.L.H. served as part of the British Eighth Army against Rommel, and then crossed the Mediterranean via Sicily to take part in the Italian Campaign. It served with distinction at Monte Casino after which it came under the command of the US 5th Army for the rest of the Italian campaign. It won battle honours in many of the fiercest battles in Italy and the Po valley. It exists today as the Light Horse Regiment, stationed in Johannesburg.

In fact, war was still avoidable at that late stage, although it hardly seemed likely to Kruger and Smuts. On the eve of the war, before any ultimatum had been delivered and while the Transvaal commandos were mustering on the Natal border, Piet Joubert simplistically, but correctly, observed that all that was required was to restore the original five-year residence for new immigrants. Milner might have been inflexible, but had Kruger or Smuts been able to talk directly with Chamberlain, they would have found him much more amenable. They mistook the face of Milner for that of Chamberlain.

The British gold imperative

The South African war has been described as a war fought primarily over South African gold. But would Britain and the Transvaal go to war for control of the gold mines and was the road to war paved with gold? Was Britain prepared to spend blood and money at the behest of the despised Randlords? The role of gold in the road to war requires scrutiny.

The first question that needs to be addressed is the extent to which gold in general, and South African gold in particular, fuelled the British Empire. Most European countries had by 1886, adopted the gold standard as the underlying value of their countries. The US was on a bi-metallic standard, but due to the declining price of silver, they were under severe pressure to join the single gold standard, which eventually, they did.[40] The gold standard was 84 shillings $11\frac{1}{4}$ pennies per fine ounce during the final decades of the 19th century up to the First World War.[41]

There is an inherent problem with having a commodity, which is itself scarce, as the underlying value of a currency. The problem is that in a monetary economy, the currency must be in sufficient supply to pay for all goods and services generated in the economy, plus accumulated wealth. Part of the First and the Second Industrial Revolution's effect was to increase production and the output of manufactured goods. The service industry grew in

tandem and all in all, the G.D.P. of nations tended to rise quite dramatically.

With the increase in value of goods and services, more money was required to pay for such goods and services. On the gold standard, this meant that more gold was continually required in order for more money to be issued. Imbalances between the growth of the value of goods and services and the growth of the total amount of available gold would thus cause severe deflation or inflation, depending upon which grew faster.

However, during the late 19th century, the growth of the total international demand for gold and the growth in the supply of gold were in reasonable equilibrium, although fears were expressed from time to time that the market would be flooded with gold. This was especially so after the Transvaal gold mines of the Witwatersrand came on stream during the last decade of the 19th century and added to the already substantial Californian and Australian outputs.

The gold market has always been an international one, meaning that there was free access to the market by all buyers and sellers. The market was centred in Paris, London and New York, with London being the main centre. All countries on the gold standard together held the ultimate reserves of the system. In theory at least, the system would allow any country that required an immediate increase in its gold reserves to issue money by manipulating its discount rate.

It was therefore with some surprise that it was later noted that, on the occasion of the South African war, British commercial banks were quick to respond to bank rate rises by reshuffling their portfolios. But very little gold was attracted to London. On the other hand, there was no real crisis of confidence on that occasion and interest rates and prices in Britain remained reasonably steady throughout the war. As a stopgap measure, however, Britain felt itself constrained to transform the Indian gold reserve into British government securities.

Britain based the defence of her monetary stability, in the event of international gold rushes, on her position as a creditor nation, but did not build up a massive gold reserve beyond what was required for the issue of currency. Indeed, the sufficiency or otherwise of Britain's gold reserves was a debate that would flare up from time to time. Nearly 30 years of peace had led to a definite bias in the international monetary system to fiduciary liquidity. International trust had developed to the point where gold reserves were not always held to the full value of the currency in circulation.

France too defended the stability of her currency based on her status as a creditor nation, but in addition, she built up a massive gold reserve as a second line of defence.[42] France, not Britain, was the greatest European purchaser of new gold for strategic purposes.

Thus, the answer to the question posed earlier seems to be that, although reliable supplies of gold were required to fuel the European monetary system, there were no compelling reasons at that particular moment for Britain to wish to control the government of the Transvaal in order to have control over its gold mines.

Whatever gold was mined in the Transvaal would in any event find its way to the international gold market and the European monetary system, to which Britain had as much access as anybody else. Moreover, whoever bought the gold had to pay the companies who mined it. The mining companies made profits from selling gold, not those who controlled the governments of the producing countries. For Britain, there would thus be enormous disadvantages in taking over the Transvaal, but no conceivable economic advantage in governing a gold-producing colony – it was a much better proposition to hold prime trading rights with a gold-producing colony. There was thus no economic imperative driving Britain to covet the Transvaal for its gold.

The second question, then, was whether Britain was squaring up to the Transvaal at the behest of the Randlords. There is evidence of supportive correspondence between Milner and Alfred Beit during Milner's exertions to precipitate a war, and there was certainly collusion between Milner and Percy Fitzpatrick during the deliberations between the parties before the war. The Corner House, to which both of these gentlemen were connected, as related earlier, was not financed by British investment. Nevertheless, many accusations of warmongering have been levelled at them as well.[43]

A thorough analysis of the business strategies of the internationally oriented controllers of South Africa's gold mines shows that they were not in any way synchronized with the imperial priorities of any nation, including Great Britain. International capitalism was in fact in competition, if not actually in conflict, with both British imperialism and Afrikaner nationalism.

Both local political developments in the Transvaal and British imperial priorities invariably operated against the needs and demands of the internationally oriented financial mechanisms and institutions that capitalized the gold mining industry in South Africa. There is the example of the Banque Française de L'Afrique du Sud that was poised to take a leading role in gold mine finance, but was put off permanently by the war and then the British presence. The last thing the capitalists wanted, or needed, in 1899 was a war, especially one instigated and won by Britain, when the industry's most prominently engaged capitalist mechanisms and institutions were French and German.[44]

Percy Fitzpatrick, who was not a Randlord anyway, involved himself with Milner from his own personal convictions and motivations. Alfred Beit's sharing of ideas with Milner should be seen more as the actions of a prudent businessman who required the good offices of whoever was going to control the country eventually.

But still, gold did play an important role in the road to war. It was a supreme irony that the backward, misanthropic and isolationist Transvaal Boers should have come and parked themselves squarely on the world's most extensive gold deposits. This, coupled with their inability to exploit it, caused the influx of great numbers of people from all over the world. The role of gold on the road to war was that it drew the *Uitlanders* to the Transvaal in great numbers within a very short period. The fear of change and their inability to compete with these strangers were what fired the animosity of the Boers.

The ultimatum and the end of the road

By the end of September, ultimatums were being prepared in both London and Pretoria. Smuts was drafting the one in Pretoria, but as the Transvaal would require Free State cooperation for its war effort, Steyn's consent was essential. It was on his insistence that the final document contained a reference to a breach by Britain of the terms of the London Convention. As a lawyer, it probably satisfied his sense of the legalities involved, but the Convention was completely irrelevant to the position of his Republic. His views were duly accommodated, but the ultimatum was designed to be unacceptable and would require Britain's response within 48 hours.

In London, meanwhile, Chamberlain was doing his own drafting in consultation with Milner. They were preparing a draft for a proposed 'final settlement', which would also serve as an ultimatum and the intention was that it be delivered to the Transvaal Government at the end of October. In essence, it now required the Transvaal to repeal all legislation detrimental to the *Uitlanders* that had been passed since 1881, representation in reasonable proportion to their numbers and the right to speak their own language in the Volksraad and courts.

It further required guarantees of the independence of the courts and the judiciary as well as 'most-favoured nation' status to Great Britain and a few other matters. In return the British Government would fully guarantee the Transvaal against any attack on its independence, whether from any British dominion or from the territory of any foreign country.[45] Kruger had earlier rejected such guarantees from Britain, as he said at the time, he did not want to become a British Protectorate. Nevertheless, nothing in the draft seemed in any way to suggest a desire by Britain to annex the Transvaal. Also, from the draft form of the document it does not appear to be an ultimatum, since no sanction is included should the reaction from the Transvaal not be favourable.

The British document would never become an ultimatum, nor would it ever be presented to the Transvaal Government, since on 9 October an ultimatum from the Transvaal government was handed to Conyngham Greene, the resident British agent in Pretoria.

It took the form of a long letter that primarily accused the British government, by its insistence on redressing the grievances of the *Uitlanders*, of interfering in the internal affairs of the Z.A.R. in contravention of the London Convention. Then it demanded the

peaceful settlement of all disputes to the parties by arbitration, that all troops on the Republic's border be withdrawn forthwith; all recently landed troops to be withdrawn to harbours and embarked as soon as possible and that all troops not yet landed be stopped from doing so. The ultimatum required a favourable British response by no later than 5 p.m. on Wednesday, 11 October 1899 otherwise the Republic would regard it as a declaration of war.[46]

Milner and Chamberlain were both relieved that a strategic problem had been solved for them. There was now no need for the as yet incomplete British ultimatum to be delivered. The road to war ended at 5 p.m. on the day after Paul Kruger's 74th birthday, the very last birthday he would ever have in Pretoria.

It was war.

CHAPTER EIGHTEEN

A SHORT WAR – A LONG BATTLE

Gelukkiger zijn zij die fielen
toen nocht de vlacht werd opgebeurd,
dan wij, die met bedroefde zielen
het zagen in het stof gesleurd *

(A lament by author unknown. I know it only from my father's recital)

The war in South Africa represents the end of the great age of Victorian peace which began at the end of the Franco-Prussian war. European powers at the time believed that war was diplomacy by other means and the threat of war was a common tool in negotiations. But they had also become expert at avoiding war. The threats were thus never translated into war.

Many of the politicians and officials in the Colonial Office and in Whitehall did not expect actual fighting to occur in South Africa, even when the war talk heated up. The actual outbreak of hostilities thus came to most officials as a nasty surprise.

The war in South Africa would also be the testing ground of a new type of warfare. Massed armies in textbook formations would no longer face each other at close quarters and shoot it out in exchanges of volleys, as had happened, for instance, at Waterloo.

---

* The following is my best attempt at a free translation:

More fortunate are those departed
when still the flag was proudly thrust,
than we, distressed and broken-hearted,
who see it trampled in the dust.

The five-shot German Mauser rifles, with which their governments had armed the Boers of both republics, were accurate up to 1,000 paces – a major advance over previous rifles. Their Maxim guns would sow death when fired from trenches at lines of advancing troops. For the first time, raking fire would be directed at an advancing enemy from cover and well-camouflaged hiding places.

The war would be the first practical field test of smokeless ammunition, magazine rifles and long-range accuracy. How would existing field tactics be amended to meet the challenge of technology? The lessons would be hard and dear. The fact of the matter was that modern weapon technology had at that stage swung the balance of power firmly in favour of the defenders. This proved true for the Boers as well as for the British forces.

For the British soldier during the initial phases of the war, the Boers would be largely an unseen enemy, bringing devastating firepower to bear on their advancing columns while themselves remaining protected from return fire and out of sight in their trenches. However, the Boers were hopeless at close quarters. When British troops managed to get close enough for a bayonet charge, the Boers were virtually defenceless.

In many ways, it would be a dress rehearsal for the First World War. The trench-warrens and earthwork fortifications used by the Boers at, among others, the battles of Modderrivier, Magersfontein and Paardeberg in the Cape and in Colenso and Ladysmith in Natal, would become prototypes of the later battles in the fields of Flanders. In the South African War, however, the British never dug themselves into opposing lines of trenches as happened in Flanders. Nevertheless, as a defensive strategy, the advantages of trench warfare would be clearly demonstrated by the Boers during the South African war.

Marwick's march – a true hero found

But the first hero of the war was not from the military. He was not a soldier risking all for the glory of his country; he was a remarkable civil servant going far beyond the call of duty – merely one human being risking all to save the lives of other human beings. He was J.S. Marwick, the agent of the Natal Native Affairs Department, stationed in Johannesburg.[1]

On the eve of war, when the massive machinery of the Rand's mines fell silent, only the black and coloured labourers were left. The managers, the engineers, all the bosses and their families had left. Nobody had arranged for the labourers to leave, to go home. Their wages had already been cut to the bone to give the mines sufficient profit, but when it came right down to it, nobody cared about them – not the Boers and not the *Uitlanders*. They were just Kaffirs.

But the blacks from the Cape and from Natal were British subjects. Seven thousand African mineworkers from Natal, about 3,000 of them Zulu, for whom the Natal government was primarily responsible, faced a severe plight. Without jobs and without any means to earn a living, there was no way that they could live on the Rand. Their only hope was to go home, back to Natal.

But if they ventured to walk that mighty distance on their own, they would surely starve. The Boers were quite content to see them starve on the veld, but ultimately, they were the also the responsibility of the High Commissioner, Lord Alfred Milner. It was a responsibility that he shirked. Marwick did not.

His pleas for help from the Natal government, via the Governor of Natal, were refused. Marwick decided that he would have to act alone, and in the only way open to him: he would personally march them back to their homes in Natal. It was a brave course of action, for the obstacles were immense, but he did not falter and he did not shrink from taking full responsibility for those in his care and his own actions.

He cabled his employer, saying that 'so that my proposed action may not embarrass you, please suspend me from office. If I get the natives through without loss of life, you could please yourself about re-instating me.' Hely-Hutchinson accepted the offer, but did not suspend him.

Before he left, Marwick prudently obtained a warrant guaranteeing him safe passage, signed by President Kruger personally. He then assembled the people, men, women and children, the healthy as well as the sick and the lame. Arrangements were made to accommodate everybody on this march, no matter what their physical condition. When the 7,000 assembled on 6 October 1899, Marwick was honoured by the Zulu in their traditional way: they always salute a great man with great words. To Marwick they said: 'Child of the Englishmen, but for whose presence no one might brave the Boers ... Gather the orphans of the Zulu.'

Then his remarkable procession left Johannesburg. They marched thirty abreast, led by a couple of inebriated ZARPs on horseback, followed by a colourfully dressed, concertina-playing group of musicians. Marwick, himself on foot, brought up the rear to make sure that no stragglers were lost. Food on the road was scarce and slowly the long march sapped their energy. Many Boers in their path fled, fearing the great body of black people, probably not realizing that they were nearing starvation. But by the 13th, they had marched the 170 miles to Piet Joubert's encampment near Majuba Hill.

Marwick then was faced with a setback. Some of Joubert's burghers stopped them and the State Artillery commander would not let them pass, despite Kruger's warrant. Eventually it was agreed to let 400 of the Zulu haul Joubert's siege guns up onto the hill facing Majuba, in return for the safe passage of the whole group.

At last, dawn on the 14th saw everybody allowed to pass through Boer lines unhindered. On the 15th the journey was almost complete. The nearly starving marchers staggered down to the creek, close to the camp of Major-General Symons at Dundee, but they were home. The people here would give them food, shelter and rest to complete their individual journeys.

They had covered more than 250 miles on foot over mountainous country in nine days. It was a triumph for Marwick: no lives had been lost. He had undoubtedly saved the lives of 7,000 people through his own, selfless action. Here was a true hero.

An unconventional conventional war

Immediately after the period of grace following the Transvaal's ultimatum, the Transvaal and Free State launched a joint offensive into Natal, with the purpose of a swift march down to Durban to seize the port. That would have been a great strategic blow to Britain. However, their forces, having driven one part of General White's divided force out of Dundee and forced them to fall back to Ladysmith, could not take Ladysmith, whereupon Botha decided to lay siege to it, thereby losing their strategic advantage.

At the same time, they launched offensives into Griqualand West from the Transvaal and into the Northern Cape from the Free State. But where British forces numbers opposed them in reasonable strength, such as at Kimberley, Upington and Mafeking, the Boers could not take the towns and consequently laid siege to them also. In this way, they tied up large numbers of their men and materials to besiege towns that had limited, to zero, strategic value. Consequently, their drive into the two colonies fizzled out. In the second phase of the war, they would be forced to limit themselves to defending the sieges – merely trying to stop relief columns from reaching the besieged towns and liberating them.

Thus, in the initial phases of the war, the new conventions of war did not favour the Boers. The Boer militia, supported by the Transvaal artillery with their modern French and German artillery pieces that substantially outperformed British ones, did not meet with any great success as attackers against fortified and determined defenders. Not one of the besieged towns would eventually fall to them. It would not be for lack of trying, however. Colonel Baden-Powell's defence of Mafeking would make a name for him throughout the length and breadth of the British Empire and even beyond. But his callous treatment of the local native population living in Mafeking, causing great numbers of them to die of starvation due to his withholding food rations from them, would not receive the same wide publicity.

The Empire falls back

Only a few miles west of the Transvaal border lies the town of Vryburg. It is the principal town of the area then known as British

Bechuanaland, previously capital of the short-lived and ill-fated Boer republic of Stellaland. It is a dry, sandy area of semi-desert known as the Kalahari, which in its vastness extends to cover most of present-day Botswana and Namibia. Vryburg straddled the railway line that connected Cape Town and Kimberley with Bechuanaland and Rhodesia. It was a link on the Cape to Cairo line, situated between Kimberley and Mafeking.

There, on the morning of 20 October 1899, the resident magistrate received by hand a courteous, but firm letter informing him that it was intended to take over his town 'in the name of the people of the South African Republic, by force if necessary'. He was advised to offer no resistance, as the author was anxious not to spill any blood if it could be avoided. The letter was signed by General J.H. (Koos) de la Rey. Since the magistrate had very little means of offering resistance anyway, he wisely complied.

The next day de la Rey's commando marched into the town. That afternoon the General addressed the townspeople at a gathering on the town square. He opined that the whole of Bechuanaland would be annexed to the Transvaal, while the whole of Griqualand West, including the diamond city of Kimberley, its main town, would be annexed to the Free State. He mentioned that some of the people of Bechuanaland were already under arms and he expressed the hope that many others would soon follow. With great bravado he added that the *Vierkleur* (the four-colour flag of the Z.A.R.) that he had hoisted over the town that day would be lowered again only over their dead bodies. An attempt was then made to sing the National Anthem of the Transvaal, but the singing was half-hearted and disappointing, for the Boers at any rate.

Much the same can be said of de la Rey's recruiting efforts. Nobody in Vryburg joined the commando, but after a few days, lists were drawn up of Boers in the countryside who might be interested in joining up. The commando forces then went around with these lists to recruit troops. It is not known what the eventual success of the recruiting campaign was, but no pressure was apparently put on those that remained adamant not to join.

The intention to annex British colonial territory was not limited to these western additions, but was repeated in the areas of Cape colony bordering on the Free State. The Free Staters had a better response to their recruiting efforts.

Crossing the Orange, now renamed the Gariep River, from the Free State, the first town on the Cape side of the border is Colesberg. A picturesque town, it is surrounded by high, rocky hills and sparse, karroo-like vegetation. Passing through it was the strategic railway line from Pretoria, via Johannesburg and Bloemfontein to Cape Town. The vastness of the expanse of country, in which the town sits almost insignificantly, is the dominant impression of this approach; the empty land stretches endlessly in all directions and into the blue forever.

A hard pounding on his front door was the first notice that Mr Wrench, the magistrate of Colesberg, had that something was afoot. It was pre-dawn on 14 November 1899, when he rushed, still dishevelled and wearing his nightclothes, to answer his door. Opening his door, he discovered standing on his front stoep, two burly, bearded men, armed to the teeth. They demanded that he hurry to the magistrate's offices to hand over the keys to the government buildings. They informed him that Chief Commandant E. R. Grobler of the Free State armed forces was busy taking over the town.

Having dressed quickly, Mr Wrench hurried himself to the government buildings. In the half-light of early dawn, he could already see that the hills around the town were alive with Free State Burghers. Commandant Grobler, who met him at the government offices, requested the keys from him. Wrench complied and he received assurances that no peaceable people would be molested or property taken without receipt. If Mr Wrench would take the oath of allegiance to the Free State, he could remain on in his post as magistrate. This honour he politely refused.

The public of Colesberg had meanwhile assembled at the court buildings. They greeted Grobler's speech and his proclamation of annexation with wild acclamation. Then he invited all citizens to join his forces. When Wrench pointed out to the crowd that the proclamation was illegal, he was nearly assaulted by the local bookkeeper, but bystanders prevented him from doing so. Then everybody repaired to the courtroom to sign up. From the following day, pressure was put on those who had not yet signed up to join the Free Staters; between 200–300 men eventually joined.

Within three weeks of the taking of Colesberg and its surrounding district, the Free Staters, in the same manner, took over four more of the large Northern Cape districts. In each case the district was taken without opposition and thereafter by proclamation annexed to the Free State, with many young men joining the Free State forces. Only the besieged towns of Mafeking, Kimberley and Ladysmith were still holding out.[2]

The Boer invasion halted

British forces started arriving in Cape Town and Durban in ever-greater numbers. Sir Redvers Buller, the appointed Commander in Chief of all British forces in South Africa, landed in Cape Town on 31 October 1899. He was followed by another troopship on 9 November before the British contingent had grown strong enough to go onto the offensive. Their first job was to lift the sieges and that was to prove a costly exercise – especially in soldiers' lives. While Buller and his forces headed for Natal, he despatched Lord Methuen with 10,000 men to relieve Kimberley. These forces were soon to prove inadequate for that task, but they did stop the spreading invasion of the Cape Colony.

As the Boers had experienced, the British now found that attackers were in a severely disadvantaged position compared to well-fortified defenders. The new technology presented battlefield situations that the military textbooks of the time had no answer to. By trial and error, General Buller eventually started to get the hang of the new battlefield situation during his approach to Ladysmith. However, before he could reach Ladysmith, he suffered a serious reverse at Colenso on 8 December 1899. He was thereupon replaced by Lord Roberts as Commander in Chief of South African forces, but Buller retained command of the forces in Natal. Lord Kitchener, the Sirdar of Egypt and Chief of Staff to Lord Robert, appeared to be a slow learner. He demonstrated this when he ordered a closed order, full-frontal attack on Cronjé's forces at Paardeberg. He would prove his worth in the war soon enough though, but not as a field commander.

At the start of the British forces' northward march, they suffered many setbacks and suffered heavy casualties. The reason for this was not merely bad leadership and a failure of command, although that certainly played a role and exacerbated the situation of the British army. The main reason for their failures and losses, especially in the early stages of the war, was the difficulty of attacking forces to succeed against defenders with modern arms, fortified in trenches. Nevertheless, British forces inched their way forward, suffering heavy casualties, but the Boers were not able to withstand the constant weight of numbers being thrown against them. Heavy losses are, of course, relative. In fact, the war in South Africa was, comparatively speaking, a small war with light losses on both sides.

While Buller and his men concentrated on lifting the siege of Ladysmith and getting the Boer forces under the command of General Botha out of Natal, Roberts launched a great outflanking move through the Cape and Free State. After many travails and Methuen's defeat by General Cronjé at Magersfontein, just north of the Modder River and south of Kimberley, General French managed to lift the siege of Kimberley on 15 February 1900, four months after the outbreak of the war.

Three days later, the battle at Paardeberg followed. There General Cronjé's army, ensconced on Paardeberg hill next to the Modder River, was surrounded by the British 6th Division under Lieutenant-General Thomas Kelly-Kenny. Kitchener, who was appointed over Kelly-Kenny by Lord Roberts personally, nearly managed to snatch defeat from the jaws of victory through his impatient interference, but eventually Cronjé surrendered on 27 February 1900, with some 4,000 burghers and their equipment. It was a turning point in the war. The Boer's conventional warfare capacity had essentially been broken.

Unconnected to the fate of Cronjé, Buller now at last tasted success in Natal. He lifted the siege and liberated Ladysmith the following day. The Boer forces, under General Louis Botha, thereafter retired further north to the Biggarsberg. In the Orange Free State, the capital Bloemfontein fell to General Roberts on 13 March; and on 15 March he issued a proclamation granting amnesty to all burghers, excluding their leaders, who laid down their arms.

On 27 March, Piet Joubert, the old Commandant General of the Transvaal and veteran of umpteen 'Kaffir wars' died from natural causes. He had already relinquished his command of the Transvaal Boer forces to General Louis Botha. On 3 May Roberts resumed his march northward from Bloemfontein, reaching the Vaal River and proclaiming the Orange River Colony on 28 May 1900.

In the meantime, Colonel Mahon, after joining up with Lieutenant Colonel Plumer outside Mafeking, managed without too much trouble, to liberate the town on 17 May. In Natal, Buller was also moving forward. After successfully manoeuvring the Boer forces off Biggarsberg, he took Volksrust and defeated Louis Botha at Berg-en-Dal. On 6 September, he took Lydenburg and the gold fields of the Eastern Transvaal.

Roberts' march, led by a huge helium balloon floating ahead of the marching columns to scout the territory ahead, had been even more dramatic. Having taken all the important towns in the Orange Free State and proclaiming the new colony, he took Johannesburg on 31 May and Pretoria two days later. And that, as they say in the classics, should have been that. But Roberts carried on the march to the Transvaal's northern border and on 25 September, Major General Pole-Carew reached Komatipoort, the northernmost Transvaal town, situated on the Limpopo River – the border between Transvaal and Rhodesia. With that, every town in the Transvaal was in British hands.

Even before the occupation of the Transvaal was complete, Paul Kruger used his long cherished railway line to Lourenço Marques for the last time, travelling in the sumptuous railway coach that had served as the seat of the Z.A.R. government after the fall of Pretoria. It was to be from that port, which he had so long held out as the Transvaal's lifeline – the one guarantee of its independence, that he left the shores of Africa forever. The Delagoa Bay railway line was to be his own lifeline to Europe, from whom he had expected so much and had received so little.

On 19 October 1900, Paul Kruger boarded the Dutch cruiser *De Gelderland*, which had been specially sent to fetch the old President, headed for France and his eventual exile in Clarence, Switzerland. There, from a large, handsome house that befitted a head of state living in exile, he spent his days looking out over the magnificence of Lake Geneva, while in the distance the blue, snow-capped Alps formed a majestic backdrop for the final scenes of his life. A strange final setting for this man who was as African as the soaring peaks and the craggy, rocky cliffs of the Drakensberg he had crossed from Natal with his family as a youngster, moving away from the British, seeking a promised land across the River Vaal.

After the exit of Kruger, Schalk Burger was appointed acting President of the Z.A.R., but the formal annexation of the Transvaal was proclaimed in Pretoria on 25 October 1900. Milner was given charge of the civilian government of the two new colonies. Life in Bloemfontein and Pretoria, as in most towns in the erstwhile republics, started returning to normal. General Buller had already returned to England the previous day. White mine employees also began returning to the Rand in droves and so did the black miners. But even by April 1902, gold production was still less than half its pre-war levels.

Milner adopted a policy of Anglicization of the two old republics and he assembled men around him that he could trust. These men actually did a great rebuilding job of the devastated countries, despite the resentment caused by the Anglicization drive. Merriman, poking some fun at Milner's Germanic gravity, dubbed them 'Milner's Kindergarten'.

The conventional war had been won in less than a year from its outbreak, but it had not yet finished. Hostilities had merely entered another phase – the phase of guerrilla warfare. The Boers no longer had the forces to oppose the overwhelming numbers and organization of the British steamroller, but Steyn, the Free State President, was still in the field and armed, like most of the young leaders, Botha, Smuts, de Wet and de la Rey. They still had substantial forces under their command and Steyn, having held out for peace as long as possible, was not for ending the war right then.

At the end of December 1900, Field Marshall Lord Roberts left South Africa for England where he succeeded Wolseley as Commander-in-Chief. Kitchener, his chief-of-staff, he left in charge in South Africa. The war held its personal tragedy for Roberts too. He had lost a son in the battle of Colenso, but he regarded his job as complete. Only some mopping up remained to be done, was his opinion.

The guerrilla war

Most wars in the European theatre would have been finished at that stage, but Boer society was not, as we have seen, an urban one. Taking their towns and cities did not destroy the fabric of their lives or their political and military organization. They could continue the war as long as they had ammunition and there were wide-open veldt and hills to live in. This they proceeded to do, attacking British supply trains, command-posts and taking whatever disruptive action they could.

Having been deprived of an economy and lacking all facilities for commerce with the outside world, they were eventually driven to wearing looted British uniforms, using captured British Lee-Enfield rifles and British ammunition. Raids on army depots and supply trains would augment even their food supplies. They could no longer take prisoners-of-war, having no facilities to keep them. Their solution was therefore, when British soldiers were caught, to relieve them of everything they had, right down to their underwear. They would thereupon release them to travel horseless, unarmed and naked across the veldt and rejoin their regiments. Unfortunately, there were also instances where prisoners were shot, and this happened on both sides.

The British at least had somewhere to send Boer prisoners. In order to make sure the Boers taken prisoner were unable to escape and rejoin their commandos, they were banished to St. Helena Island and others to Ceylon.

Many of the young Boer hotheads still saw their salvation in the rising of the Afrikaners in the Cape. They had not yet given up hope of driving the British into the sea. In this spirit, Kritzinger took his commando into the Cape on 16 December 1900 and between 10–28 February, Christiaan de Wet also led his commando on an incursion into the Cape Colony.

A peace bid fails

At this stage some Boers would have liked to end the war. Many of them realized that actually reversing what had already happened was, at best, a long shot. Many, like Christiaan De Wet's brother Piet De Wet, who had fought bravely and effectively, had already recognized the warning signs and had surrendered in July 1900. After a number of false starts to get Botha to even discuss peace, Kitchener made a breakthrough. He approached Louis Botha's wife and she agreed to reach her husband in the field. Her message was that the agenda for peace discussions were open, except for the annexation of the two erstwhile republics. This was regarded as a *fait accompli* and was not on the agenda. Botha reacted positively to his wife's representations and the talks were scheduled for 28 February, 1901, to be held at Middleburg in the Transvaal. Kitchener had already conveyed his draft proposals to London. The Boers were to be offered reasonably generous terms, including self-government for the new colonies and grants to assist burghers in re-establishing themselves.

But, as might have been expected, negotiations failed on the question of rights for people of colour. To be sure, it was not the only point of disagreement. The Boers were not happy with the proposed treatment of Cape rebels and wanted total amnesty for all of them. But the main point was the native franchise and on that issue Chamberlain insisted from London that 'we cannot consent to purchase a shameful peace by leaving the coloured population in a position in which they stood before the war with not even the ordinary civil rights which the government of the Cape Colony has long conceded'.[3]

Boer race attitudes always were, and would always remain wholly intractable, even to their own death and destruction. There is thus justification for the contention that in the second phase of the war, the Boers were fighting mainly to retain their racial supremacy as it existed in the old republics, their political independence having already been destroyed and *Uitlander* rights already given. Most of them realized by then that they had lost the fight for independence and against *Uitlander* rights. This is confirmed by their acceptance of the basic conditions of surrender offered by Kitchener at Middleburg. The main term that they rejected and on which the negotiations eventually floundered must thus be taken to be the only thing that they were fighting for after that. They were fighting only to 'keep the Kaffirs in their place'. * This part of the war they were destined to win.

The guerrilla war thus continued and while Kritzinger and his commando were driven out of the Cape Colony on 12 August, Smuts and his commando invaded it again on a long incursion that would take him almost to the Atlantic Ocean. For people who were ostensibly concerned about the lot of the Cape rebels, this invasion was rather reckless. If Cape citizens were caught under arms, they were not regarded as prisoners-of-war, but as rebels-in-arms. They were therefore subject to trial and execution. Eventually, approximately 1 in 50 of captured Cape rebels were shot.

Amnesty for Cape rebels would not have been required were it not for Boer recruitment drives into the colony in the first place. Now, after the failure of the peace bid, another drive was undertaken into the Cape, further aggravating the lot of Cape rebels. In the end, the Boer incursions into the Cape met with only a small measure of recruiting success, while it made absolutely no impact on the course of the war. In December 1901 the National Scouts were founded. This division consisted of Boers who had decided that it would be better to join the British against the 'bitter-enders' – Boers who would fight until nothing remained, as it were. The National Scouts were under the command of General Andries

---

* A favourite and ubiquitous phrase in pre-1995 South Africa. What 'their place' was, was always far beneath the station of any white person, but the exact degree of desired servility depended pretty much on the particular preferences and degree of race rabidity of the person using it.

Cronjé, the brother of the general who had surrendered at Paardeberg, ably assisted by Piet De Wet, the previously mentioned brother of Christiaan.

Sowing the seeds of bitterness

Heroic as these attacks, incursions and battles of the guerrilla war might have been, they were to no avail. The extension of hostilities merely gave rise to the start of the worst phase – the truly tragic, ugly and disastrous phase of the war. Kitchener realized that, although the guerrillas had no hope of dislodging him and his forces from the ex-republics, there would be no peace and a return to full civilian administration until the commando members were all either captured or dead. He therefore embarked on a scorched earth policy.

Scorched earth policies were of course nothing new in European warfare, but it was a shocking idea to the Boers, who knew very little or nothing of it. Its most recent use had been by the French against the invading Germans in 1870, and before that by the Russians against the invading armies of Napoleon. Notably, it is a defensive strategy designed to deny the invader the use of the defender's supplies. Kitchener, no longer being the invader, now used it to the same purpose against the resident and non-invading Boer commandos.

He also realized that every Boer homestead was not only a potential supply depot for commandos, but also a haven where commandos could obtain all manner of succour. It would also be of little use to 'scorch the earth' and then leave those who would replant and restock it *in situ*. He therefore decided to adopt an additional strategy that had been employed, with some success, by the Spanish in the Cuban war, some six years earlier. This entailed removing the 'enemy-friendly' population from the countryside and housing them in 'concentration' camps spread over the length and breadth of the country.

The removal to camps not only involved Boer women and children, but also the black farm labourers and their families, who would otherwise still be available to work the farms and supply the commandos. In deference probably to Boer race attitudes, the blacks were kept in separate camps from the whites. After removal of a farm's occupants, their homes were immediately destroyed, the crops burnt and the animals slaughtered, mostly being left to rot where they were killed. The stark devastation of such a deserted farmstead, with the smell of death hanging over it, must have been a demoralizing sight for any commando to come upon in the hope of getting supplies or even for a visit home.

In addition to these strategies, Kitchener started building lines of stone forts, called blockhouses, all over the country. The idea was originally Milner's, but the execution and armaments were Kitchener's. The blockhouses were connected to each other with barbed wire to which empty tin cans had been attached. The tin cans were an improvised alarm system. If the wires were interfered with, they would rattle, thus alerting the guards on duty in the blockhouses. They were also connected by field telephones all along the line.

The purpose was to form a total grid, like a giant net cast over the territory of the two erstwhile republics, so that commandos would find themselves hemmed in and could be hunted down by patrols operating within the grids. Since the grids could be systematically cleared of Boer commandos, they also served to create growing 'clean and peaceful' areas from the centres of Bloemfontein, Pretoria and the Rand respectively.

A large part of this grid was eventually put in place, with more than 8,000 blockhouses being built over a distance of some 3,700 miles. Many of the original stone blockhouses stand to this day and, while travelling through what used to be the Free State, Transvaal and Northern Natal, they can often be observed still standing solidly on some koppie, silent sentinels now, ever-watchful over the long peaceful veldt. They eventually proved to be very effective for what they were intended to be, although they were unable to deliver the *coup de grâce* that Kitchener so fervently hoped for.

By the end of October 1901, the grid system had changed the strategic map of South Africa dramatically. Natal had been cleared of Boer commandos. In the Cape Colony the Boer forces could only operate in the semi-desert areas of the far west and northwest. In the Transvaal and the Orange River Colony the Boer forces were dispersed and unable to attack even the remotest railway stations. Most of the central areas of the colonies were 'clean'. Only three areas of Boer activity remained – the north-eastern corner of the Orange River Colony (Steyn and De Wet); the semi-desert area of the Transvaal west of the Magaliesberg (De la Rey) and the Eastern Transvaal to where Botha had been forced to retire from Natal.

Slowly but surely these measures were having a strangling effect on Boer efforts. De Wet and Steyn were nearly caught and they were lucky to escape with their lives. The demoralizing effect of the fencing-in and especially the fate of the woman and children were exacting their toll. There is no doubt that the blockhouse grid system helped to restrain the mobility of the commandos and assisted greatly in tiring and demoralizing Boer militiamen. Taking into account what was reported during the discussions among Boer leaders that led to their eventual surrender and peace, the strategy played a major part in ending hostilities.

Kitchener's experiment with concentration camps was not such a great success. While some of the camps were well run, others were ineffectively organized and incompetently run. They were all plagued by disease such as typhus and dysentery. In the beginning these diseases ran rampant in the camps, exacting a horrifying death toll. Many Englishmen and women, especially Emily Hobhouse, whose statue and memorial is a central feature of the Women's Monument in Bloemfontein, made strenuous efforts to render assistance and to relieve the plight of the women and children.

The policy of burning down farms had already been stopped in November 1900, by order of the British government. Now, almost one year later, Kitchener stopped his policy of removing women and children from the country areas to the concentration camps. In fact, although it pacified the Liberals in Britain, it was a less humane policy, but it paid dividends in military terms. This was confirmed by the later discussions of Boer leaders at Vereeniging that took place before peace was concluded.

Milner took over the administration of the concentration camps and John Buchan, later to become the well-known author, landed the job of clearing up the mess left by the military administration of Kitchener. Assisted by two experts brought over from India, he succeeded in bringing the death toll in the camps under control, and then dramatically, within five months, he brought it down in the white camps to 3 per cent and in the black camps to 6 per cent. Life in the camps was also improved. Apart from knitting lessons and organized cultural activities, schools were organized. By November 1901 more than 12,000 children received schooling in the camps of the Orange River Colony which compares very favourably with the highest number (8,900 pupils) ever reached under the administration of the Free State Republic.

The improvement in camp administration and health facilities meant that Boer woman and children were now safe under the protection of the British. Not so for those Boer families left on the farms. The rapidly tiring, under-equipped, thinned-out ranks of the Boer commandos were no longer in any position to feed or to protect them effectively. They became an added burden to the already harassed commandos.

The Boer communities of the Transvaal had always been plagued by restive black populations, which only accepted Boer authority under duress. They had been remarkably quiet during the war years, but the Boers were beginning to fear for the families left unprotected on their isolated farms. Rumours were circulating that the Zulu were planning to reclaim some territory in southeastern Transvaal that the Boers had previously taken from them. These, and other similar concerns, pressed heavily, especially on the Transvaal burghers when, on the initiative of their acting State President, Schalk Burger, the leaders went to Pretoria to discuss peace with Kitchener and Milner for a second time.

The 'shameful peace' concluded

By this time, the deteriorating military situation, from the Boer point of view, made the peace negotiations more fruitful. The Free Staters, Steyn and De Wet were still wholly intractable.

They wished to continue the fight, but when questioned by the Transvalers in conference, they could not say to what end and with what strategy for victory. Indeed, Boer forces had long ago run out of any overall military strategy. They could harass, plunder and kill, but they had nothing with which they could hope to gain eventual victory, unless the British just tired of the war, packed up and went home. But by that time, both new colonies had already become financially self-sufficient under the competent administration of Milner. Not for nothing had he become famous for his financial abilities.

Kitchener was actually tired of the war and so was Whitehall. Roberts' premature declaration in December 1900 that the war was over was a bad mistake – many had believed him. Public enthusiasm for the war had waned in Britain and the War Office wanted to withdraw troops. Everybody wanted to end it sooner rather than later. The financial burden of the war was becoming irksome and insufferable to the Exchequer and Kitchener personally had an important new job as Commander-in-Chief waiting for him in India. Such were the factors that would drive the peace negotiations from the British side, causing them to throw away in the peace so much that they had accomplished in the war.

Negotiations followed in Pretoria and a concept agreement was arrived at. It would be terms of surrender, rather than a peace agreement. They were not much different from the ones that had been offered 14 months previously: the conditions regarding financial assistance to assist burghers in re-establishing themselves were tweaked and better amnesty terms were agreed to for Cape rebels. Their punishment would be loss of the franchise for five years. The terms were worse in one important respect. At Milner's insistence, the Dutch language would no longer be treated on equal terms with English in government, the courts and in education. Milner wanted completely Anglicized colonies, which he thought, would solve all the problems in South Africa conclusively.

To avoid the previous sticking point of extending the franchise to people of colour, Kitchener repeated the suggestion, so eloquently quashed by Chamberlain on that occasion, which he had wanted to make at Middelburg. His suggestion was that the franchise would not be given to natives until after the grant of self-government to the colonies. It was Smuts, not Milner, who so cleverly pencilled into the draft an innocuous amendment. The sentence in the draft now read: 'the question of granting the franchise to natives will not be decided until after the introduction of self-government'.[4] These words then were contained in the final draft sent from Pretoria to London for the British Government's approval.

The meaning and implications of the sentence on the native franchise were not lost on the Colonial Office. They knew what it meant and what it was intended to mean – the natives would never receive the franchise, not then, not later and not ever. There was an internal debate whether the words should be changed or left as they were. Eventually it was decided to leave the wording as it stood, but the Boers would not be able to negotiate any further. They would have to say yes or no to the final draft now telegraphed to Pretoria. Chamberlain's 'shameful peace' was now on the table; the Butcher of Modderfontein had won the day.*

To establish their legitimacy as peace negotiators, the Boer leaders sought an opportunity to consult their forces in the field. The opportunity was granted and the forces duly elected deputies to advise their leaders. Although there had been no final *coup de grâce* administered, no final defeat inflicted, it was clear that the Transvaal forces at least, had been fought to a standstill. From most areas, the reports were the same: it would be either a negotiated peace or they would be forced into a total surrender. The Free State agreed that they could not continue the fight alone. Botha and Smuts spoke to Steyn and De Wet long and earnestly; they agreed to accept the terms of surrender as proposed.

---

* This refers to Jan Smuts who was in charge of the commando that, at his command, wiped out the whole population of the black town of Modderfontein on January 1901. In this century that action would have landed him before the International War Crimes Tribunal in The Hague, not as happened later in his case, in the War Cabinet of a British Prime Minister (Churchill). But he was not the only one who 'shot Kaffirs like dogs'.

By train, the Boer leaders travelled to Pretoria, to Kitchener's headquarters. They went to put the final seal, their signatures, on a document they would have preferred never even to have been drafted, much less signed by them; a document that, in their perception, made them the losers. It was, after all, the terms of their surrender. But the real losers were not even there; the majority of the residents of the new colonies were not represented at any talks, had no opportunity to express their concerns, nobody to present their proposals to. They were shadowy figures in a white man's world.

Schalk Burger signed the document first on behalf of the Transvaal, followed by De Wet for the Free State. Kitchener and Milner signed last. Thus, the curtain came down on the last act of a terrible war, and a drawn-out battle that ended in a shameful peace.

It was 31 May 1902. The agreement was named the Peace of Vereeniging and the die had been cast. But the long battle that could have ended then, was set to continue for another three generations ...

EPILOGUE

The last imperial war?

Was the South African war the last great war of imperial conquest? Were the Boer fighters the brave opponents of greedy imperialists, the indomitable defenders of the high principles of republicanism against the onslaught of imperialism? However much many Afrikaner historians have tried to cast the events of the South African war in that mould, the answer to all these questions are undoubtedly no.

There is not the slightest doubt that Rhodes, Milner and Chamberlain and many others were all imperialists. But they each had a different perception of Empire and imperialism. Rhodes was an imperial dreamer, Chamberlain a pragmatist and wheeler-dealer, but Milner was an uncompromising practical imperialist. Although he believed in the destiny of the British race and much of the mysticism that that entailed, he regarded British political institutions as making for weakness and inaction. Political parties had to pander to public opinion and that always led to compromises. Compromises were what undermined the Empire and kept it from realizing its full potential, he believed.

Milner realized that certain compromises were inevitable, but he would keep them to the absolute minimum. He knew, for instance, that in a war with the Transvaal, it would be necessary to keep the loyalty of the Cape Afrikaners to prevent an Afrikaner uprising in the Colony, but there were limits. 'It is the old policy of keeping on good terms with the Colonial Dutch – the bulk of them – AT ALL COSTS which has got us into this mess.' He regarded the 'left wing' of the Afrikaners as 'Republicans and rebels out and out'. The rest were loyal up to a point; as long as they could govern according to Afrikaner ideals they would willingly listen to 'God Save the Queen' and make a small contribution to the British Navy.[1] Milner had clearly set his face against the weak, vacillating policies of the past and he would not repeat them, even if it meant war.

But the sum of all the factors still does not make the war one of imperial conquest. As it appears from the events recounted on the road to war, it is evident that there was no reason for Britain to conquer the Transvaal, much less the Free State, which was never even in contention until they brought themselves into it. When Lord Salisbury wrote to Lansdowne that the war would bring neither profit nor power to Britain, he was correct, but only insofar as it would not increase its profit or its power, but it would retain that which it had in South Africa. The question that thus remains is not how, but why the British government had allowed itself to be drawn into this costly war.

The events actually speak for themselves. The South African colonies had grown and developed from their own internal dynamics, never from any expansionist need of the imperial power. For many decades the only advantage to Britain of having a colony at the southern tip of Africa had been its strategic position, protecting the sea route to the jewel in the crown – India. But holding onto that strategic position was expensive for Britain and up to the discovery of diamonds and later gold, none of the colonies were financially self-sufficient. Their administration had always required money to flow from Britain into the colony.

But when the rich, inland mineral deposits were discovered, it brought growing prosperity to the region. British interests were then involved in at least two important ways: first, the colonial governments could become financially independent and so relieve the financial burden of their administration on the home country and, second, Britain's great investment of blood, time and money over many decades could now finally pay dividends.

The dividends that Britain expected from the Southern African countries, as she did from all her colonies and countries within the Empire, were those that flow from them as markets for her manufactures. In imperial terms she required prime, although not exclusive, access to these markets. This primacy was the true meaning behind terms like 'suzerainty', 'hegemony' and 'paramountcy'. Britain did not want to compete with her European contenders on the open market in regions she regarded as falling within her Empire. In the never-delivered ultimatum, Britain's true requirement was correctly expressed for the first time: she required 'most favoured nation' status.

Thus from the British point of view, the war was not one of imperial conquest. The dynamics of Empire did not require this conquest in any way. The war was an imperial one only insofar as Britain was an imperial power seeking to protect her existing imperial interests. But for this contention to be valid, the existing imperial interests must have been under threat. While it is debatable to what extent these interests were credibly under threat, it cannot be denied that all those involved from Britain's side perceived her interests to be under a credible threat; more often than not, perception is reality.

With the success of gold mining on the Rand, the economic balance in South Africa had swung dramatically and irrevocably in favour of the Transvaal. The future prosperity of the two South African colonies would largely depend on their economic interaction and cooperation with the Transvaal.

With that background, the perceived threat had many facets. The drifts crises had demonstrated not only the Z.A.R.'s ability, but also their willingness, to act to the economic detriment of the Cape and British industry in the matter of imports. Rampant Afrikaner nationalism and the often publicly expressed policy of Kruger and even the Transvaal Progressives for a South Africa, united under its own flag, were a direct threat to British interests, although its practicality might have been in some doubt. But these open challenges must at least have shaken British confidence in the prospect of continuing good relations. As it turned out, the challenges were not merely rhetorical, but were even more feasible than the British at first realized.

Even the question of *Uitlander* rights constituted a facet of the threat. Apart from the fact that the imposed constitutional disabilities and differential taxation were perceived as insulting and considered a breach of the London Convention, it was also seen as part of the pattern of hostility against British interests.

Therein, too, lay further confirmation of the total threatening circumstance.

The problems caused to the mining industry by Kruger's obstructionism and his government's general incompetence illustrate another facet of the threat. The gold mining industry was still in its infancy and thus very vulnerable. It represented a great deal of international, including British, investment. If it were to flounder as an industry, it would not only squander the capital involved, but the region's promising economic prosperity would be destroyed. That eventuality, too, was a threat to British interests.

British officials in South Africa perceived the threats posed by the Z.A.R. and Afrikaner nationalism as very real and not without reason, as it turned out. When the two Boer republics attacked the colonies of Natal and the Cape, it was clearly not merely a pre-emptive war. They did not enter the war merely for the much-vaunted purpose of protecting their independence; they must be taken at their word – they intended to permanently annex large parts of British colonial territory and fully incorporate them into their republics. It is what they said and it is what they did. Whether they would have gone so far as to try to annex the Cape Colony as a whole is an open question, as it must perforce remain, since they never had the opportunity of extending their annexations.

It is in this light then that Milner's instructions to restore and secure British hegemony should be seen. But if Britain's participation in the war was to secure and protect her imperial interests, were the Boers not fighting imperialism? Such a claim would credit the Boers with much greater depth of principle than they possessed. They were never against imperialism as such. They never objected to German, French, Portuguese or Belgian imperial adventures in Africa. The famous European 'scramble for Africa' took place during the life of the two Boer republics. Neither one of them ever raised its voice in protest. In fact, we have seen how Kruger tried to be cosy with the Kaiser and attempted to use German imperial ambitions as a counterpoise to British ones in South Africa.

The Boers did not even oppose British imperialism in the Zulu war, which took place on their doorstep. They were only opposed to British imperialism when they perceived themselves to be at the receiving end of it. Their objection to British imperialism was never principled in any way; their only principle was self-interest. After all, they themselves did to the local black population exactly what they alleged the British wanted to do to them, the Boers − except that Boer actions against the natives were much worse than even the worst accusations they ever levelled against the British.

However, when the causes of the war are considered, one must not lose sight of the Boer perspective on these matters. There is not the slightest doubt that there was a general and pervasive welling of solidarity and sense of a shared cultural identity among many of the Cape Afrikaners and the Boers of the Republics. This was not a benign growth; it fed on a strong anti-British sentiment, a shared feeling of injustice and persecution, cosseted and nurtured for at least four generations. Taking the pamphlet entitled *A Century of Wrong** as a basis, it is clear that virtually every complaint and accusation, every real issue between Boer and Brit, had at its heart the question of the equal, merely even the fair and equitable, treatment of people of colour. The problem did not arise from the fact that the British were such great humanists; it was merely that the Boers were such incredible Negrophobes.

The 'equality' that the British were accused of wishing to establish for the natives was not even equality in any real sense of the word. It was merely equality in civil and criminal law, and the basic fairness of adjudication and procedure. But even the assertion that black people could enjoy any rights at all, especially as against white people on whatever grounds, has the ability to set many

---

* This propaganda was issued as a thin booklet, almost contemporaneously with the Transvaal's ultimatum. Given under the name of F. W. Reitz, the State Secretary, it contains a synopsis of every Afrikaner complaint, accusation of injustice and persecution ever held against the British by Afrikaners, from the first annexation of the Cape through to the outbreak of the war. It was to serve as justification for the war declaration against Britain and was reputedly the work of Jan Smuts. This has been shown to be incorrect. The content was written by Roos, an attorney friend of Smuts. Smuts was asked to comment and he apparently made some alterations and additions to the Introduction. However, it was not Smut's work, but at the time he undoubtedly identified himself with its contents and sentiments.

Afrikaners foaming at the mouth, while the mention of 'human rights' tends to cause temporary insanity.*

To them the British and their sense of justice thus presented a permanent threat. They foresaw that the British would continually interfere in their affairs, if not on behalf of *Uitlanders*, then on behalf of the natives. They would never be allowed to run the country according to their own lights. The only way to get the British, and with them their hated attitude to people of colour, out of the way forever would be to drive them out altogether. Many of the Boers, misled by their successes at Majuba and against Jameson, were convinced that they could achieve this. They believed that their modern weaponry, supplied through the newfound economic power of the Transvaal, added to their superiority as warriors, in their own estimation at least, would give them the upper hand. Among Milner's papers, there is the following letter, written by F. N. Blignaut, the brother of the Government Secretary of the Orange Free State, to an unidentified addressee. The letter was written at Kroonstad, Orange Free State on 25 September 1899, just before hostilities began. How it came into Milner's possession is not known, but the extract is quoted as saying:

> ... The only thing we are afraid of now is that Chamberlain, with his admitted fitfulness of temper, will cheat us out of the war, and consequently the opportunity of annexing the Cape Colony and Natal, and forming the Republican United States of South Africa; for in spite of (S. J. du Toit) we have forty-six thousand fighting men who have pledged themselves to die shoulder to shoulder in defence of our liberty, and to secure the independence of South Africa.[2]

Thus no analysis of the causes of the South African war can be complete without the perspective of an aggressive nationalism, ambitiously launching itself against the Southern African dominions of the British Empire. It might not have been the first cause, or even the proximate cause of the war, but it certainly was one of the very

---

*This is from my own observation. Thankfully these attitudes no longer represent the view of the vast majority of modern Afrikaners.

important underlying dynamics of the war. Without it as a driving force behind Boer ambitions, the search for further mutual accommodation, which was far from over, could well have been profitably continued. Too soon, for their own good, were the Boers prepared to say enough is enough.

It is also from this aggressive nationalism that the military alliance between the Transvaal and Free State was most likely born. Only in a joint military drive could they hope to achieve the United South Africa, free from British domination, that they sought. Afrikaner nationalism then, was the altar on which the independence of the Free State was offered, an independence that was never in jeopardy before the Free Staters themselves placed it there.

Would not peace now reign supreme?

It is said that the peace made at the end of one war contains the seeds for the start of the following one. In a sense that was true of the Peace of Vereeniging, but in a rather roundabout way. Britain never fought another war in South Africa and the country loyally supported the allies in the two World Wars that followed. The peace accord contained the seeds of further conflict inasmuch as it only brought the war between the warring white factions in South Africa to an end. The war had been simmering for some time before it became a hot war, but nobody in South Africa, least of all the natives, escaped its action or its consequences. But the peace accord went even further. By leaving the native franchise issue completely open, it cast the dice for the future and they came up 'snake's eyes' for the natives and all people of colour in South Africa.

It had been an expensive war for all concerned. On the British side there were contingents from all over the Empire: South Africa, Australia, New Zealand and Canada. In all, some 82,000 soldiers from the colonies participated. British troops numbered more than 365,000. More than 100,000 casualties were suffered, of which just over 22,000 found their last resting place in South Africa.

The Boer numbers are not as well recorded. According to the best estimates, some 87,000 men were in the field, of which 2,120 were volunteers from France, the US and a number of other European countries. It also included 13,300 Cape rebels. Some 7,000 Boers under arms were killed, but it is not known what the total casualties were. It is also not quite certain how many women and children died in the concentration camps. Estimates vary between 18,000 and 28,000.[3] Proportionally, the suffering of the Boers were much greater.

Technically, the black people of the country were not parties to the war, but in fact, they were. When they fought, they fought willingly for the British, expecting a better deal for themselves from them. But when they suffered, they suffered at the hands of both belligerents. In Kimberley, Baden-Powell armed some 2,000 blacks from the local township. He referred to them as his 'Black Watch' and they were well treated, but in the later stages of the siege, he withdrew rations from most of the other black people living in the township. That black township was just as much besieged as the white town was; the Boers shot anybody whom they saw trying to leave it. Nevertheless, Baden-Powell told them to head 70 miles north, on foot, to Fullers' command where they would be able to obtain rations. Many died in the veldt, either because they could not slip through Boer lines successfully, or from starvation. But still, many did make it to the northern garrison.

At least 10,000 blacks were armed by Kitchener to act as scouts, guides and to man the blockhouses as guards. Then there were upwards of 30,000 unarmed black people who acted as muleteers, wagon drivers, labourers, batmen and so forth. It is unknown how many of these died. The Boers openly admitted to fusillading any armed blacks that they came across, but there is also much published evidence that they shot unarmed ones as well. Then there were the blacks that worked for the Boers. Many of them died in the concentration camps, but nobody really kept a record. It is estimated that some 7,000 of them died.

In total, the war cost just over 22,000 British lives, 25,000 Boer lives and 12,000 black lives, although the figure for blacks must be the most uncertain of them all. In monetary terms, it cost Britain more than £200 million, and the lives of more than 400,000 horses, mules and donkeys. In reparations to the Boers, as promised in the peace treaty, another £3,000,000 was spent, but to that a further £30,000,000 was later added in loans. Reparations were paid to both white and black claimants, but the blacks were paid on a lower scale than whites. It must be one the very few wars in all of history, if not the only one, where reparations were paid by the victors to the vanquished.

As envisaged by the peace treaty, the two new colonies became self-governing very soon after the agreement, and in 1910, the Union of South Africa was formed out of the two old colonies plus the two ex-republics. True to the wording of the peace treaty, the constitution of the Union did not introduce the franchise for natives to the Transvaal and the Free State, although the existing franchise arrangements for blacks and coloured people in the Cape and Natal were retained.

Thus in the bigger picture, the fate of 20th-century South Africa had virtually been sealed. After the negotiations on the constitution of the Union of South Africa had been finalized, General Smuts remarked, apropos to the native franchise, that it was a question he would leave for the next (white) generation to address. He could hardly have chosen a worse arbiter. The united South Africa that so many had looked forward to previously, had come about at last. It was a Union under the British flag as Paul Kruger had feared, but it was also an Afrikaner State, as Milner had feared. In a sense, it was the worst of both worlds.

The numbers of Afrikaners and English speakers in South Africa as a whole, and in the Transvaal in particular, were pretty much evenly matched after the war. This fact Milner discovered in the census of 1904. He was thus unable to gain success in his Anglicization policy, because the numbers of Anglos just were not there. Nor could he by any means entice sufficient English-speaking immigrants to flood the country. There was no real incentive to come to South Africa – the rush for gold was long over and the new rush was to the new world – the US.

Thus, when self-government was granted to the two new colonies, General J. B. M. Hertzog became leader of the Orange River Colony and General Louis Botha became Prime Minister of the Transvaal with Smuts his deputy. This put the lie to Paul Kruger's fears of domination by the *Uitlanders*, on the altar of which he had sacrificed his whole republic and that of the Free State. He died in 1904, in the year of that census.

This state of affairs was confirmed and continued at the first general elections held after Union, when the South African Party, under General Louis Botha with Smuts again as his deputy, was elected to govern the new country. They were elected on a platform of reconciliation between the two white races. In essence, being a conciliatory party, it had to make some compromises with English feelings of fair play and justice for all, although that does not translate to equality for all. Under such leadership, the development of civil rights for the natives were thus not entirely excluded; in the Cape, coloured people enjoyed full political rights until the middle of the 20th century, when the National Party under Dr D. F. Malan finally succeeded in disenfranchising them, despite the original constitutional guarantees.

But the intractables, represented by General J. B. M. Hertzog and his National Party, were the official opposition from the beginning. Over the next few decades they would rout the politics of conciliation and a new, even more rigid domination by Afrikaner Nationalism would begin; the scourge of South Africa as a whole, even more virulent than it had been in the old Z.A.R., and now supported by a much stronger economy and a much more efficient administrative machinery. For the greater part of the South African population, peace with dignity, true peace, would be a fading prospect for many decades.

The insoluble problem

The Z.A.R. was the first failed experiment in Afrikaner political philosophy and statecraft, although it might not then have been seen as such. It failed in statecraft inasmuch as it was unable to develop and establish an efficient, reasonably honest and effective government and administration. It also failed to deal successfully with the complex problems and challenges of international diplomacy. But its greatest failure was perhaps the one least visible at the time, its failure as political philosophy. This failure stemmed from the basic premise on which the state was founded. That premise forced it to keep a black labour force in servility, and through the political chicanery of Kruger, to use the knowledge, labour and expertise of immigrant whites for its own benefit in much the same way as it did those of the local black population.

They used it to the full, taxed them as much as the market would bear, but gave them no meaningful political say in how the society within which they operated was run and in how their tax monies were spent. This was race exclusivity driven to extremes. Moreover, taxation without representation was always a dangerous road.

It is difficult to feel sorry for the often rich and well-paid *Uitlanders*, or to see them as underprivileged helots as Milner described them in one of his more emotional despatches to Chamberlain. They were none of these in any socio-economic sense. But because the *Uitlanders* were mostly well educated and politically sophisticated, they felt their political disability and the directly stated discrimination against them so much more acutely.

But to argue, or imply, as some have done, that such generally well-to-do people had for that reason nothing to complain of, is tantamount to arguing that people who enjoy financial success are not entitled to political rights and that keeping them from it can hardly be regarded a hardship. The Boers could get away with discriminating against the blacks for a long time, but not against the *Uitlanders*.

In evaluating this part of South African history, it is always easy to forget that when dealing with the Z.A.R. of the 1880s, one is not dealing with a long-established country, suddenly overrun by fortune-seekers who try to take over the reigns of state. In the 1880s, the Z.A.R. was never more than a collection of admittedly growing, but still far-flung, isolated communities. Due to their greater access to modern weapons, they could dominate to subjugation their surrounding black communities, extracting labour from them as tribute, but not much more.

The Z.A.R. was only regarded as a state because Britain, for its own purposes, had seen fit to recognize it as such, and that recognition only pre-dated the arrival of the first *Uitlanders* by five years. Even then, all are agreed that the Z.A.R.'s independence was conditional and that it lacked sovereignty.[4] There is no good reason why people, coming to what can at best be described as a nascent state, perennially indigent, with no industry, no commerce or economy, and no expertise to change that situation, should be denied full participation in that state by those whose only claim was that they had arrived a few years earlier. Even more so, when those earlier arrivals had in the space of those years not achieved anything constructive, except for the fact that they had survived.

Thus, the Transvaal cannot be said to have been a true state in the internationally accepted sense of the word, at least not until the exertions and expertise of the newcomers had made it so. It was never truly independent either, because it never had or developed the means to be self-sufficient – not even in food production. Nor was it ever a true republic, nor was it ever sustained by republican ideals. It was always a mere race oligarchy, even to the exclusion of other white peoples whom they found inassimilable. Even when it developed an economy, it was not a free economy – a fundamental principle of republicanism. It was based on concessions and monopolies, which are features associated with absolutist monarchies and autocracies.

It might be that in some way Milner had perceived this fundamental weakness, which is why he wanted to destroy it totally, never to rise again. But he proved to be no great champion of justice and fair play when it came to black people either. The fundamental, philosophical problem of the Afrikaner state goes much further than mere racism. The Boers were not the only people in the world, or in South Africa for that matter, who regarded themselves as racially superior to people of colour.

A good example of racist attitudes by English speakers is supplied by the activities of the Rand Pioneers. It was an exclusively white, English-speaking association formed in 1903, shortly after the fall of Johannesburg to Roberts. They regarded the Transvaal as 'white man's country' and thus took upon themselves the task of 'preserving to the uttermost the rights of the white population of this country'. Consequently, they were continuously complaining and petitioning against any act they perceived as an extension of the rights to people of colour. They complained about shared railway facilities and too light sentences handed to blacks in the criminal courts; they complained about Chinese people using taxis and even about black people being allowed to walk on the pavements.[5]

Beyond mere race attitudes lies the basic and insoluble problem of an Afrikaner state: the insupportable premise upon which it is founded. The roots of the problem lie deep in the Afrikaner psyche, as this narrative shows; the insupportable premise is the fundamental contradiction inherent in the Afrikaner's total dependence on servile, non-Afrikaner labour and his simultaneous desire for political supremacy in an exclusively Afrikaner state. It is surely stating the obvious, but a racially or culturally exclusive state, whatever its size, absolutely demands self-sufficiency in all aspects of socio-economic life.

Even more, it needs to start with a single, contiguous territory to which it has an unassailable and uncontested right. None of these prerequisites was ever present in the Z.A.R. A state cannot be independent and dependent at the same time. Apart from the moral reprehensibility, it is fundamentally impossible to keep people, on whom the polity as a whole is dependent for their contribution to the common good, in a state of servile rightlessness indefinitely. This proved true for the Z.A.R. in respect of the *Uitlanders*, as it would also prove true for the later Republic of South Africa in respect of all its people of colour.

And yet, these dubious principles, the inherent contradictions and the fundamental, insoluble problem were carried over from the Boer republics and imported wholesale into the constitution of the Union of South Africa. This was the true South African inheritance. An inheritance bestowed on it by a shameful peace. It would only be disavowed and purged by the efforts of the South African people, mostly by those of colour, albeit with substantial assistance by the international community. But it would take many decades; much humiliation, pain and suffering would still have to be endured before the whole country could become a republic founded on true democratic principles.

Even now, at the time of this writing, the new Republic has not yet existed long enough to prove its resilience and its long-term commitment to the principles of democracy and republicanism. It can only be trusted that the scars of the past do not run so deep as to disfigure the face of liberty in what is still the financial heart and the economic engine room of Africa.

BIBLIOGRAPHIC NOTES

Chapter 1

1. *The Circumnavigation of Africa*, by Ciaran Branigan, in the *Classics Ireland*, Volume 1, 1994, published by the University College Dublin, Ireland. The footnote to the story reads: 'Sataspes may have reached Cape Palmas. He may have been caught in the doldrums off the Cape Verde coast of Senegal and hence unable to proceed further. Some of the Arab voyagers down the west coast of Africa in medieval times reported that at a certain stage they could go no further, ... Herodotus and possibly Hanno report dwarves in West Africa. Sataspes' dwarves have been identified as early Bushmen, still found in South Africa but which may have been found further north 2,500 years ago. Pygmies were also found in the Cameroons, Hyde op. cit. pp. 242–4.'

2. The legend of Prester John is well told by Robert Silverburg in *The Realm of Prester John*, New York, 1972. Also, *The Land of Prester John*, New York, 1944, by Elaine Sanceau makes fascinating reading.

3. For an authoritative history of the Portuguese trade and movement down the East Coast of Africa, see *The Slave Trade* by Hugh Thomas, (London, 1997).

4. *A History of South Africa* by Frank Welsh, (London, 2000), revised edition, p. xxiv and authorities quoted by him. I am, *inter alia*, indebted to his scholarly work for much of what follows.

5. *South Africa: A Modern History* by T. R. H. Davenport, 4th edition, 1991, p. 9.

6. Paul Maylam, *A History of the African People of South Africa* (Cape Town, 1986), p. 44.

7. Frank Welsh, op. cit., p. 53.

8. T. R. H. Davenport, op. cit, p. 12.

9. Paul Maylam, op. cit., p. 54.

10. Ibid., p. 54.

11. Davenport, op. cit., p. 16. Prof. Davenport also notes that despite mainstream anthropologists' and historians' assumption that enslavement of people was alien to northern Nguni tradition, it seems quite clear that most chiefdoms of the area, including the Zulu, became involved in this trade, both as hunters and as hunted.

Chapter 2

1. Frank Welsh, op. cit., p. 2.
2. T. R. H. Davenport, op. cit., p. 19.
3. Ibid., p. 20.
4. Ibid., p. 24.
5. *Afrikaner Political Thought*, by A. du Toit and H. Giliomee (Vol. 1, Berkeley, 1983) at 3.3.
6. *History of the Army*, by J. W. Fortescue, Vol. 4, Part 1, (1990) AMS Press, Cambridge, p. 402.
7. T. R. H. Davenport, op. cit., p. 37.
8. A. du Toit and H. Giliomee, op. cit. [n. 2.4]. Although some historians, such as Beyers, Idenburg and Schutte have emphasized the links of the Kaapsche Patriotten (Cape Patriots) with liberal continental Hollanders and Beyers argued that they had actually assimilated the liberal doctrines of their European mentors, recent historians are justifiably sceptical. Du Toit and Giliomee, on the evidence of representative documents prepared at the Cape from 1778 to 1784, point out that the Patriotten differed in their views from the new European liberalism. For example, they displayed no interest in universal rights, popular sovereignty or even independence. Indeed, with substantial individual exceptions, the history of the Afrikaner right up to the end of the 20th century, displays a total blind spot for the universality of the concepts of rights and justice and a special disdain for popular sovereignty.
9. T. R. H. Davenport, op. cit., p. 37, referring to V. T. Harlow and W. M. Macmillan in the *Cambridge History of the British Empire* VIII (1963), pp. 169–238.
10. V. T. Harlow and W. M. Macmillan, op. cit., pp. 249–65.
11. *Money and Empire: The International Gold Standard, 1890–1914*, by M. de Cecco (London, 1974), pp. 20–1.
12. Frank Welsh, op. cit., p. 117.
13. Ibid., p. 235.
14. *Reluctant Empire* by J. S. Galbraith (Berkeley, 1963) for a general economic discussion on the growth of the British Empire in South Africa.

Chapter 3

1. T. R. H. Davenport, op. cit., p. 20.
2. *The Shaping of South African Society 1652–1820*, by R.H. Elphick and H. Giliomee (eds) (2nd edition, London, 1989) [n. 2.1.] p. 365.
3. *The Encyclopaedia Americana* (Vol. 14) entry under 'Imperialism', by R. W. Winks (New York, 1963), at p. 320.

4. T. R. H. Davenport, op. cit., p. 26.

5. Ibid., p. 27.

6. Ibid., p. 27.

7. Frank Welsh, op. cit., p. 109 – the quote is actually from the aims of the London Missionary Society, but could probably stand for the intention of all Christian missionaries.

8. Ibid., p. 110.

9. Ibid., p. 113.

10. Ibid., p. 114.

11. Quoted by Welsh, op. cit. p. 122 and endnotes thereto. In 1809, the elder *Landdrost* Stockenström described these people as vagabonds in a letter to Colonel Collins, probably the best-informed authority on frontier affairs. He wrote of them that they were 'de la plus basse classe. Le plus grande nombre sont des bâtards' – meaning that they were low class people of mixed blood – a rather sad comment, given the later elevation of these Bezuidenhouts to the Afrikaner pantheon.

12. T. R. H. Davenport, op. cit., p. 40.

13. *Kaapland en die Tweede Vryheidsoorlog*, by C. J. Scheepers Strydom, published in 1937 by Nasionale Pers, Cape Town as part of a series entitled *Ons Geskiedenis – Serie* (Our History – Series). The book is a reworked version of a doctoral thesis accepted by the University of Cape Town for a PhD degree.

14. *Geskiedenis van Suid Afrika* I, by A.J.H. van der Walt, J. A. Wiid and A.L. Geyer (eds) NASOU, Capetown p. 135; *Die Trekboer in die Geskiedenis van die Kaapkolonie, 1659–1842*, by P. J. van der Merwe, pp. 245 – 247.

15. C. J. Scheepers Strydom, op. cit., p. 4.

16. *Afrikaners in die Goudstad, Vol. I: 1886–1924*, by Dr J. J. Fourie – Prof. dr. E. L. P. Stals (ed.) (Johannesburg, 1978), p. 1 and further for what follows. This is the first volume in a series initiated by the Rand Afrikaans University in 1968 as the first project of its Department of History.

17. *A History of South Africa – Social and Economic*, by C. W. de Kiewiet, (London, 1966), p. 13.

18. Du Toit and Giliomee, op. cit., 3.8. They quote from the petition to the Burgher Senate, 10 July 1826, recounting how the burghers of Stellenbosch found their 'Nerves and Bowels in agitation' at the 'revolting ... shuddering idea' that a slave could bring his master to court. This reaction is at once surprising, because Roman Law allowed such rights to slaves, albeit under limited circumstances, and yet the reaction is also not unexpected. It might be that they had good reason to fear such rights if given to their slaves and labourers under circumstances where the courts were less than wholly partial in their favour.

19. *Vir Vryheid en Vir Reg*, by Generaal J.C.G. Kemp, second impression published by Nasionale Pers Beperk in 1942, (Cape Town, 1942), pp. 4–5. The book forms part of the *Ons Geskiedenis – Serie*. The author apparently rose to generalship during the South African War (Boer War) of 1899 to 1902. The poor man is innocent of all history, even his own. It is, however, not as

history that this tome is significant. What is significant is that such drivel could be published, which in turn indicates the extent to which such views were acceptable, prevalent and even authoritative among Afrikaners in the 20th century. In his naïve bombast the author exposes the true character of those Afrikaners who later imposed the system of apartheid, but who then tried to justify it with much less candour. The verbatim quote from the book is as follows:

> Die basis van hierdie beleid was dat wit en swart, beide daarbo in die hemel en hier op die aarde, gelyk is op alle gebiede. Dit was die pogings om hierdie teoretiese gelykheid in Suid-Afrika toe te pas wat sommer uit die staanspoormoeilikheid veroorsaak het; want hierdie beleid het reëlreg ingedruis teen dié van die koloniste, wat deur die ondervinding van anderhalf eeu geleer het om die naturel te beskou en te behandel as 'n op geestelike gebied minderbevoorregte en op 'n maatskaplike gebied minderwaardige. Dis dáárom dat ons voorouers daarin geslaag het om te midde van miljoene inboorlinge 'n blanke aristokrasie te vorm en te behou. Die basters in ons land is grotendeels te wyte aan persone wat die tipies Engelse naturellepolitiek prakties wou uitvoer.

20. The quote is from *A Hundred Years of Wrong*, or *Een Eeu van Onrecht*, published under the name of F. W. Reitz, the State Secretary of the Z.A.R. at the start of the South African War. It was intended as a propaganda piece justifying the Boer declaration of war on Britain. Originally attributed to Gen. J. C. Smuts, later research revealed an attorney, H. Roos, as the author. Smuts and Roos were apparently friends and Smuts was shown the draft for his comments before publication. He suggested some minor changes to the beginning and end and generally associated himself with its contents.

Chapter 4

1. Welsh describes him as a 'picturesque, hard swearing, opinionated and gifted fighting veteran of the Peninsular War' – Welsh, op. cit., p. 157.
2. Despatch dated 26 December 1835, quoted by Welsh, op. cit., pp. 160–1.
3. 'Hoeveel Kaapse Koloniste het Voortrekkers geword?' by G. D. J. Duvenhage, *Historical Journal* no. XXI, 1 (1976) 2–14.
4. Paul Maylam, op. cit. p. 111.
5. T. R. H. Davenport, op. cit., p. 69.
6. Quoted in Welsh, op. cit., p. 162.
7. Ibid. p. 178.
8. Quoted in C. W. de Kiewiet, *British Colonial Policy*, (London, 1945), p. 19.

Chapter 5

1. T. R. H. Davenport, op. cit.

Chapter 6

1. Paul Maylam, op. cit., p. 123.
2. Cf. *Die Tweede Vryheidsoorlog – Deel 1: Voorspel tot die Stryd*, by J. H. Breytenbach (Cape Town, 1948). The book is a publication of the author's doctoral thesis and fairly represents an era of Afrikaner historiography wherein the main purpose was to justify the claims of Afrikaner nationalism rather than to conduct scientific study. Although many facts from the period have been researched and incorporated in the work, they are viewed and dealt with from unproven and undisclosed premises, which do not stand up to scrutiny. There is unfortunately a great body of work, which has done a similar disservice to Afrikaner academic standards.
3. 'Die Pastorale Aard en Leefwyse van die Afrikaner tot 1886', by Dr. J. J. Fourie in *Afrikaners in die Goudstad*, Part I, op. cit., p. 3 for most of what follows.
4. *The Urban Trek: Some Comparisons of Mobility in American and South African History*, by R. B. Ford, (Berkeley, 1985), p. 22.
5. *De Zuid-Afrikaansche Republiek en hare bewoners*, by H. Blink, p. 64. Written in Dutch, the original passage is as follows:

   > De spoorweg zal een gehele omkeer brengen in het economisch leven der Republiek. Hij zal de Boeren wakker schudden uit hun rust; hij zal hen bezielen met ijver in den strijd om het bestaan. Hij zal den Zuid-Afrikaner maken tot een concurrent van meer ontwikkelde volken en hem daartoe aangorden met ondernemingsgeest. De oude methoden van landbouw en veeteeld, half natuur-, half roofbouw, zullen dan moet plaats maken voor cultuur.

6. Ibid., p. 54: 'Deze algemeene beoefning der verschillende bedrijven tot eigen behoefte was noodzakelijk, doch bracht hen niet tot groote bekwaamheid in eenig vak.'
7. Ibid., p. 66: 'Wetenschappelijke specialiteiten vraagt men er niet, en zullen als zoodanig weinig success in dit land hebben.'
8. *World Economic Primacy, 1500–1990*, by Charles Kindleberger (New York, 1996). He argues convincingly that, given the aims of colonial policy as a whole, the effect of the terms of this perpetual alliance and trade agreement was to make Portugal effectively a British colony. The strength of this alliance would also be demonstrated at the time of the South African War.
9. Paul Maylam, op. cit., p. 122.
10. *Valley of Gold*, by A.P. Cartwright (Cape Town, 1973), p. 21.

11. *The Complete Story of the Transvaal — from the 'Great Trek' to the Convention of London*, by John Nixon. Originally published by Sampson Low, Marston, Searle, and Rivington of Fleet Street, London, in 1885. The quote is from a facsimile reprint by C. Struik (Pty) Ltd. Cape Town in 1972, p. 31. This gem of a book is a fascinating account by a contemporary observer, present in the Transvaal during the Presidency of Burgers, the annexation of the Republic by Sir Theophilus Shepstone, The First Anglo-Boer War and the Retrocession. Although he is not a disinterested historian, being very much at pains to support the 1877 annexation by Shepstone and to condemn the subsequent retrocession, his treatment of the material is fair and balanced. He makes a detailed and unanswerable case proving the widespread practice of slavery among the Boers in the Transvaal; practised both with and without the consent and cooperation of the government. His facts are corroborated by so many other sources that the verisimilitude and integrity of his narration cannot be faulted.

12. A. P. Cartwright, op. cit., p. 26.

Chapter 7

1. A. P. Cartwright, op. cit. p. 29 – 30.
2. Ibid., p. 32.
3. Ibid., p. 35.
4. Ibid., p. 35.
5. Ibid., p. 46.
6. Ibid., p. 48.

Chapter 8

1. Paul Maylam, op. cit., p. 92.
2. T. R. H. Davenport, op. cit., p. 141.
3. Ibid., p. 143.
4. Paul Maylam, op. cit., p. 95.
5. Delius, op. cit., pp. 184 – 6.
6. Nixon, op. cit., p. 35.
7. T. R. H. Davenport, op. cit., p. 144.
8. A. P. Cartwright, op. cit., p.71.
9. Nixon, op. cit., p. 36.
10. T. R. H. Davenport, op. cit., p. 144.
11. Osborn, the resident Magistrate of Newcastle, in Natal, who later became the British Resident in Zululand, gives a vivid picture of the manner in which Boers got their way with native chiefs. In a report presented to Sir

H. E. Bulwer in 1876 (contained in C.1748, p. 196), he describes the land encroachment process in detail and adds: 'This, I have no hesitation in saying, is the usual method by which the Boers obtain what they call cessions to them of territories by native chiefs. In Sikukune's (sic) case, they allege that his father, Sikwato (sic) ceded to them the whole of his territory (hundreds of square miles) for 100 head of cattle.'

12. Paul Maylam, op. cit., p. 131.
13. Ibid., p. 175.
14. A. P. Cartwright, op. cit., p. 72.

Chapter 9

1. *Die Protesbeweging van die Transvaalse Afrikaners 1877–1880*, by M. C. van Zyl (Pretoria, 1979).
2. T. R. H. Davenport, op. cit. p. 101.
3. Frank Welsh, op. cit., pp. 256–7.
4. *Hansard's Parliamentary Debates 244, Third Series*, pp. 1652–3.
5. Unbeknown to Nixon, of course, Lord Carnarvon had written to his Prime Minister, Lord Beaconsfield, on 20 September as follows (P.R.O. 30/6/11, pp. 151–2.):

   I propose to send out by the mail of Friday Sir Theophilus Shepstone, the man who has the most intimate knowledge of S. African affairs and the greatest influence alike over Native and Dutch, with a secret despatch empowering him to take over the Transvaal Govt. and Country and to become the first English Governor, if circumstances on his arrival render this in any way possible. Should any new or unforeseen change have occurred, as unfortunately is possible, tho' I hope not likely, he will hold his hand and I shall give him instructions suitable to the case. But I have every confidence in his judgement and capacity and courage, and knowing my mind he will under almost any circumstances I believe act rightly.

   These words express a much clearer preference on Lord Carnarvon's part for annexation than do the *ipsissima verba* of Shepstone's commission. Nevertheless, this communication does not make a case for concluding that the overt reasons for the annexation were mere subterfuge. It merely establishes that Carnarvon's preferred solution was annexation; this preference was probably not entirely unconnected to its agreeable implications for his plans in the longer term.

6. John Nixon, op. cit., p. 41.
7. Cf. *Great Britain and South African Confederation, 1870–1881*, by C. F. Goodfellow (Cape Town, 1966), pp. 204–9.
8. M. C. van Zyl, op. cit., p. 20.
9. Ibid., p. 58.

10. John Nixon, op. cit., p. 93.
11. Frank Welsh, op. cit., p. 257.
12. M. C. van Zyl, op. cit., p. 58.
13. Frank Welsh, op. cit., p. 270.
14. John Nixon, op. cit., pp. 91 – 2.
15. Quoted by Frank Welsh, op. cit., p. 270.
16. Ibid., p. 271.

Chapter 10

1. Paul Maylam, op. cit., pp. 131 – 3.
2. The essential works are to be found in the annotated bibliography in *Studies in the Theory of Imperialism* (London, 1972), by E. R. J. Owen and R. B. Sutcliffe (eds.), pp. 331 – 8. The works quoted therein are not exhaustive of the subject, but represent a fair sample.
3. The reinterpretation of imperial history in the light of economic fundamentals starts with the seminal study of J. A. Hobson, wherein he proposes his 'surplus capital' thesis in *Imperialism: A Study* (London, 3rd edn, 1938). This was followed by a succession of other studies such as *The Theory of Capitalist Imperialism*, by D. K. Fieldhouse (ed.) (London, 1967); and *Europäischer Finanzimperialismus vor 1914: Ein Beitrag zu einer Pluralistischen Theorie des Imperialismus*, by W. J. Mommsen, published in *Historische Zeitschrift*, CCXXIV (1977), pp. 2 – 81.
4. Cf. M. de Cecco, op. cit., pp. 23 onward for an authoritative analysis of the economic history of that period.
5. *The Evaluation of the Sterling System*, by D. Williams, quoted by M. De Cecco, op. cit., pp. 20 – 1.

Chapter 11

1. *The Commandant General – The Life and Times of Petrus Jacobus Joubert of the South African Republic*, by Johannes Meintjies, 1st edn (Cape Town, 1971), for the narrative of the siege that follows.
2. *The Randlords*, by Geoffrey Wheatcroft, published by Weidenfeld & Nicholson (London, 1985), pp. 124 – 5.
3. Dr. J. J. Fourie, op. cit., p. 4.
4. Ibid., p. 3.
5. As reported by Wheatcroft, op. cit., p. 79, Nellmapius had not only been granted the concession, but also a farm every fifteen miles along the route to rest man and animals. The land grant alone accounted for some 3,000 morgen (about 2,400 hectares) in all.

6. A. P. Cartwright, op. cit., pp. 74–6.
7. Ibid., pp. 5–7.
8. *A History of South Africa Social and Economic*, by C. W. de Kiewiet, 9th imprint (London, 1966).
9. *'Die Arm Blanke' in die Suid Afrikaanse Republiek tussen die jare 1822 en 1899*, by A. N. Pelzer, published in *Historiese Studies* 2, No. 3, of January 1941, p. 126.
10. A. P. Cartwright, op. cit., p. 76.

Chapter 12

1. Dr J. J. Fourie, op. cit., pp. 4–8 and authorities quoted by him for the situation on the Witwatersrand before the discovery of gold.
2. Stipulations in a contract of lease between S. W. J. Meyer (lessor) and P. C. van der Walt (lessee) dated January 9, 1886, quoted by Dr J. J. Fourie, op. cit., p. 7.
3. Geoffrey Wheatcroft, op. cit., p. 41 *et seq.* for the background of Kimberley and the particulars of the main personalities mentioned in what follows.
4. A. P. Cartwright, op. cit., p. 78.
5. Quoted in *Payable Gold: An Intimate Record of the History of the Discovery of the Payable Witwatersrand Goldfields and of Johannesburg in 1886 and 1887*, by James Gray, (Johannesburg, 1937), p. 49.
6. *Recollections of the Discovery of Gold on the Witwatersrand and the Early Development of the Gold Mines*, written by J. B. Taylor at the request of the Director of the Africana Museum, W. R. Morrison in October 1936, p. 5.
7. Ibid., p. 8.

Chapter 13

1. James Gray, op. cit., p. 110.
2. Ibid., p. 112.
3. Ibid., p. 91.
4. J. B. Taylor, op. cit., p. 8.
5. James Gray, op. cit., p. 105.
6. *Randlords*, by P. H. Emden (London 1935), p. 69.
7. J. B. Taylor, op. cit., pp. 6–7.
8. Geoffrey Wheatcroft, op. cit., p. 113.
9. Ibid., p. 114.
10. J. B. Taylor, op. cit., p. 9.
11. Cf. Geoffrey Wheatcroft, op. cit., pp. 120–1.
12. J. B. Taylor, op. cit., p. 9.

13. Geoffrey Wheatcroft, op. cit., p. 123.
14. *The Foundations of the South African Cheap Labour System*, by Norman Levy (Johannesburg, 1982), p. 20.
15. *The Gold of the Rand*, a publication of the Chamber of Mines, op. cit., p. 70.

Chapter 14

1. Frank Welsh, op. cit., p. 289.
2. Ibid., p. 299.
3. Ibid., p. 305.
4. *Paul Kruger – Deel II: 1883–1904*, by D.W. Krüger (Johannesburg, 1963).
5. 'German Capital, the Netherlands Railway Company and the Political Economy of the Transvaal, 1886–1918', by J. J. van Helten, *Journal of African History*, 19, 1 (1978), p. 370.
6. *Chamber of Mines Annual Report*, (Johannesburg, 1890), p. 16.
7. J. J. van Helten, op. cit., pp. 377–9.
8. Frank Welsh, op. cit., p. 305.
9. 'Natal, the Transvaal and the Boer War', by Ritchie Ovendale, *The Journal of Imperial and Commonwealth History*, Vol. VIII (3), May 1980, p. 228.
10. Frank Welsh, op. cit., p. 312.
11. Ritchie Ovendale, op. cit., p. 228.
12. J. J. van Helten, op. cit., p. 377 and authorities quoted by him.

Chapter 15

1. Cf. *Studies in Social and Economic History Of the Witwatersrand 1886–1914, (1.) New Babylon* and, *(2.) New Nineveh*, by Charles van Onselen (Johannesburg, 1982).
2. *Johannesburg onder die Zuid-Afrikaansche Republiek*, by M. S. Appelgryn (University of South Africa), *Historia* vol. 3, no. 2. p. 9.
3. Ibid., p. 9.
4. Cf. D.W. Krüger, op. cit., p. 116.
5. Charles van Onselen, *(1.) New Babylon*, op. cit., p. 114.
6. Charles van Onselen, *(2.) New Nineveh*, op. cit., p. 113.
7. D.W. Krüger, op. cit., p. 97.
8. Ibid., p. 96. Krüger states that the President made these remarks at the end of his speech in a jocular spirit. Nobody seems to have appreciated the humour, if such was actually intended. His paternalistic remarks no doubt also did nothing to endear him to his worldly-wise audience.
9. James Gray, op. cit., p. 231.

10. Ibid., p. 231.
11. D.W. Krüger, op. cit. p. 97.
12. Ibid., p. 97.
13. Ibid., p. 96.
14. Ibid. pp. 108 and 135.
15. *Staats-Courant der Z. A. Republiek*, 13 February 1889.
16. D.W. Krüger, op. cit. pp. 105–6.
17. Volksraad minutes of 29 may 1889, art. 303.
18. D.W. Krüger, op. cit. p. 109.
19. Ibid. p. 107.
20. Ibid., p. 108.
21. James Gray, op. cit., p. 194.
22. J. B. Taylor, op. cit., pp. 11–12.
23. Quoted by Geoffrey Wheatcroft, op. cit., p. 129.
24. Ibid., p. 131.
25. Ibid., p. 128.
26. D.W. Krüger, op. cit. p. 117.
27. Quoted by J. J. van Helten, op. cit., pp. 378–9.
28. *Staats-Courant der Z. A. Republiek*, 4 September 1895.
29. D.W. Krüger, op. cit. p. 151.

Chapter 16

1. Details of this enterprise are to be found in *Crown and Charter*, by J. S. Galbraith (Berkeley, 1974), Chapter 5.
2. Frank Welsh, op. cit., p. 313.
3. D.W. Krüger, op. cit., p. 134.
4. Quoted by Frank Welsh, op. cit., p. 313.
5. Geoffrey Wheatcroft, op. cit., pp. 160–1 for all the bribery and corruption.
6. Ibid., p. 177.
7. Ibid., pp. 178–9.

Chapter 17

1. D.W. Krüger, op. cit., p. 167.
2. Frank Welsh, op. cit., p. 320 for most of the aftermath and the background of Milner.
3. *History of South Africa*, by Eric A. Walker (Cape Town, 1963), p. 471.
4. *Die Dinamietontploffing te Braamfontein op 19 Februarie 1896*, by J. J. Fourie, taken from *Geskiedenisnavorsingsprojek, Die Geskiedenis van die Afrikaner*

    aan die Rand, 1886–1961, R. A. U., Nr. 2, Oorsig 1973, for the history and events surrounding the explosion.

5. *The Milner Papers: South Africa 1897–8* (2 Vols, London, 1931), by Cecil Headlam Vol. 1, p. 31 for most of the background and the appointment of Sir Alfred Milner.

6. Transvaal secret archive quoted by Frank Welsh, op. cit., p. 319.

7. Ibid., p. 164.

8. Ibid., p. 224.

9. J.J. van Helten, op. cit., p. 378.

10. Ibid. p. 386 and authorities quoted by him.

11. Quoted by Cecil Headlam, op. cit., p. 28.

12. Ibid., pp. 47–8.

13. Ibid., pp. 45–6.

14. Gen. J. C. G. Kemp, op. cit., p. 2.

15. D. W. Krüger, op. cit., pp. 172–3 for the glowing eulogy on Paul Kruger and the rousing espousal of Afrikaner Nationalism.

16. Cf. especially *The Boer War*, by Thomas Pakenham (London, 1979).

17. Frank Welsh, op. cit., p. 312.

18. Cf. the previously referred to analysis of De Cecco.

19. *The Power of Gold: The History of an Obsession*, by Peter L. Bernstein, (New York, 2000), pp. 257–8.

20. Memorandum to Sir Alfred Milner by General Goodenough dated 5 May, 1897. Cecil Headlam, p. cit. pp. 46–7.

21. Quoted by Thomas Pakenham, op. cit.

22. Cf. Frank Welsh, op. cit., p. 274.

23. Eric A. Walker, op. cit., p. 473.

24. All references to the findings of the Transvaal Industrial Commission and the follow-up commission have been taken from their reports as published in full in its English translation in the 1897 *Yearbook of the Chamber of Mines.*

25. Cf. D. W. Krüger, op. cit., p. 221 and Eric A. Walker, op. cit., p. 470.

26. The Deutsche Bank's views were taken from CO. 537/59 by Frank Welsh, op. cit., and quoted on p. 304 of his book. When the British occupied Pretoria in 1900, the Transvaal's secret Archives were captured and extracts reproduced in the mentioned documents of the British Colonial Office.

27. J. J. van Helten, op. cit., p. 386.

28. Eric A. Walker, op. cit., p. 471.

29. Cf. *Kölnische Zeitung*, 26 May 1898, 22 September 1898 and 3 November 1898.

30. D. W. Krüger, op. cit., p. 224.

31. Cf. Eric A. Walker, op. cit., pp. 471 to 473 for a concise summary of the election and the reactions of Kruger and Milner and the 'of course you are loyal' speech.

32. Thomas Pakenham, op. cit.

33. Ibid.

34. Ibid.

35. R. Taylor, *Lord Salisbury* (London, 1975), p. 178.

36. Frank Welsh, op. cit., p. 328.

37. Ibid., p. 327.

38. Thomas Pakenham, op. cit.

39. Ibid.

40. De Cecco, op. cit., p. 239.

41. *The Gold of the Rand 1888–1923*, a brochure published by the Transvaal Chamber of Mines in 1924.

42. M. de Cecco, op. cit., pp. 123–4.

43. J. S. Marais, op. cit., p. 324.

44. *Economic Imperialism in Theory and Practice*, by R.V. Kubicek, (Durham, USA, 1979), pp. 203–4. It is impossible to do justice to this authoritative and persuasive study in a book of the present nature. Readers who are really interested in the dynamics of economic imperialism are encouraged to read this work.

45. *Die Tweede Vryheidstryd – 1 – Voorspel tot die Drama*, by J. H. Breytenbach (Cape Town, 1948), p. 335.

46. Ibid., p. 375.

Chapter 18

1. Cf. Thomas Pakenham, op. cit., pp. 120–1. The story is not well known and deserves a retelling.

2. For the detail of the invasion of these colonial towns I am much indebted to C. J. Scheepers Strydom, op. cit., pp. 63–70.

3. Frank Welsh, op. cit., p. 339.

4. Frank Welsh, op. cit., p. 340.

Epilogue

1. Headlam, op. cit., p. 477.

2. Ibid., p. 545.

3. The numbers are all taken from the Epilogue of Thomas Pakenham's book, op. cit.

4. Cf. D.W. Krüger, op. cit., p. 225.

5. *Die Politieke Aktiwiteite van die Rand Pioneers Vereniging Gedurende Sy Vroeë Bestaansjare*, by A. J. Potgieter (S. W. A. Broadcasting Corporation Windhoek), *Historia* vol. 3, no. 2, p. 12.

BIBLIOGRAPHY

Appelgryn, M. S. (1986). Johannesburg onder die Zuid-Afrikaansche Republiek, *Historia*, **3**, 2.

Atmore, A., and Marks, S. (1969). The Imperial Factor in South Africa in the 19th Century: Towards a Reassessment, *Journal of Imperial and Commonwealth History.*

Axelson, E., (1962). *Portugal and the Scramble for Africa*, London.

Bernstein, P. L. (2000). *The Power of Gold: The History of an Obsession*, New York.

Blainey, G., (1964–5). Lost Causes of the Jameson Raid, *Economic History Review*, 2nd series, XVIII.

Blink, H. (1890). *De Zuid-Afrikaansche Republiek en Hare Bewoners*, Amsterdam.

Branigan, C., (1994). The Circumnavigation of Africa, in *Classics Ireland*, Volume 1, Dublin.

Breytenbach, J. H., (1948). *Die Tweede Vryheidstryd – 1 – Voorspel tot die Drama*, Cape Town.

Cartwright, A. P., (1973). *Valley of Gold*, Cape Town.

Chamber of Mines, (1890). *Annual Report*, Johannesburg.

Coleman, F. L. (ed.), (1989). *Economic History of South Africa*, Pretoria.

Davenport, T. R. H., (1997, 1991). *A Modern History of South Africa*, London.

De Cecco, M., (1974). *Money and Empire: The International Gold Standard, 1890–1914*, London.

De Kiewiet, C. W., (1937, 1965). *The Imperial Factor in South Africa*, London.

De Kiewiet, C. W., (1945). *British Colonial Policy*, London.

De Kiewiet, C. W., (1966). *A History of South Africa – Social and Economic*, 9th imprint, London.

Delius, P., (1983). *The Land Belongs to Us*, Johannesburg.

Denoon, D. J. N., (1980). Capital and Capitalists in the Transvaal in the 1890s and 1900s, *The Historical Journal*, **23**, 1.

Duminy, A. H., (1973). The Political Career of Sir Percy Fitzpatrick (unpublished thesis), University of Natal

Du Toit, A. and Giliomee, H., (1983). *Afrikaner Political Thought, Vol. 1*, Berkeley.

Duvenhage, G. D. J., (1976). Hoeveel Kaapse Koloniste het Voortrekkers geword?, *Historical Journal*, **XXI**, 1.

Elphick, R. H. and Giliomee, H. (eds), (1971, 1989). *The Shaping of South African Society 1652–1820*, Cape Town and London.

Emden, P. H., (1935). *Randlords*, London.

Fieldhouse, D. K. (ed.), (1967). *The Theory of Capitalist Imperialism*, London.

Fieldhouse, D. K., (1973). *Economics and Empire, 1830–1914*, London.

Ford, R. B., (1985). *The Urban Trek: Some Comparisons of Mobility in American and South African History*, Berkeley.

Fortescue, J. W., (1940). *History of the Army*, Vol. 4, Part 1 AMS Press, Cambridge.

Fourie, J. J., (1978). *Afrikaners in die Goudstad*, Vol. I: *1886–1924*, Johannesburg.

Galbraith, J. S., (1963). *Reluctant Empire*, Berkeley.

Galbraith, J. S., (1974). *Crown and Charter*, Berkeley.

Gifford P. and Louis, W. R. (eds) (1967). *Britain and Germany in Africa*, London.

Goodfellow, C. F., (1966). *Great Britain and South African Confederation, 1870–1881*, Cape Town.

Gray, J., (1937). *Payable Gold: An Intimate Record of the History of the Discovery of the Payable Witwatersrand Goldfields and of Johannesburg in 1886 and 1887*, Johannesburg.

Headlam, C., (1931). *The Milner Papers: South Africa 1897–8*, 2 Vols, London.

Hobson, J. A., (1938). *Imperialism: A Study*, 3rd edn, London.

Kemp, J. C. G., (1942). *Vir Vryheid en Vir Reg*, Cape Town.

Kindleberger, C., (1996). *World Economic Primacy, 1500–1990*, New York.

Kotze, D. J. (ed.), (1958). *Letters of the American Missionaries 1835–1838*, Cape Town.

Krüger, D. W., (1963). *Paul Kruger – Deel II: 1883–1904*, Johannesburg.

Kubicek, R. V., (1972). Randlords in 1895: A Reassessment, *Journal of British Studies*, **XI**, 2.

Kubicek, R. V., (1979). *Economic Imperialism in Theory and Practice: The Case of South African Gold-mining Finance, 1886–1914*, Durham, USA.

Levy, N., (1982). *The Foundations of the South African Cheap Labour System*, Johannesburg.

Marais, J. S., (1961). *The Fall of Kruger's Republic*, Oxford.

Marks, S. and Atmore, A., (1980). *Economy and Society in Pre-industrial South Africa*, London.

Maylam, P., (1986). *A History of the African People of South Africa*, Cape Town.

Meintjies, J., (1971). *The Commandant General: The Life and Times of Petrus Jacobus Joubert of the South African Republic*, Cape Town.

Mendelsohn, R., (1978). *Blainey and the Jameson Raid: The Debate Resumed*, Institute of Commonwealth Studies Collected Seminar Papers, University of London, 8

Mommsen, W. J., (1977). Europäischer Finanzimperialismus vor 1914: Ein Beitrag zu einer Pluralistischen Theorie des Imperialismus, *Historische Zeitschrift*, CCXXIV.

Nixon, J., (1885). *The Complete Story of the Transvaal – from the 'Great Trek' to the Convention of London*, [reproduced in a facsimile version 1972], London and Cape Town.

Ovendale, R., (1980). Natal, the Transvaal and the Coming of the Boer War, *Journal of Imperial and Commonwealth History*, **VIII**, 3.

Owen, E. R. J. and Sutcliffe, R. B. (eds), (1972). *Studies in the Theory of Imperialism*, London.

Pakenham, T., (1979). *The Boer War*, London.

Pakenham, T. (2001). *The Scramble for Africa 1876–1912*, London.

Pelzer, A. N., (1941). Die 'Arm Blanke' in die Suid Afrikaanse Republiek tussen die jare 1822 en 1899, *Historiese Studies*, **2**, 3.

Potgieter, A. J., (1986). Die Politieke Aktiwiteite van die Rand Pioneers Vereniging Gedurende Sy Vroeë Bestaansjare, *Historia*, **3**, 2.

Roos, H., (1899). *A Hundred Years of Wrong* (originally *Een Eeu van Onrecht*), [originally published under the name of F. W. Reitz, State Secretary of the Z.A.R.], Pretoria.

Sanceau, E., (1944). *The Land of Prester John*, New York.

Silverburg, R., (1972). *The Realm of Prester John*, New York.

Strydom, C. J. Scheepers, (1937). *Kaapland en die Tweede Vryheidsoorlog*, Cape Town.

Taylor, J. B., (1936). Recollections of the Discovery of Gold on the Witwatersrand and the Early Development of the Gold Mines, [unpublished work, written at the request of the Director of the Africana Museum].

Thomas, Hugh, (1997). *The Slave Trade*, London.

Transvaal Chamber of Mines, (1924). *The Gold of the Rand 1887–1923*, Johannesburg.

Van der Merwe, P. J. (1995). *The Migrant Farmer in the History of the Cape Colony 1657–1842* (originally *Die Trekboer in die Geskiedenis van die Kaapkolonie, 1657–1842*), Athens, USA.

Van Helten, J. J., (1978). German Capital, the Netherlands Railway Company and the Political Economy of the Transvaal, 1886–1918, *Journal of African History*, **19**, 1.

Van Onselen, Charles, (1982a). *Studies in Social and Economic History of the Witwatersrand 1886–1914, (1.) New Babylon*, Johannesburg.

Van Onselen, Charles, (1982b). *Studies in Social and Economic History of the Witwatersrand 1886 – 1914, (2.) New Nineveh*, Johannesburg.

Van Winter, P. J., (1937). *Onder Kruger's Hollanders*, Amsterdam.

Van Zyl, M. C., (1979). *Die Protesbeweging van die Transvaalse Afrikaners 1877–1880*, Pretoria.

Walker, E. A., (1963). *History of South Africa*, Cape Town.

Welsh, F., (2000). *A History of South Africa*, London.

Wheatcroft, G., (1985). *The Randlords*, London.

Wiid, J. A. and Geyer, A. L. (eds), (1974). *Geskiedenis van Suid Afrika, Vol. 1*, Cape Town.

Winks, R. W., (1963) *British Imperialism: Gold, God and Glory*, New York.

Index